THE FRENCH CANADIANS
OF MICHIGAN

Great Lakes Books

*A complete listing of the books in this series
can be found at the back of this volume.*

Philip P. Mason, Editor
Department of History,
Wayne State University

Dr. Charles K. Hyde, Associate Editor
Department of History,
Wayne State University

THE
FRENCH CANADIANS OF
MICHIGAN

THEIR CONTRIBUTION *to the* DEVELOPMENT *of the*
SAGINAW VALLEY *and the* KEWEENAW PENINSULA,
～ 1840–1914 ～

Jean Lamarre

Wayne State University Press   Detroit

TRANSLATED BY HOWARD KEILLOR AND HERMIONE JACK.

Library of Congress Cataloging-in-Publication Data

Lamarre, Jean, 1958–
    [Canadiens français du Michigan. English]
    The French Canadians of Michigan : their contribution to the development of
the Saginaw Valley and the Keweenaw Peninsula, 1840–1914 / Jean Lamarre ;
[translated by Howard Keillor and Hermione Jack].
        p.   cm. — (Great Lakes books)
Includes bibliographical references and index.
    ISBN 0-8143-3158-0 (paper : alk. paper)
    1. French-Canadians—Michigan—Saginaw River Valley—History.
2. Saginaw River Valley (Mich.)—History.   3. French-Canadians—Michigan—
Keweenaw Peninsula—History. 4. Keweenaw Peninsula (Mich.)—History.
I. Title.   II. Series.
    F572.S2L3613 2003
    9774'99004114—dc21   2003002252

♾ The paper used in this publication meets the minimum requirements of
the American National Standard for Information Sciences—Permanence of
Paper for Printed Library Materials, ANSI Z39.48-1984.

Contents

Acknowledgments

A number of people assisted me in the preparation of this study. I must first thank Bruno Ramirez of the University of Montréal, my Ph.D. director and friend, who helped me find the sensibility required to understand the migrants. I owe a great deal to the stimulating friendship of John P. DuLong of Berkley, Michigan, with whom I shared my discoveries. Thanks are also due to Jean-François Cardin, whose judicious comments helped me to improve the text. I am grateful to the American embassy (ASUSI) for supporting part of my research in Michigan. And I extend warm thanks to Theresa Sanderson Spence, director of the Copper Country Historical Collection at the Michigan Technological University in Houghton, Anna Mae Maday of the Hoyt Public Library in Saginaw, and Leroy Barnett, reference archivist at the State Archives of Michigan in Lansing. I would like to thank the entire editorial staff at les Éditions du Septentrion in Quebec City, especially Gaston Deschênes, for judicious comments. My thanks go also to Jane Hoehner, acquisitions editor who, right from the start, believed in this project. With her energy and dynamism, she has been an inspiration to me. I would like to thank also the whole team at WSUP, particularly Adela Garcia, Renee Tambeau, and Robin DuBlanc for their help and care. Finally, I would like to thank Dr. Ron Weir, dean of research at the Royal Military College of Canada in Kingston, Ontario, Dr. Joel Sokolsky, dean of arts, and especially Dr. E. J. Errington, head of the history department, who had confidence in me and gave the financial support to allow this publication.

Introduction

From the time the French first settled in North America in the early seventeenth century, French colonists never ceased to blaze new trails across the continent. Their taste for adventure, fascination with the fur trade, and desire to improve their circumstances all contributed to the expansion of New France—with the result that barely a century after its founding, it had become a vast empire stretching to the far north, westward beyond the Mississippi, eastward to the English colonies, and southward as far as the Gulf of Mexico.

The fur trade was the driving force behind this movement. From the early seventeenth century to the beginning of the nineteenth, French Canadians actively participated in all phases of the trade. As canoeists, traders, and voyageurs, they played a vital role in this commerce centered around the Great Lakes, always pushing back the frontiers of the colony. In so doing, they came into contact with Amerindian peoples, with whom they formed such strong bonds that some decided to integrate into Amerindian societies.

This scattering of the population over such a wide area may have posed a threat to the survival of New France, but the scores of small, isolated French Canadian communities throughout the continent proved remarkably hardy. In spite of peace treaties, shifts of allegiance, and the decline of the regional fur trade at the beginning of the nineteenth century, they somehow managed to sustain themselves. The territory known as Michigan changed allegiance at least twice in the eighteenth century: first, after the victory of England over France in 1760, and again after the Jay Treaty of 1794 when the territory officially switched from England to the United States. But these changes did not seem to alter the way French Canadians lived in this region.

The industrialization of the continent during the nineteenth century and the market economy that disrupted the agricultural way of life caused various problems and inspired renewed interest in migration among some French Canadians who had problems adjusting to the new economic reality of the open market. Many borrowed money to invest in mechanization in order to produce a surplus to sell on the market, but were met with bankruptcy when they failed to find the necessary buyers. This wave of migration from Quebec, which began before the 1860s, was directed in roughly equal streams toward the New England states and the American Midwest. The latter movement, principally to the state of Michigan, is not surprising, as the colonists associated with the fur traders had taken this same route earlier: the arrival of these new migrants replenished and stimulated communities long established in the region, instilling in them new vitality.

In 1890, there were 537,298 people of French Canadian origin living in the United States. Of this number, the great majority, some 72 percent, lived in the states of the Northeast. Nevertheless, 137,168 French Canadians, or 26 percent of all those living in the United States, resided in the Midwest, and 58,377, or 43 percent of these, lived in Michigan.[1]

This book analyzes French Canadian immigration from 1840 to the beginning of the twentieth century to two regions of the state: the Saginaw River Valley, including the counties of Bay and Saginaw, and the Keweenaw Peninsula—aptly named Copper Country—which includes the counties of Houghton, Keweenaw, and Ontonagon. These regions were selected for examination because they were affected by the forestry and mining industries, respectively—the two major economic pillars of industrial development in nineteenth-century Michigan—and because they were the two regions of the state, outside of Detroit, that attracted the greatest number of French Canadians. The period under study coincides with the beginning of industrialization, which changed both regions and favored the influx of thousands of migrants. My study ends in 1914, the year that marked the end of the most important strike ever seen in the Keweenaw Peninsula. The conflict was decisive in several respects, and its outcome brought a profound change to social relations in the communities of the region.

This book emphasizes that the process of French colonization on the continent continued to make its mark long after the Conquest, the victory of England over France in 1760. It seeks to give an account of this phenomenon, especially as it concerns the region of Michigan which, conveniently adjacent to the Great Lakes, served for a long period as the hub of the fur trade and saw the founding of a good number of small French Canadian and Métis communities. The sizable minority of French Canadian emigrants that headed to Michigan in the nineteenth century was continuing a tradition of mobility that had characterized the lives of French Canadians since they first settled on this continent.

I have also tried to learn who these immigrants were, where they came from, what prompted them to set out for Michigan, how they adapted to industrialization, and what strategies they adopted to achieve this. I sought to re-create their world in French Canada, to reconstruct their itineraries, and to describe the social environment to which they had to adapt in Michigan. Finally, in light of this new information, I have reexamined the overall movement to the United States in order to clarify and reevaluate certain aspects of it such as the behavior of French Canadian workers, the relationship between the clerical elite and the parishioners, and the economic integration of the migrants.

The study shows that French Canadians participated in pushing back the frontiers of the continent and highlights their exceptional geographic mobility. It also opens a window onto a hitherto neglected regional dimension of the general migratory movement that led thousands of French Canadians to move throughout North America.

The first chapter presents an overview of developments in French Canada in the nineteenth century in order to portray the socioeconomic context of migration. The second chapter offers a brief analysis of the socioeconomic evolution of the two regions under study, explaining why they were attractive to French Canadians. Chapters 3 and 4 analyze the migrations themselves (first in the Saginaw Valley and then on the Keweenaw Peninsula), the development of the immigrant communities, and their subsequent decline.

Chapter 1

Quebec in the Nineteenth Century

It is common knowledge that Lower Canada has been poorer in the last two or three years than at any time in the past half century. Cash has disappeared; there is no credit; real estate is mortgaged to the hilt; bankruptcy is the order of the day; trade is dead and agriculture threatens to follow it to its grave. What have we left? Factories? They have been smothered in their cradles. Logging? It has hastened the ruin of the country. All that we have left, I tell you, is poverty. [1]

Thus J. B. A. Ferland, the principal of Nicolet College, described the economic situation prevailing in Quebec in the mid-nineteenth century. He was responding to a questionnaire prepared by the committee of inquiry set up in 1849 by the Legislative Assembly of the Province of Canada to analyze the reasons for migration to the United States—the extent of which was cause for alarm among the political elite. But this observation could have been voiced by thousands of French Canadians, wherever they resided, who had witnessed—and fallen victim to—the deterioration of the economy.

Between 1760 and 1850, French Canadian society underwent profound socioeconomic and demographic transformations that engendered economic problems affecting the entire population. The unabated worsening of socioeconomic conditions confronted French Canadians with an endless series of challenges, continually obliging them to adapt to new situations and devise different strategies to limit the consequences of the situation. Several options were available—seasonal employment in the fur trade, temporary work in logging camps, leaving the land, colonizing undeveloped regions, and migration to the United States.

1

These options, all of which involved geographic mobility, served as strategies of survival for thousands of French Canadians seeking to mitigate the deterioration of their living conditions.

THE SOCIOECONOMIC DEVELOPMENT OF QUEBEC

The British conquest of New France in 1760 appeared to sound the death knell for the survival of the French Canadians in North America. In the 150 years of the existence of New France, its population had grown to only seventy thousand. Under the provisions of the Treaty of Paris and later of the Royal Proclamation of 1763, the disappearance of French Canadian society seemed to be but a matter of time.[2]

Yet the reality was quite different. The meager numbers of British immigrants to Quebec, along with the social and political disturbances in the American colonies and the fear of their possible spread northward, soon altered London's attitude toward its new colony. The Quebec Act, passed in 1774, followed by the Constitutional Act in 1791, allowed the French Catholic population and its religious and economic elites to regain certain prerogatives essential to preserving economic, linguistic, and religious identity. The Quebec Act supported French Canadian institutions by recognizing the seigneurial system and French civil law, legalizing the Catholic Church, and guaranteeing the right of French Canadians to practice their religion. Furthermore, with the aim of curbing the rebellious American colonies' desire for westward expansion, the Quebec Act placed under the colony's administration a vast territory west of the Appalachians, around the Great Lakes, which became an integral part of Quebec's geopolitical reality. The Constitutional Act divided the province into two political entities, Upper and Lower Canada, and reaffirmed the intent of the Quebec Act. However, it did make an amendment to one section of the 1774 act, inserting a clause stipulating that all new concession of lands would henceforth be made in "free and common socage," thus restricting the seigneurial system to the regions then within its jurisdiction.[3]

Constitutional changes were not the only factors that enabled the French Canadian community to sustain itself. In fact, from the beginning of the eighteenth century, the population of Quebec experienced spectacular demographic growth.[4] It increased at a remarkable rate, doubling every twenty-seven years, with an average birth rate hovering around fifty per thousand between 1760 and 1850. In spite of a high mortality rate, the net result was still a natural growth rate of about twenty-five per thousand.[5] This high rate carried the Quebec population to record levels, increasing from 70,000 in 1765 to 161,000 in 1790, then to 335,000 in 1814 and 697,000 in 1844, finally reaching 890,000 inhabitants in 1851, 75 percent of whom were of French Canadian origin.[6]

However, by the beginning of the nineteenth century, demographic pressures had begun to create problems in certain seigneuries: from 1784 to 1844, the population had increased by 400 percent while the area of occupied land had grown by only 275 percent.[7] The younger generation of French Canadians was forced to settle in the marginal regions of the seigneuries. Although lots were still available in the seigneuries, the opening up of territory for settlement was not achieved without difficulties. The seigneurs, wishing to profit from the positive effects of demographic pressure on the price of land and the emergence of an increasingly lucrative timber trade at the beginning of the nineteenth century, were more exacting with regard to the obligations (*cens et rentes*) of their tenants and more reluctant to grant new lands to individuals. This situation forced many French Canadians to seek new regions of settlement.

At the beginning of the nineteenth century, French Canadians could move into the northern and southern extremities of the seigneuries in the St. Lawrence Valley. However, these lands, generally of poor quality and isolated from transportation routes, held little attraction. The Eastern Townships offered another possibility.[8] This region, opened to British colonization at the end of the eighteenth century, still afforded opportunities for settlement, but several factors discouraged French Canadians. It was a relatively undeveloped region at the time, with rudimentary transportation routes. Also, the character of the Eastern Townships remained solidly English and Protestant. The isolation in which French Canadians would have found themselves in the region partly explains their reluctance to settle there in large numbers.[9] But it was the system of land sales applied in the area that especially deterred French Canadians, few of whom had easy access to the capital required to buy land. Nevertheless, many did settle there. In 1831, the ten thousand French Canadian inhabitants represented only 20 percent of the population,[10] but poor economic conditions in the seigneuries through the 1830s and 1840s prompted more to join them and the Francophone population reached fifteen thousand inhabitants in 1844 and thirty thousand, or 37 percent of the total population of the Townships, in 1851.[11] In spite of these opportunities for settlement, it may be said that at the beginning of the nineteenth century French Canadians were experiencing serious difficulties in finding new land.

Beginning in the early nineteenth century, many families sought to alleviate this problem by means of the gradual subdivision of their landholdings.[12] The recourse to subdivision seemed a valid option to many and the practice was increasingly widespread in Quebec from the 1820s on.[13] However, in the longer term, it proved highly disadvantageous, increasingly reducing the arable land area per family and thus diminishing productivity.[14]

The repeated application of this method led to the gradual emergence of a new territorial unit in the seigneuries—the emplacement. These emplacements were small areas, sufficient to accommodate a building and a plot of land only large enough for supplementary cultivation and certainly inadequate for providing all that a household required to survive. These circumstances turned farmers into agricultural laborers, seeking wages on the job market to supplement their income because they were not able to farm on a large scale. During the 1820s a rural proletariat thus emerged, made up of an increasing number of *emplacitaires*, reduced to looking for remunerated work on neighboring farms or in small villages nearby. But the demand for labor in the agriculture and trade sectors was low and irregular.[15] Lacking land and unable to reliably sell their labor as farmhands, these French Canadians became prime candidates for migration as a means of finding employment.

From 1760 to 1850, the majority of the French Canadian population maintained an essentially rural, agricultural life. In 1760, 75 percent of the population lived in rural areas. In 1851, the rural population still represented 70 percent of Quebec's inhabitants, while Montreal and Quebec City accounted for about 30 percent.[16]

Economically, Quebec had developed within a colonial system where fur was the primary commodity of exchange. Nevertheless, agriculture—especially the cultivation of wheat—could provide farmers with economic self-sufficiency.[17] But an examination of the development of wheat production and the importance of this product in agricultural exports during the first half of the nineteenth century reveals a distinct downward trend. As the century advanced, the proportion of wheat in total agricultural exports shrank continually.[18] Moreover, not only did wheat fall behind in relation to other agricultural exports, but wheat production itself declined. In 1827, it stood at 2.9 million bushels. By 1844, it was down to 942,829 bushels.[19]

After 1833, Quebec's fluctuating production of wheat plummeted.[20] The fact that Quebec was obliged to import wheat from Upper Canada and the United States during the 1830s in order to meet its needs clearly demonstrates the gravity of its agricultural problems. This collapse of wheat production was aggravated by a number of natural scourges during the 1830s and 1840s in Quebec. The invasion of the wheat fly destroyed harvests in many places. The result in the short term was increased hardship—food shortages and poverty—for numerous farmers.

Another effect of the situation was to increase farmers' debt load. Since the beginning of the century, some farmers had borrowed money with the aim of mechanizing their means of production in order to keep or increase their market share.[21] But the economic difficulties of the 1830s and 1840s pushed debt levels to alarming proportions.[22] It was increasingly hard for farmers to honor their loans and many had to divest themselves of their land.[23] Such farmers, forced to sell their property, created a new labor pool that swelled the ranks of those already suffering from the subdivision of lands and increased the total number of candidates seeking work for wages.

SURVIVAL STRATEGIES

French Canadians were thus obliged to find solutions—this time outside the agricultural sector. These included migrating to urban centers, colonizing undeveloped lands, temporary employment in the fur trade, seasonal work in logging camps, and migration to the United States. Many French Canadians tried all of these, but only the latter three options will be discussed here.

All the strategies attempted by the French Canadians shared a common feature in that they relied on geographic mobility, on a propensity for movement, either within or beyond political boundaries. This factor was a constant source of support in developing strategies of survival. The reliance on mobility constitutes a distinctive, and even recurrent, trait in the socioeconomic and cultural life of French Canadians. Its origins go back to the very beginnings of French colonization on the continent, and it must be carefully considered as a means of better understanding the nature of the solutions chosen by French Canadians in times of crisis.

Paradoxically, the evidence of this geographic mobility and its repercussions have long been neglected by historians, especially as regards the period 1760–1930.[24] The image traditionally associated with the French Canadians, especially after the British conquest, has been one of an essentially rural people, conservative, and above all sedentary—the only characteristics, according to the ideology of "survival" advocated by the clerical elite, that could ensure the endurance of a French Catholic identity and the survival of French Canadians as a distinct people in an English Protestant North America. Nevertheless, recent studies has demonstrated the central role and strength of migratory movements within French Canadian society throughout its history.[25] They have concluded that the mobility of the French Canadians was a fundamental trait that demands examination if the continuity of the Quebec identity is to be fully understood.[26]

This propensity of the French Canadians to move throughout the continent owes its origins to their participation in the fur trade.

The Fur Trade

The fur trade was the heart of the economic, geographic, and social development of Quebec from the seventeenth century to the beginning of the nineteenth century. Though a rudimentary agriculture occupied a good proportion of the colonial population in the St. Lawrence Valley, the fur trade and its profitability attracted a significant number of the inhabitants.

At first, organization of the trade was simple, and the activity was accessible to all. Although the export of furs had almost always been in the hands of various monopolies until the British conquest, every settler was free to trade directly with the Amerindian groups who periodically came to Montreal, Quebec City, and Trois-Rivières to exchange their furs for merchandise.[27]

As the hunting territories gradually moved farther away from the St. Lawrence Valley, Amerindian peoples came less frequently to the colony, obliging the colonists to travel to their villages.[28] In undertaking such an expedition, they would change their settlers' clothes for the outfit of the coureurs de bois, and adopt the fur traders' way of life, becoming acquainted with the geography, waterways, culture, and language of the Amerindian tribes.

The increasingly distant location of the trading territories led some merchants to establish way stations on the major trading routes between Montreal and the Great Lakes. A great number

of posts were founded in this way, including Detroit, Michilimackinac, Sault Sainte Marie, Fort Michipicoten, Fort Cam-
anistigoyan, Fort Kaministiquia, Grand Portage, and Baie des
Puants. Further south, Fort Miami was established in Indiana, and
Vincennes and Kaskaskia in Illinois. At first these posts merely
served as supply stations for the expeditions, but they acquired
strategic importance as transit points where furs from the West
were brought before being sent on to Montreal.[29] These outposts
became the bases from which the trade penetrated further into the
hinterland. Starting out with very few inhabitants, they grew into
small islands of semipermanent settlement whose development
continued into the early nineteenth century.[30] The few residents
of these posts engaged in subsistence farming, enabling them to
support themselves and feed the traders.

The transportation network of the fur trade soon forged close
ties between Quebec (especially Montreal) and the Great Lakes
region, the main trading area. As the trading regions continually
receded, the Great Lakes became the hub around which the fur
trade revolved. However, this close relationship between Montreal and the Great Lakes region was disturbed several times by
political changes up until the beginning of the nineteenth century. In different ways and to different degrees, the Treaty of Paris
(1763), the Quebec Act (1774), the American Revolution, the
Jay Treaty (1794) and the Treaty of Ghent (1814) all modified
the close ties between Montreal and the Great Lakes. But the
relationship persisted, and French Canadians continued to play a
role in the fur trade into the first third of the nineteenth century.

Beginning in the late eighteenth century, work in the fur trade
served as a specific response to problems in the agricultural sector. Farmers, especially the young sons of farming families, joined
the ranks of the traders. This willingness of youth to participate
in the rough life out West may be explained by "the need of
large numbers of young people to earn their living and the in-
adequacy of incomes from agriculture."[31] At the end of the eighteenth century, frequent departures for the *Pays d'en Haut*, as the
Great Lakes region was then called, were so common that in some

regions of Quebec they were considered a completely ordinary occurrence.[32]

Because of their long experience in this type of work and their excellent knowledge of the river routes, the French Canadian canoeists were a highly prized labor force. In 1798, for example, the North West Company, founded by Scottish merchants in 1785, employed 1,257 workers as interpreters and guides, but especially as canoeists. The great majority of these workers were of French Canadian origin.[33]

This relationship between the French Canadians and the fur trade began to weaken in 1821 as the trapping routes of the North West Company moved ever further westward, where the Hudson's Bay Company had concentrated its activity for many decades. Once it was far from Montreal, its point of export, the North West Company soon had difficulty competing with the Hudson's Bay Company. The situation worsened to such an extent that the directors of the North West Company were obliged to accept a merger with the Hudson's Bay Company in 1821. The merger marked a turning point in the participation of French Canadians in this labor market. The disappearance of the North West Company shut down an important source of supplementary employment for the many French Canadians who had dominated the workforce until then. From then on, "the West was no longer accessible in the context of organized economic activity."[34]

In spite of these upsets, French Canadians retained a place in the fur trade. Until the 1840s, the American Fur Company maintained a policy that favored hiring them.[35] From 1827 to 1846, "not only are there many Canadian hired laborers and voyageurs in the service of the American Fur Company, but also many Canadian traders and company representatives."[36] The French Canadians demonstrated a high degree of mobility in the regions of the Northwest, especially in Michigan. They never confined themselves within the geographical limits of a national territory, but showed a consistent lack of "border consciousness" in their movements, going wherever the activities of the fur trade took them and maintaining direct access to the Great Lakes. But by the early

1830s, the principal fur trading areas had definitively moved west of the Great Lakes, and activities in the territory of Michigan itself had almost ceased. In this situation, many French Canadians working in the trading posts in the Great Lakes region decided to settle there. And thus "the descendants of French-Canadian traders, factors and voyageurs became settlers on American soil who melted into the rest of the population."[37]

The participation of the French Canadians in the fur trade is significant in several respects. In the beginning, their presence in this market represented a survival strategy to which they periodically resorted to improve their living conditions. But beyond this, the experience opened up new economic horizons for them. It allowed them to move freely through the Great Lakes region, become familiar with its transportation routes, make contact with trading posts, and evaluate the resources available to them. It therefore served to broaden their geographic awareness and define an economic territory that extended well beyond the borders of Quebec.

This experience was no doubt a contributing factor when, during the 1830s and 1840s, as Quebec encountered serious economic hardship and internal strategies of survival were exhausted and as many French Canadians turned to migration, a good number of them moved westward—most notably to Michigan—looking for better opportunities.

When employment opportunities in the fur trade began to decline in the 1830s, just as agricultural problems were being felt more keenly in Quebec, French Canadians had already developed new strategies to alleviate the deterioration of their living conditions. For several years, one of these strategies had been to set off for the logging camps.

The Lumber Industry

Before the nineteenth century, the lumber industry had represented only a minor sector of the economy in Canada. In spite of the availability of large timber reserves, the lumber industry was

limited to a small number of modest sawmills distributed throughout the territory. The high costs of transportation between the
mother country and its North American colony hindered the development of a thriving lumber industry. England preferred to
obtain its lumber in the Baltic region, where timber was easily
accessible and less expensive.[38] It was not until the beginning
of the nineteenth century, when the political climate of Europe
was destabilized by the Napoleonic wars, that London adopted a
protectionist trade policy that encouraged the start of the timber
trade in Canada.[39]

The development of timber resources was begun by American,
Canadian, and British entrepreneurs, some of whom had come
from the Baltic region, moving their operations to Canada to take
advantage of the favorable economic climate opening up there.[40]
Several regions of Canada were eventually developed, but it was
in the Ottawa Valley that the first lumber firm was launched.[41] At
this time the Outaouais region covered an immense territory, including the basin of the Ottawa River and the entire area linking
the Ottawa Valley to the Georgian Bay, including Lake Nipissing.
The region thus stretched from the Long-Sault dam to the gateway to Hudson Bay and the Great Lakes. The Outaouais region
was the country of the *coureurs des bois* and the fur traders, the
heart of the route taken by the furs as they were brought from
the West to the St. Lawrence Valley.[42] The region was favored
with immense timber resources and a system of rivers suited to
the transport of logs, all of which quickly transformed this virgin
territory into the dominant logging region of Canada.[43]

Development of the Ottawa Valley's resources was started
by Philemon Wright, an American entrepreneur from Woburn,
Massachusetts, who came to explore the region in 1797. In 1800,
he returned with several American lumberjacks recruited in New
England and settled there. He established the initial infrastructure
of what would become the city of Hull on the eastern bank of the
Ottawa River, and put up the first sawmill in 1801. By 1807, the
first raft of square timber from Wright's mill had left the Ottawa
Valley, headed toward the port of Quebec, leading the way for

the thousands of rafts that would follow it through nearly a half-century, destined for the markets of Great Britain.

The beginnings of the lumber industry had little effect on the settlement of the region, however. Until 1814, the Ottawa Valley remained very sparsely populated. With the end of the European wars, Britain's demand for colonial wood increased. This favored the growth of the forestry sector and created new employment opportunities that attracted new workers, many of whom were French Canadians. Because the lumber was sent to Quebec City for export, close ties formed between the two regions. In fact, several counties in the St. Lawrence Valley became the principal sources of labor for the logging camps. In the economic climate of the first half of the nineteenth century, "logging became a gateway of escape from the many problems assailing the St. Lawrence Valley."[44]

To supplement their inadequate agricultural earnings, farmers made seasonal trips to the logging camps. Several communities in the St. Lawrence Valley experienced a seasonal cycle of migration—not the one of former days leading to the trading posts of the Great Lakes in summer, but a new one leading to the logging camps of the Ottawa Valley in winter.[45] Some farmers participated in this seasonal migration, but it was mainly the farmers' sons—those who had difficulty finding work in the winter and wished to save money in order to settle on a piece of land—who were most numerous in the logging camps of the Ottawa Valley.[46] French Canadians had little problem adapting to the work demanded of them in the logging camps. All farmers, young and old, were used to handling an ax, as they often had to clear their own land. Their camp duties were a natural extension of their own work culture.

French Canadians soon predominated in the workforce of the logging camps.[47] During the 1830s, the majority of workers in all the large logging operations in the valley were French Canadian.[48] According to Wright's accounting books, between 1832 and 1840, French Canadians constituted no less than 90 percent of the 230 workers employed in his various camps. From the 1810s to the

1840s, French Canadians always accounted for more than 50 percent of the labor in the Ottawa Valley logging camps.[49]

Beginning in 1835, the lumber industry in the valley benefited from the gradual opening of the American market to Canadian products. Until that time, the needs of American cities had
been adequately met by the timber resources of New York and
Pennsylvania. But as these resources were showing signs of depletion, some American entrepreneurs took an interest in Canadian products.[50] However, the American market was looking for
sawn lumber to supply its rapidly growing urban centers. American demand hastened the establishment of better-equipped, more
efficient sawmills in the early 1840s. Sawn lumber gained increasing importance as an export commodity, and by the 1850s it had
replaced square timber as the principal product of the Ottawa
Valley.[51]

This transformation required a larger and more stable workforce. The seasonal migration of workers tapered off, and small
French Canadian communities were established on either side of
the Ottawa River. A great number of French Canadians, especially
from Montreal and the counties west of Montreal, came to the region to establish communities in the 1840s. Some settled north of
the Ottawa River, in the counties of Pontiac and Outaouais, others to the south in the counties of Glengarry, Prescott, and Russell,
and some even formed small pockets of settlement in Carleton
County, which included the city of Bytown (Ottawa). In 1844,
the estimated population of French Canadians in the four counties was 3,400, and by 1850, the estimate had risen to 10,248, an
increase of 300 percent in six years.[52]

The economic depression of 1837 forced Britain to reevaluate
its trade policies, and in 1842 it reduced its protection for Canadian lumber by lowering taxes on foreign lumber by one-quarter.[53]
This decrease cut exports by one-third between 1841 and 1842.[54]
But more significantly, the decline in exports left entrepreneurs
unable to sell surplus production, causing a marked slowdown of
activity in the logging camps.[55]

By the middle of the decade, however, increased British

demand brought greater stability to the sector. Canadian exports to Great Britain picked up, attaining the record level of nearly 500 million board feet.[56] But in February of 1846, after a budget vote, British authorities imposed new cuts on lumber tariffs. These provisions made the British market more accessible to foreign products and consequently reduced the export levels of Canadian lumber, which by 1848 had dropped back to 350 million board feet. The Canadian lumber industry then entered a period of depression whose effects were felt until 1850.

This depression had a disastrous effect on thousands of French Canadian households. Overproduction had forced entrepreneurs to reduce their activities, laying off many workers. Young men—the farmers and laborers who had become used to going to the logging camps every winter—saw their supplementary income disappear. For many who had settled in the region, this depression meant the loss of their only revenue.[57]

In the early 1850s, the situation in the forestry sector stabilized. Later, it would again be subject to further tariff reductions that completely liberalized the British market in 1866, but the growing needs of the American market compensated for this.[58] The decade from 1850 to 1860 saw the consolidation of the industrialization process with the arrival of many entrepreneurs from Maine and New York.[59]

The development of the lumber industry in the Ottawa Valley had thus opened up another option to French Canadians. In a period of economic instability in Quebec, the forest represented the only dynamic sector capable of providing employment. The depression that struck the sector in the 1840s therefore had especially disastrous effects. French Canadians were obliged to revise their strategies and look elsewhere for solutions to their economic problems. For many, migration to the United States seemed increasingly to be the only alternative. Much of the testimony collected during the inquiry of 1849 revealed that during the 1840s many workers, laborers, and log drivers who had settled in counties bordering the Ottawa Valley had left the region and moved to the United States. L. Letellier, a Quebec City notary, pointed out that "after they have been to school at the logging camps around Bytown, they move on to our [American] neighbors."[60]

Migration to the United States: New England

Migration to the United States was, in fact, a strategy many French Canadians adopted very early.[61] New England, the Midwest, and even distant California all seemed to hold promise for them in the first half of the nineteenth century.[62] Whether their intention was to find temporary employment, acquire fertile land at good prices, or strike it rich prospecting for gold, a great number of French Canadians were attracted to the United States early in the century. The New England region, which borders on Quebec, had the strongest appeal of various possible destinations.

Since the beginning of the nineteenth century, many French Canadians had acquired the habit of crossing the border to take advantage of seasonal jobs in the agriculture and forestry sectors in northern New England. As early as 1809, heads of families and their sons living in Saint-Jean and Missisquoi, south of Montreal, would travel to Vermont on a regular basis to find work. Following the Richelieu River and Lake Champlain, they would stop in communities on the lake and hire on for the season as farmhands or lumberjacks. Likewise, French Canadians from the Beauce would travel down the Chaudière, Penobscot, and Kennebec Rivers into Maine and take work in the logging camps there. Others from Quebec City and the counties of the lower St. Lawrence region would go to Maine by means of the Temiscouata Portage to work in the fields or forests.[63]

This migratory movement was still modest in scale at the beginning of the nineteenth century. In 1840, there were a total of 8,700 French Canadians in the six New England states. Of this number, 8,000 (90 percent) were concentrated in Maine and Vermont, the two American states bordering on Quebec. The other four southern New England states (Connecticut, Massachusetts, New Hampshire, and Rhode Island) shared a population of 700 French Canadians (see table 1.1).

TABLE 1.1
French Canadian Population of New England, 1840–60

State	Number			Increase (%)	
	1840	*1850*	*1860*	*1840–50*	*1850–60*
Connecticut	50	250	1,980	400	692
Maine	2,500	3,680	7,490	47	103
Massachusetts	500	2,830	7,780	466	174
New Hampshire	50	250	1,780	400	612
Rhode Island	100	300	1,810	200	50
Vermont	5,500	12,070	16,580	119	37
Total	8,700	19,380	37,420	120	93

Source: Roby, *Les Franco-Américains de la Nouvelle-Angleterre 1776–1930*, 18.

This migration was for the most part temporary. Migrants went to the United States with the objective of working for a period of time and then returning home with their savings to buy a new piece of land, upgrade their equipment, or settle their debts. In some cases, however, these seasonal migrations, often repeated every year, gave birth to semipermanent colonies with small populations. In Vermont, for example, small concentrations of migrants grew up in the forest regions of Burlington, Winooski, and St. Albans, while in Maine they appeared in the agricultural regions of Madawaska and Aroostook and in the forest regions of Waterville, Skowhegan, and Augusta.[64]

The geographic concentration of the population clearly shows that before 1840 geographic proximity, seasonal employment opportunities, and natural transportation routes strongly influenced the pattern of French Canadians' migrations into American territory.[65]

Beginning in the 1840s, New England went through a period of profound economic changes which, coupled with the depressed economy of Quebec, provided new stimulus for migration and reoriented the destination of the migrants. The American economy was experiencing a remarkable upswing. Industrialization burgeoned after the depression of 1837, giving rise to a strong

American manufacturing sector. Southern New England (Massachusetts, Rhode Island, Connecticut, and New Hampshire), where the majority of the cotton, wool, and shoe industries were located, benefited greatly from this development, bringing the establishment of new factories and an increase in the demand for labor.

The proliferation of factories and the fierce competition developing between them led many entrepreneurs to resort to bold measures to increase their market share. While raw materials and technology were available to all factory owners at about the same price, workers' wages were the only factors over which these owners had any real control. Therefore, the labor force in these factories—at this time consisting mainly of young farmers' daughters and other members of farming families—was subjected to repeated salary cuts during the 1840s, which, together with increased mechanization of production, created strong resentment, led to several strikes, and caused a large part of the workforce to quit. The jobs they left vacant, as well as new jobs created by factory expansion, required few skills and paid low wages. They were filled at first by Irish immigrants who had recently arrived in the region in great numbers, and later by French Canadians, who joined them in the 1850s.

The agricultural sector was also changing rapidly. New England had never been an ideal region for agriculture. The poor quality of the soil, along with a topography ill suited to cultivation and limited mainly to wheat growing, had consistently kept productivity low and restricted the inhabitants to subsistence farming. By the start of the nineteenth century, the soil was showing signs of depletion, having been continuously and intensively cultivated for many decades. Wishing to improve their lot, many farmers decided to sell their farms in the East and move to the West, where lands recently opened for settlement had become more easily accessible since the completion of the Erie Canal in 1825 and the introduction of steam navigation on the Great Lakes.

Wheat production from the West gradually came to present strong competition to the lower-quality grain produced in the

Northeast. The constant departure of farmers for the West added
to the difficulties of the remaining farmers in the Northeast. Not
only did the influx of products from the West limit sales of local agricultural products, but the departure of so many farming
families deprived farmers in the Northeast of the seasonal workforce they relied on during sowing and harvesting. In addition,
the demand for labor in the developing manufacturing industries,
in numerous construction projects, and in the building of canals
and railways lured an increasing number of agricultural laborers,
who deserted the countryside to take advantage of these employment opportunities. Although some French Canadians benefited
from this scarcity of labor, taking seasonal work on the farms in
the Northeast, the agricultural sector entered a period of crisis
that would worsen as production from the West increased. As a
result, demand for seasonal agricultural workers declined, virtu-
ally eliminating this sector as a source of employment for French
Canadians.

The forestry sector in New England was also undergoing a
transformation. The lumber industry was concentrated in Maine,
known as the "Pine Tree State," which had been the nation's pre-
eminent producer of white pine until 1840.[66] The lumber industry
drew on neighboring farming communities for a part of the seasonal labor it required in the logging camps. The westward migration of American families thus deprived the industry of a portion
of its workforce, giving French Canadians—already used to being
hired there—greater access to jobs in the logging camps of Maine.

However, in the 1850s, the lumber industry of Maine entered a period of structural reorganization when depletion of its
pine reserves forced entrepreneurs to turn to the harvest of other
species, especially spruce, that were less in demand on the market.[67] This situation created problems for many entrepreneurs,
who decided to leave the region and move west where pine was
more easily accessible. Although the lumber industry continued
to operate in Maine throughout the nineteenth century, the departure of entrepreneurs reduced opportunities for employment in

the sector. According to testimony recorded during the inquiry of 1857, young French Canadians, who had become used to working in the logging camps of Maine every winter, stopped going there after 1855 after many of them returned with no wages because their employers had gone bankrupt.[68]

The numerous socioeconomic changes that took place in New England from 1840 to 1860 greatly modified employment opportunities and shifted centers of economic development, creating a large demand for seasonal labor that was met, in part, by a greater influx of French Canadians. Between 1840 and 1850, the French Canadian population in New England more than doubled, reaching 19,380 in 1850, an increase of 120 percent. This demographic pattern continued, though at a somewhat slower rate, between 1850 and 1860, reaching a population of 37,420 people. With the emergence of new centers of development, French Canadians began to reorient their migratory movements to the United States. Although Maine and Vermont saw their French Canadian populations grow steadily from 1840 to 1860 in absolute numbers, in terms of percentage their attraction decreased in favor of the southern New England states, although this change should not obscure the fact that they maintained their dominance over all other states as the principal destination for French Canadians migrating to New England. These states were host to over 80 percent of all French Canadians living south of the border in 1850, and nearly 65 percent in 1860.

The lumber industry, and to a lesser extent the agricultural and manufacturing sectors, continued to attract French Canadians until the Civil War.

Migration to the United States: The Midwest

The "emigration of French Canadians to New England was only one facet of their remarkable geographic mobility."[69] The American Midwest—consisting of the states of Indiana, Illinois, Michigan, Minnesota, Ohio, and Wisconsin—also held an attraction for

many of them. As early as 1836, the *Gazette* of Montreal pointed
out that a large number of Canadians had abandoned the shores
of the Richelieu and gone to settle in Michigan.[70]

It should not be surprising that there was a migratory movement to the Midwest before the Civil War. Even though this region, unlike New England, was a considerable distance away from
Quebec, that had never been an obstacle for the French Canadians who made their way there regularly in earlier days for the fur
trade and established small communities in the region.

Moreover, in light of the agricultural situation of the 1830s
and 1840s in Quebec, the possibility of acquiring fertile land at a
good price in the West was perceived as a godsend by many farming families who wanted to escape poverty without completely
abandoning farming as a way of life.[71] Since there was no fertile land to settle in Quebec and no Canadian "Midwest," many
families saw migration to the American Midwest as a valid, and
even natural, solution. Such a migration was all the more logical since the high productivity of the wheat fields of the Midwest
was partly responsible for the economic problems experienced by
French Canadian farmers at home. Using the same reasoning as
that of American farmers in the Northeast, some French Canadians decided that the future of farming lay in the Midwest and
they headed in that direction. Although some young men had
been going out to take temporary work in the logging camps of
Michigan and Wisconsin before 1860, the migratory movement
to the West before the Civil War was of a permanent and familial
nature, centered around the acquisition of land with the intention
of maintaining an agricultural way of life.[72]

In spite of the distance separating Quebec from the Midwest,
traveling conditions to the Great Lakes region were good. The
opening of the Erie Canal in 1825 made the once-dangerous journey to the West considerably faster and safer. Depending on where
they were starting from, French Canadians could take several possible routes to their destination. Some followed the Richelieu
River, Lake Champlain, and the Hudson River to Albany and
boarded one of the boats that regularly plied the Erie Canal to

reach Lake Erie and then the West. Others took the steamships and sailing vessels that plied the "traditional routes" to the Great Lakes region, following a southwest direction up the St. Lawrence River, through Lake Ontario, and then to the Welland Canal, which had opened in 1829, to reach Lake Erie. From there they could set out for the Ohio or Illinois territories.[73] Yet others took the northern passage, along the Ottawa River to Georgian Bay and Lake Huron, and thence to Lake Michigan via Michilimackinac to Wisconsin, Illinois, and Indiana.[74]

Before 1850, those who wished to migrate to the Midwest enjoyed better conditions than those migrating to New England. While those who lived near a major waterway leading into the northeastern states could travel there in reasonable comfort, migrants coming from more isolated areas had to make a long journey by horse-drawn cart that could take three to four weeks.[75] The majority of French Canadians who lived near the St. Lawrence River could easily reach the vast Great Lakes region by taking one of the many boats that sailed upriver.

Nevertheless, the Midwest was not accessible to everyone. Families who wished to settle on a piece of land had to have a certain amount of capital. Only those who were better off, or who could count on the help of friends or relatives already established in the region, could successfully settle there.

This migration gave birth to a number of communities. One of them developed in Illinois around the farming village of Bourbonnais, in Kankakee County, south of Chicago. This colony was founded in 1830 by Noël Levasseur, a French Canadian who settled in the region after having worked in the fur trade for a time in the early part of the nineteenth century. The demographic growth of the village was slow until the beginning of the 1840s, when Levasseur made a successful trip to Quebec to recruit settlers. Nearly a thousand French Canadian families responded to his appeal.[76]

The attractiveness of migration is confirmed in the conclusions reached by the committee formed in 1849 by the Legislative Assembly to study emigration to the United States. Having examined the observations of the clerical elite of the Montreal and

Quebec City dioceses for the period 1844–48, the members of the committee concluded that the lands in the American West had attracted a significant number of French Canadian families during the second half of the 1840s. According to the testimony received, the majority of the thousand families who had left the diocese of Montreal between 1844 and 1848 had chosen go to the Midwest. Their three preferred destinations were the large Chicago-Bourbonnais region; St. Louis, Missouri; and Wisconsin. Of the four thousand parishioners who had left the diocese of Quebec City, roughly half of them had gone to lands in Illinois and the other half to Maine, Vermont, and New York.[77]

This movement to the Midwest continued through the 1850s. The conclusions of a second study on emigration in 1857 indicated that migration was then almost equally divided between the eastern and the western states. The majority of families that moved to the Midwest settled in Illinois and took up agriculture, while a minority of them, especially the younger ones, worked in the logging camps, sawmills, and iron mines around Lake Superior in Michigan.[78]

The improvement of transportation routes during the 1850s encouraged the migratory movement to the Midwest. The completion of the Illinois Central Railroad (1853), which stopped in the French Canadian community of Kankakee, Illinois,[79] and the opening of the Sault Sainte Marie Canal (1855), which provided easier access to Lakes Superior and Michigan as well as to the Upper Peninsula of Michigan and to Wisconsin, both greatly facilitated migration into the region. The recruitment efforts of the controversial Father Charles Chiniquy among his ex-parishioners in the counties of Bellechasse and L'Islet also helped to increase the contingent of French Canadians in Illinois.[80]

By the middle of the nineteenth century, the Midwest had well-organized French Canadian communities. The French Canadian population in Illinois was estimated at close to eight thousand inhabitants in 1851 and close to twenty thousand in 1859.[81] In Bourbonnais itself, there were approximately seven thousand people in 1856.[82] In Wisconsin there were nearly eight thousand

French Canadians in 1850. Ten years later, their estimated population was eighteen thousand.[83]

This attraction for the Midwest diminished with the outbreak of the Civil War and the unstable economic conditions. Researchers unanimously agree that from 1860 on, New England supplanted the West as the favored destination of French Canadians.[84] They point out that the settlement of lands in the West would have required significant capital, that the journey by boat or train would have been long and costly, and that the Midwest lacked both a strong development of its railway system and massive industrialization—two phenomena that were creating new employment opportunities in the northeastern states, steering French Canadians away from the western prairies toward the factories of the American Northeast.

Though it is generally agreed that it was only after the start of the Civil War that the New England states became more attractive than the Midwest, the reasons given are not satisfactory. The causes usually cited were already present in the 1850s. In this decade, as early as 1851, New England had inaugurated a new rail link between Montreal and Portland, Maine. Obstacles to migration westward were present before 1860 and had long been part of the hardships that migrants had to face. Moreover, between 1840 and 1860, when migration seems to be equally divided between the two regions, New England already enjoyed both a geographic advantage over the Midwest and a more diversified economic development. All these factors together should have made it a destination much preferable to the West in those decades. The reasons for the increased migration to New England after 1860 are to be found elsewhere.

One of the reasons is related to the fact that the agricultural frontier, which for some French Canadian families was the goal of their migration, had shifted between 1840 and 1860 to regions such as the Dakotas, Montana, and Kansas, which were much farther and difficult to reach than the Midwest.[85] Considering the distance and the expense of such a move, it is understandable that the American agricultural frontier now held less appeal for French

Canadians and that many of them had to give up their dream of farming and settle for the factory jobs available in the New England states.

Another explanation lies in the fact that French Canadian agriculture recovered after the Civil War by gradually reorienting toward the dairy industry.[86] The profitability of this activity depended on farmers' ability to acquire the equipment necessary for the transition. Farmers who had a certain amount of capital—the very ones who might have decided to move west before the Civil War—had the choice of remaining in Quebec and taking a more active role in the new orientation of agriculture. As for farmers who were less well off, they could not really participate in this restructuring and had to resign themselves to moving to the northeastern states to find work.

Some clarification is also necessary regarding the supposed lack of economic development in the Midwest in the middle of the nineteenth century. Like New England, the Midwest began a process of industrialization in the 1840s, though it was different in nature from that of the Northeast. This growth was sustained by a marked improvement in transportation routes, as well as by the development of forestry and mining resources.

Finally, the opening of a "Canadian West" to settlement in the 1870s, following the acquisition of Rupertsland from the Hudson's Bay Company and the creation of the Province of Manitoba by the Canadian government, provided a new option for French Canadians who wished to remain in the agricultural sector. The possibility of settling in Manitoba answered the needs of those who might have been tempted to strike out for the American agricultural frontier.[87]

These explanations help to better understand the attraction of New England. However, this situation did not put an end to the appeal of the Midwest, whose advantages became more diversified after the Civil War. Though they represented a marginal phenomenon compared to the dominant migratory current to New England, increasing numbers of French Canadians headed to the

Midwest, with different objectives than those of their predecessors in the region.[88]

Within the Midwest, Michigan was the favored destination of French Canadians throughout the nineteenth century. In terms of French Canadian migration, Michigan was to the Midwest what Massachusetts was to New England. While at mid-century Wisconsin and Illinois had a combined French Canadian population of about eight thousand, Michigan could already count nearly twenty thousand.[89]

Around the middle of the nineteenth century, the greatest concentration of French Canadians in Michigan was found in the regions that had once served as centers of the fur trade, especially in the southeast part of the state, around Detroit. The agricultural county of Monroe, bordering on Lake Erie, had at this time between seven thousand and eight thousand French Canadians, while the neighboring agricultural counties of Macomb and St. Claire, north of Detroit, had between four thousand and five thousand. Wayne County, which includes the city of Detroit, had close to eight thousand. There were also some smaller concentrations of French Canadians elsewhere, notably at Michilimackinac, a former fur trading post on the shores of Lake Superior, where a few copper and iron mines were in operation.[90] All together, around 1850, there were almost twenty thousand French Canadians in Michigan, fourteen thousand of whom had been born in Canada.[91]

As one of the strategies to which the French Canadians had recourse in the eighteenth and nineteenth centuries as they sought solutions to their recurrent economic and agricultural problems, migration to Michigan was an option that reflected a perfect continuity with the past, while at the same time offering a new range of opportunities.

The French Canadians, a primarily rural people, experienced marked economic hardship during the first half of the nineteenth century. Intensive demographic pressures and limited availability of land presented them with serious problems. Not content with passive endurance, they developed various strategies for improving their living conditions.

At first, French Canadian farmers chose to focus on "internal" solutions, which did not always produce the desired results. They then opted for other solutions. They tried participating in the fur trade and later in the fledgling lumber industry—both strategies reflecting a propensity for movement. Structural transformations in the fur trade in the 1820s, together with changes in British tariff policy in the 1840s, made these strategies less appealing. French Canadians were then obliged to resort to migration to the United States on a larger scale. This strategy was not at all new, but more and more French Canadians adopted it.

While economic and geographic considerations came first in the choice of a destination, previous work experiences also played a role. The migrants selected places based on their culture of work, their family structure, considerations of geographic accessibility, and the economic objectives they had set for themselves. New England was an attractive destination. But the Midwest, especially Michigan, was also well suited to their purposes. Migration to Michigan was perfectly logical given the economic situation faced by French Canadians in the nineteenth century—all the more so in that it was consistent with the continental tendency leading the population of the East inevitably toward the land available in the West.

It is important to note that French Canadians' participation in the fur trade did more than improve their living conditions. It enabled them to become familiar with the whole western region, especially that of the Great Lakes. At ease with moving across the continent, they gained valuable knowledge of the Great Lakes and these experiences were present as common subjects of everyday discussion. Also, the territory of Michigan had long been an integral part of the geopolitical reality of Quebec. In spite of the numerous treaties to which it was subject, Michigan remained a territory to which French Canadians had free access over a long period of time. Migration to this region was therefore never considered an expatriation, but rather a relocation within a French Canadian sphere—to which the territory of Michigan belonged.

The high productivity of the wheat lands of the Midwest was a major factor in some of the agricultural problems experienced by French Canadians in the mid-nineteenth century. Just as the Americans of the northeastern states had left their underproductive land in the East to seek better land in the West, the French Canadians, lacking a West of their own, carved out a portion of the Americans' West for themselves. The French Canadians who went to work as day laborers on the farms of New England at the beginning of the nineteenth century became aware that American farmers were facing problems similar to theirs. If the solution of moving west was valid for the Americans, it must have seemed just as valid for them. Finally, it is worthy of note that their work experience in the lumber industry of the Ottawa Valley predisposed them to follow that industry as it moved to new regions of operation, in particular to Michigan.

If Michigan proved to be an attractive region for French Canadians during the 1840s and 1850s, it was because the state possessed both agricultural and industrial potential that corresponded to their work culture and the objectives that many of them had set. Michigan was a natural destination for French Canadians, whose life and work experience were compatible with that environment.

In Michigan, the French Canadians settled particularly in two regions: the Saginaw Valley and the Keweenaw Peninsula. Both these regions underwent rapid industrial development after 1840 based on the exploitation of their forest and mining resources.

Chapter 2

The Development of the Saginaw Valley
and the Keweenaw Peninsula, 1840–1914

In a few years these impenetrable forests will have fallen; the sons of civilization will break the silence of the Saginaw; the banks will be imprisoned by quays; its current, which now flows on unnoticed and tranquil, through a nameless waste, will be stemmed by the prows of vessels. We are perhaps the last travelers allowed to see the primitive grandeur of this solitude.

ALEXIS DE TOCQUEVILLE, 1831

THE DEVELOPMENT OF THE SAGINAW VALLEY, 1840–1900

It was in these highly prescient terms that Alexis de Tocqueville, on a journey to the Saginaw Valley in 1831, foresaw the future development of the region.[1] He saw correctly. In the half-century that followed, the valley would witness encroaching settlement which, along with the beginnings of forestry development, radically changed its physiography and transformed this frontier zone into a major region in the Michigan lumber industry.[2]

Settlement of the Valley

With its immense forest resources and its proximity to the vast network of the Great Lakes, Michigan was well placed to become a primary force in American lumber production.[3]

The Saginaw Valley, which lies at the heart of this forested area in eastern Michigan, had all the elements required to grow into one of the state's most important lumbering centers. Located at the mouth of the Saginaw Bay, the valley possessed a

29

network of waterways ideal for this type of development. Numerous well-nourished tributaries drained an area of nearly 6,000 square miles (8,880 km^2), heavily forested in white pine, before emptying into the leisurely flowing Saginaw River, whose 20-mile (30 km) length was a perfect site for sawmills.[4] Also, the Saginaw Bay offered direct access to Lakes Huron and Erie, enabling the production of the valley to easily reach the markets of the East.[5] But until the middle of the 1830s, there was no incentive to develop the valley, since the first lumber-producing states, such as Maine, New York, and Pennsylvania, could furnish all the wood that was needed,[6] and several more years passed before the right set of conditions arose across the continent to stimulate development of the valley's timber resources.

The Saginaw Valley was settled gradually. Established as a county and opened to settlement in 1822, the valley had only 892 inhabitants in 1840.[7] The difficult access to the heavily wooded and swampy region and its reputation for unhealthiness discouraged settlers from moving there in significant numbers before the 1830s.[8] Still, some settlers dared to move there early in the nineteenth century, among them many of French Canadian origin.[9] As early as 1815, Louis Campau, in the service of the American Fur Company, was assigned to Saginaw City to establish commercial relations with Amerindian tribes and set up a trading post. Campau built the first building in the valley.[10] Several months later, as trade with Amerindian peoples picked up, the management of the American Fur Company sent Jean-Baptiste Desnoyers, another of its French Canadian employees, to Saginaw City to assist Campau in his activities.[11] Alexis de Tocqueville, passing through the region in 1831, reported that the population was limited to about 30 white settlers of Canadian, British, and American origin, living in four or five log houses.[12] The population of the valley, although it had more than doubled from 1830 to 1837, was still under 1,000 in the latter year, having risen from 400 to only 920 inhabitants.

Many of these new arrivals in the 1830s were of French Canadian origin. For example, Jos Tromble, from Wayne County in the southeast part of the territory, settled in the valley in about 1828–30.[13] Having come to work in the fur trade, he acquired a piece of land north of Saginaw City on the eastern bank of the Saginaw River, near the mouth of Saginaw Bay. This location was first called "Lower Saginaw" and was later renamed "Bay City" in 1859.[14] He set up a general store and his business seems to have been profitable. Following Jos, Leon Tromble came to settle in 1831. An inhabitant of Detroit and a former fur trader, Leon worked as an agricultural officer for the American government. He built a house on his own near the Saginaw River, and his family came to join him the following year. In 1834, Benjamin Cushway and John B. Trudell, both former fur traders, also came to settle in Lower Saginaw. Trudell built a house close to that of Leon Tromble, as did Cushway, who also built Trudell a forge to serve the Amerindian bands and the traders.[15]

In 1835, Jos and Mader Tromble, two nephews of Leon, arrived in Lower Saginaw by boat. Of French Canadian origin, they are considered the true founders of Lower Saginaw, as they were the first to exploit the economic potential of the region.[16] The Tromble brothers acquired over three hundred acres of land on the east bank of the river and tried to encourage new settlement there. In 1836, Benoît Tromble arrived in the region and bought a piece of this land from Jos Tromble, and in 1838, a professional hunter named Jos Marsac, also of French Canadian origin, settled in Lower Saginaw.[17]

This first phase of settlement saw the arrival of several promoters from the East who showed an interest in the advantages of the valley. One of the most important was Norman Little. A native of the state of New York, Little was the son of Dr. Charles Little, who had visited Saginaw City in 1822. Dr. Little had bought several acres of land with the idea of developing the region.[18] However, it was his son, a decade later, who sought to realize his father's dream. Norman Little settled in Saginaw City in 1835 and in 1836, for the sum of fifty-five thousand dollars, he acquired holdings in Saginaw City that had belonged to Dr. Abel Millington of Ypsilanti.[19] Little built the first village infrastructures that a frontier town needed if it hoped to receive promoters, speculators, and settlers with suitable amenities.[20]

Lower Saginaw also developed during the 1830s, but at a slower rate. After the Tromble brothers, Marsac, Trudell, and others had become established there, promoters and speculators came to settle in the region. Albert Miller, appointed county judge of Saginaw, acquired a property south of Lower Saginaw in 1836 at the mouth of a river he named Portsmouth and tried to attract investors.

In 1837, James Fraser, a recently arrived Scottish immigrant, moved to Lower Saginaw and founded the Saginaw Bay Land Company to develop the region. This company acquired a large share of the lands belonging to John Riley, a Métis who owned nearly 640 acres on the east bank of the river opposite Lower Saginaw, which had been granted him by the treaty of 1819. In 1843, Fraser decided to restructure the Saginaw Bay Land Company by forming an association with James G. Birney of New York and his brother-in-law, Daniel H. Fitzhugh, who launched the phase of significant development that began in Lower Saginaw in the 1850s.[21]

The Beginnings of Forestry Development in the Lumber Industry, 1840–60

This early settlement, limited as it was and lacking an organized plan, prompted the first efforts to develop the lumber industry in the valley.[22] It was in response to local demand that the first sawmills were founded in the 1830s, initiating the preindustrial development of timber resources.[23] In 1832, the brothers Gardner and Ephraim Williams, who had settled in the region in 1827, erected the first steam-powered sawmill in Saginaw City.[24]

A second sawmill was put up in 1836. Nicknamed the "Big Mill," it was built on the east bank of the Saginaw River in a small village named Buena Vista and financed by three New York entrepreneurs—Mackie, Oakley, and Jennison.[25] Finally, another sawmill was built in Portsmouth in 1837 in which Judge Miller was one of the investors.[26] These first sawmills were small-scale operations with a very limited production capacity. The mill set up in 1832 by the Williams brothers had a daily capacity of only two thousand board feet, while Michigan sawmills at that time were capable of producing up to ten times that quantity per day.[27]

These modest developments were hampered by the economic depression of 1837. Mackie, Oakley, and Jennison, as well as Judge Miller, had to close down their sawmills.[28] The economic recovery of the mid-1840s once again stimulated the interest of promoters and settlers from the Northeast, giving rise to modest islands of population around Saginaw City, East Saginaw, and Lower Saginaw.[29]

On the west bank of the Saginaw River, three small pockets of settlement developed and merged in 1877 to form West Bay City. These included the village of Banks, founded in the 1830s by Joseph Tromble and his brother Mader, and the village of Salzburg, founded by Daniel Fitzhugh in 1859–60, just as salt was beginning to be mined near Saginaw City. The third village was Wenona, built by Henry W. Sage, who in 1863, together with John McGraw of New York, bought a hundred acres of land between Salzburg and Banks for twenty-one thousand dollars to build a modern sawmill that began production in 1865.[30]

Thus, from 1830 to 1860 the Saginaw Valley was developed largely through the efforts of promoters and entrepreneurs who managed to create an infrastructure that attracted settlers to Saginaw City, East Saginaw, and Lower Saginaw (Bay City). By 1860, the respective populations of these towns stood at 1,699, 3,000, and 810.[31]

But beyond the efforts of these promoters, the central impetus for the second wave of development of the valley was the beginning of industrial exploitation of its timber resources. This attracted a massive influx of new settlers.[32]

Changes in the Lumber Industry

The years following the depression saw major economic transformations in the valley. Preindustrial operations gave way to large-

scale industrial enterprises. This came about as the lumber industry was obliged to find new locations for the logging of pine, thus
stimulating massive development of timber resources in the Saginaw region.[33]

The lumber industry of North America had moved progressively across the continent since its inception. At the start of the
nineteenth century, the first pine frontier was in the northeastern region. But gradually—following the natural pine belt that
stretched from Maine to Minnesota, passing through New York
and Pennsylvania on the American side, and New Brunswick,
Quebec, and Ontario on the Canadian side, all the way to Hudson Bay—the timber frontier moved from east to west as easily
accessible stands of pine became depleted.[34]

Table 2.1 traces the evolution of the American timber frontier. Until the 1830s, Maine, the "Pine Tree State," dominated
national production.[35] During the 1840s and 1850s, New York
displaced Maine in the first position, and in 1860 Pennsylvania
surpassed New York. In 1870, Michigan became the top national
producer, a position it retained until the 1890s.

The succession of different states to the title of largest national
producer in the forestry sector clearly illustrates the retreat of the
pine frontier. Declining production in these regions did not mean,
however, that lumber activity ceased entirely.[36] The marginalization of certain states was the result of the increasing inaccessibility
of the pine resources in their areas. When resources are difficult
to access, production costs are higher, making it more difficult to
sell the product on the market and reducing profitability. With
this in mind, many entrepreneurs planned their future activities,
looking toward the next timber frontier. A number of them acquired timberlands at low prices further west and built sawmills
there in order to be well placed when the development of the
lumber industry had reached that far.[37]

In the early 1840s, lumber entrepreneurs in the eastern regions of the continent showed a marked interest in the Saginaw
Valley's resources and were prompted to make large investments
there. Their arrival had a notable effect on the nature of lumber

TABLE 2.1
Most Productive States in the Forestry Sector, 1840–1900*

| | | | Rank | | |
Years	First	Second	Third	Fourth	Fifth
1840	New York	Maine	Pennsylvania	Virginia	South Carolina
1850	New York	Pennsylvania	Maine	Ohio	Michigan
1860	Pennsylvania	New York	Michigan	Maine	Ohio
1870	Michigan	Pennsylvania	New York	Wisconsin	Indiana
1880	Michigan	Pennsylvania	Wisconsin	New York	Indiana
1890	Michigan	Wisconsin	Pennsylvania	Minnesota	Washington
1900	Wisconsin	Michigan	Minnesota	Pennsylvania	Arkansas

Sources: These data are taken from the appendix to Lewis, *Lumberman from Flint.* Lewis prepared the statistics from Steer, *Lumber Production,* 11).

*Production measured in dollar value and number of board feet

operations in the valley. No doubt the best illustration of this is the 1846 purchase by two entrepreneurs—Curtis Emerson of Vermont and Charles Grant of New York—of an old sawmill that had closed down during the depression. They bought the mill for six thousand dollars from Mackie, Oakley, and Jennison. They also acquired 175 acres of standing pine in the area and invested ten thousand dollars to update the mill's obsolete equipment and raise its yearly productive capacity to 3 million board feet, thus transforming a modest sawmill into a modern lumber-producing operation that could supply a vast market.[38]

By 1847, the Emerson Mill's first shipment of pine left the valley for the C. P. Williams & Company docks in Albany, New York. Albany, along with Buffalo and Tonawanda, was one of the most important centers of lumber distribution in the East.[39] As a result of the excellent reception given the Emerson shipment, eastern entrepreneurs showed increased interest in the valley.[40] This initial shipment marked the real beginning of the lumber manufacturing industry of the region.[41]

At the beginning of the 1850s, the *Bangor Daily Whig and Courier* of Bangor, Maine, informed entrepreneurs in the region that ten thousand acres of pine forest were for sale in the Saginaw Valley.[42] Through the 1850s and 1860s, businessmen from Maine, such as Murphy, Dorrs, and Leadbetter, ventured west to the valley and invested there.[43] Charles Merril, who had run a sawmill in Lincoln, Maine, settled in the valley in the mid-1850s, as did C. K. Eddy just after the Civil War.[44] Others from Vermont, among them Ammi W. Wright and Ezra Rust, also invested in the region and managed lumber mills there in the 1850s.[45]

Lumber entrepreneurs from New York also became interested in the valley's resources. Samuel Webster in the 1850s, and Daniel Hardin, A. T. Bliss, W. S. Green, Albert F. Cook, James Tolbert, and Wellington R. Burt in the 1860s were among those who invested in the region.[46] The best-known figure was certainly Henry W. Sage, a businessman from Ithaca, New York. In 1864, he moved his lumber operation from Lake Simcoe, Ontario, and with his partner, John McGraw, set up the most productive sawmill in the valley at Wenona.[47] Even Canadian investors were attracted to the valley. A. H. Mershon (Marchand), who had worked in the lumber industry in New York before returning to Canada to run a large sawmill, settled in the Saginaw in 1851. With the help of Jesse Hoyt, he built the first sanding factory in the region.[48] The arrival of these entrepreneurs meant that more capital was locally invested, newer and more productive sawmills were built, and labor was in high demand.

In 1840, Saginaw County had only six sawmills and $18 000 in invested capital, for an average of $3,000 per mill. Ten years later, the number of sawmills had increased to eight, but invested capital had reached $103,000, averaging $12,950 per mill, a rise of more than 300 percent. From 1850 to 1855, the number of sawmills rose from eight to nearly sixty. In the same period, production went from 7 million board feet to close to 100 million board feet, and the number of workers increased from about 100 to 843.[49]

The eastern industrialists also equipped the new mills with the latest technology. Steam became the main energy source for the mills, powering more that 90 percent of them in 1860.[50] More effective saws were also introduced in the 1840s and 1850s, including gate saws, mulay saws, and circular saws, which improved productivity and quality of cut.[51]

The industrial exploitation of timber resources presented hiring problems for the entrepreneurs. These problems were not new. Every time the timber frontier had advanced into isolated, thinly settled regions, lumber companies had had to come to terms with the issue.[52] The development of agricultural communities in the valley had made it possible to partially meet this new demand.[53] But in the 1850s, the local community was not sufficient. In 1854, the *Saginaw Times* published an advertisement announcing that the opening of new sawmills in the region required five hundred new workers in the valley immediately.[54]

To help compensate for this lack of local manpower, the entrepreneurs of the Northeast had established a hiring strategy of bringing qualified workers from their former workforces in the eastern forestry centers to the new regions they were developing in the West.[55] As early as the 1830s, many entrepreneurs in Maine were already recruiting workers from the Northeast to help them in their relocation to the West.[56] In 1838, some of them advertised in Bangor's *Daily Whig and Courier* that they required the services of workers familiar with the use of circular saws, as well as teamsters and lumberjacks, to work in the pine forests of the West.[57] Many workers employed in the forests of Maine, Vermont, and New York thus found themselves relocating to Pennsylvania and Michigan.[58] This hiring strategy transformed lumber workers into migrant workers, moving west with the westward advance of the timber frontier, like the industry to which they were attached.[59]

It is difficult to estimate how many lumber workers in the Saginaw Valley came from the eastern states. But it seems that the great majority of skilled workers were recruited there.[60] Conditions were certainly favorable to this process. The depletion of resources in workers' places of origin gradually reduced employment opportunities and they soon found themselves faced with a problematic choice: to become a farmer in a sector in decline in the Northeast, to become a worker in the fledgling manufacturing industry, or to remain a lumber worker and follow the industry as it relocated. Many experienced workers chose the latter option, which offered them continuity of employment.[61] In this way, a market base of migratory labor in the lumber industry was created, forging direct relations between the older and newer regions of development.

Before the Civil War, the great majority of lumber workers in the Saginaw Valley came from the eastern states, particularly Maine, Vermont, New York, and Pennsylvania, while a few came from neighboring Ohio.[62] These Americans were not the only ones, however, to contribute to the workforce. In progressive waves, thousands of immigrants of German, Irish, and Scandinavian origin, as well as both Anglophone and Francophone Canadians, joined the valley's workforce.[63]

In this period, work in the forestry sector was often merely a source of supplementary income. The majority of the population of the region made their living primarily from agriculture, seeking extra income in the winter by working in the woods or by selling the products of their land-clearing efforts to the nearby sawmills. This complementary relationship between agriculture and lumber work functioned extremely well before the Civil War. However, after the war, the sawmills' greater demands for lumber extended the duration of cutting operations to the point where this complementarity was no longer so well balanced. This situation forced lumber companies to look for larger supplies of labor and also for laborers more closely linked to the industry.[64]

Work and Working Conditions in the Lumber Industry

The activities of the lumber industry may be divided into three distinct categories: felling trees, transporting logs to the sawmills, and transforming the logs into boards at the sawmill. Whatever the type of activity, however, the labor force throughout the nineteenth century was essentially masculine and adult, as the great majority of operations required strenuous physical effort of which women and children were rarely capable.

The duration of the logging season could vary according to weather conditions, but it generally began in early fall and ended early in the spring.[65] Before the Civil War, the logging camps were rudimentary structures. Since the pine forests were not far away, the first camps were located close to villages and generally also to a river. Activities at this time were simple, consisting of felling the trees, cutting them into logs, and transporting them to a nearby mill or riverbank so that after the spring thaw they could easily be floated to the sawmill.

Activities associated with log driving in the valley did not begin until the 1850s, as before then the proximity of logging and processing sites made it unnecessary. It was in the springtime, once melting ice had raised the water level enough, that log driving began. At first, before 1850, the log drivers were recruited primarily among the lumberjacks who had been working in the camps during the winter. Soon, however, the lumber companies turned to specialists for this well-paid work, which earned a logger $2.50 a day on average.[66] The first step in their work was freeing the logs, which had been stored near the river during the winter and were still imprisoned under the snow and ice. Next, the drivers had to control the direction of the logs on these fast-flowing rivers by means of poles, so that the logs reached the sawmill as quickly as possible. The log-driving season ran from mid-April to mid-November, but the duration of this activity could vary, depending on the quantity of logs to be delivered.[67] Once it began, there was no possibility of taking a break; since there was no way to interrupt the flow of water, the drivers had to work continuously until the end of the season. The development and diversification of lumber activities in the 1850s, when several companies arrived in the valley, led Charles Merril, the owner of a lumber company in the region, to establish a private log-driving firm on the Tittabawassee River in 1856 to transport logs to his sawmill in East Saginaw on the Saginaw River.[68]

Once the logs reached the sawmill, the final task was to transform them into boards. Until the mid-1870s, sawmills in the valley were built right by the Saginaw River, because river transportation was the only way to bring logs to the sawmill. As the logs arrived near their respective mills, they were removed from the water by a system of pulleys and ropes that raised them to a ramp near the first floor, where they were cut lengthwise into boards. The boards then received a preliminary sanding, after which they were set out to dry on the companies' docks near the river, ready to be loaded onto ships for transportation to the markets in the East. These processing operations began in April or May and ended in September-October.[69]

At first, the workforce in the sawmills consisted mainly of local farmers or sons of American or immigrant farmers. Although some of these workers rapidly learned the basics of sawmill work, in the 1850s, a number of entrepreneurs decided to rely increasingly on experienced, specialized workers who were already employed in the East.[70] Until the 1870s, the logging camps were generally small and their output modest. The largest could handle from twenty to thirty workers, though many employed fewer than that, and produced only 1.5 to 3 million board feet per season.[71] The camp workers worked from sunrise to sunset six days a week, and rested on Sunday.[72]

As a rule, before the end of the 1850s, working conditions in all phases of the lumber industry were difficult. Isolated as they were, workers in the logging camps were at the mercy of their employers. Workers refusing to work longer than usual hours could be thrown out of the camps, often unable to find other logging jobs in the middle of the season. Their wages could be lowered at will by an employer because of a bad season. In addition, serious accidents could occur during the felling phase. Indeed, deep lacerations and fractures caused by falls from trees were common among the lumber workers, as were contagious diseases (smallpox, typhoid fever), and the felling areas were usually so distant from any place where medical help could be obtained that some initially minor wounds or illnesses proved fatal. As some woodsmen said at the time, "going to the pineries [was] like going to the war."[73] Logging was so dangerous that it was long described as a "widow-maker."[74] It is thus not surprising that the workers' main demands concerned the improvement of safety on the job and better hygiene and more sanitary conditions in the camps. It was primarily in their strong tendency to move from one camp to another that workers expressed dissatisfaction with their working conditions.

Camps that employed many workers generally had better working conditions. Given the major initial investment required to set up the camp, entrepreneurs did not want to risk having production disrupted by excessive fluctuations in the labor force.[75] To discourage their workers from leaving, some companies established bonus plans, which could add up to 10 percent to a season's earnings, and which were reserved for workers who remained with the company for a whole season.[76]

The wages earned by lumberjacks depended on their qualifications. Before the Civil War, the average wage fluctuated between $20 and $26 a month—about a dollar a day, with food and lodging included.[77] Payment was in the form of time checks, which could be cashed at the company's offices in the neighboring village.[78] In some cases, companies paid their workers partly in cash and partly in merchandise, using vouchers that could be exchanged at the company's general store.[79] Of course, purchases made by the workers during the logging season, such as those for tobacco, clothing, or new boots, were carefully noted and deducted from the wages paid at the end of the season.

In the sawmills, wages also varied according to workers' qualifications. About 1850, the average wage of a common laborer was $1 a day. In 1860, it was $1.122,[80] or between $30 and $50 a month, but the workers had to pay for their food and lodging.[81] Before 1880, the working day was twelve hours. Women and children could easily find employment in the sawmills, whereas they could not in the log-cutting and driving operations. Boys were often hired for general services or as messengers or sweepers and were paid half the salary of an adult male. Women were employed primarily as clerks, with salaries between 25 percent and 30 percent that of men.[82] Depending on the employer, sawmill workers might be paid weekly, twice a month, or—typically—once a month.[83]

The Civil War and the Consolidation of the Lumber Industry, 1860–80

The Civil War greatly disrupted the development of the lumber industry, creating financial difficulties for the companies and causing market contraction, a serious scarcity of labor, and a decline in production.[84] By 1863, the situation had improved, and production reached nearly 134 million board feet, more than 10 percent above the 1860 level. But it was in the 1870s, as table 2.2 shows, that the number of sawmills stabilized while production rose steadily, reaching a record level of more than a billion board feet in 1882. This rise in output increased the companies' demand for labor. In 1860, sawmills in the valley employed 14.2 workers on average. By 1870, the average number of workers per mill had reached 46.1.[85]

The Saginaw Valley became the center of lumber production in Michigan after the Civil War. This development was made possible by the introduction of new technology, which raised productivity but which also affected the hitherto relatively harmonious relations between entrepreneurs and workers.

The logging camps were the first to undergo major changes. As timber resources near the villages became exhausted, the entrepreneurs began to set up their camps deeper in the interior of the lands, which made them less accessible. During the same period, several factors also increased the efficiency and productivity of the camps, including a technological improvement (the saw, which was more rapid and easier to handle, gradually replaced the ax), a more rigorous division of labor, and the employment of specialized workers. The workers still labored twelve hours a day, six days a week. Wages continued to vary according to the type of work done. In general, however, they continued to average about twenty to twenty-five dollars a month, ranging from fifteen dollars for common laborers to thirty to forty dollars for skilled workers.[86]

The ethnic composition of the labor force, which was relatively homogenous before the Civil War, became much more diverse thereafter. The Americans, Germans, Irish, and handful

TABLE 2.2

**Number of Sawmills and Production of Pinewood in Millions
of Board Feet in the Saginaw Valley 1850–92**

Year	Number of Sawmills	Production	Year	Number of Sawmills	Production
1850	8	8	1872	—	602
1852	—	90	1874	—	583
1856	—	110	1878	64	574
1858	43	106	1880	57 or 61	873
1860	57	125	1882	70	1,011
1862	77	128	1884	70	964*
1864	77	215	1886	64	785
1866	—	349	1888	63	863
1868	89	457	1890	58	815
1870	83	577	1892	—	708

Sources: The information in this table comes from various sources. Although there is agreement on the evolution of production, the authors disagree on the number of sawmills in operation in the valley in different periods (Dunbar, *Michigan*, 397; Sweet, "Brief History of Saginaw County," 499–500; Leeson, *History of Saginaw*, 383, 389; Benson, "Logs and Lumber," 210; Lewis and Headley, *Annual Statement of the Business of Saginaw Valley*, 3–4; *Industries of the Saginaws*, 32–39.

*Data based on the annual review of the Saginaw Board of Trade, which from 1880 to 1892 published a résumé of the economic activities in the valley. Before 1884, the board of trade listed the production of pine and hardwood separately. Subsequently it combined these types of production, which gives a higher figure and explains why my figures are sometimes different from those generally given for the production of pine. For the year 1890 in particular, it was impossible to separate the two types of production.

of Canadians were joined by Swedes, Poles, and a few Amerindian workers, followed later by increased numbers of English and French Canadians.[87]

The slight improvement in working conditions did not succeed in eliminating the recurrent problem of high labor mobility that faced entrepreneurs. Working conditions remained difficult, and the quality of the food and of sanitary conditions were often still poor.

The introduction in the 1870s of railroad logging—the use of narrow-gauge railways as an alternative to the rivers for transporting logs to the sawmills—transformed the lumber industry.

No longer dependent on climatic conditions, the industry could produce all year round.[88] This prolongation of the logging season, combined with the policy of the lumber companies, whose motto often seemed to be "Cut all you can and get out," rapidly exhausted the timber resources and accelerated the westward advance of the pine frontier.

But it was work in the sawmills that was most affected by the modernization of the means of production. The first step in this modernization process was the introduction of more effective saws, which greatly increased productivity.[89] In 1860, a sawmill had to employ one worker for every thousand board feet that it aimed to produce per day; in 1888, with the same labor force, the sawmill could produce three times as much.[90] Wages rose considerably—from $1 a day in 1850 for common labor to $2.19 in 1873, the highest point wages reached.[91] Table 2.3 shows the changes in wages for sawmill workers.

In the course of the 1870s, structural unemployment became a factor in the economic landscape. Previously, periods of inactivity had been short and concentrated in the springtime, at the end of logging operations, and in the fall, when activities in the sawmills came to an end.[92] But technological innovation had lengthened both the logging and processing seasons. Given that the lumber processing companies hired all their workers at the outset of their activities, all their positions were filled by the time the loggers returned from the forests.[93]

As the lumber industry grew, the small towns in the region developed rapidly, becoming multiethnic urban centers where many related economic sectors grew up: shipbuilding, manufacturing, railroad construction, and public services.[94] As table 2.4 shows, the population of the lumber towns grew significantly after the Civil War.

Throughout the nineteenth century, the population of Saginaw City was much larger than that of Bay City. Beginning in 1880, however, Bay City experienced a spurt of growth that considerably reduced the gap with Saginaw. In the period after the Civil War, these towns ceased to be simple way stations for

TABLE 2.3

Wages (in Dollars per Day) for Sawmill Work in the Saginaw Valley, 1860–77

	Year			
Type of work	1860	1873	1874	1877
Supervisor	1.75	5.00	4.00	3.50
Planer	2.50	4.38	3.50	3.00
Mechanic	1.75	4.68	3.75	3.25
Circular saw operator	2.00	5.00	4.00	3.25
Multiple saw operator	1.50	4.07	3.25	0.50
Finisher	1.125	3.13	2.50	2.00
Common laborer	1.122	2.19	1.75	1.25

Sources: Lumberman's Gazette, August 16, 1877, 100.

*According to the author's calculations, the wages for 1873 are calculated on the basis of the figures for 1874. During 1873, the managers of the sawmills decided to lower the pay scale by 12.5 percent. Thus, the wages indicated by the *Lumberman's Gazette* for 1874 have already been lowered by this amount, and the figures for 1873 are 12.5 percent higher than those for 1874. Note that wages did not rise equally for all workers. The salary of a supervisor increased by 185 percent, while that of a common laborer rose by only 60 percent between 1860 and 1873.

the workers. They became places where people wanted to settle, places where stable communities could grow up with their own social institutions. This demographic development was the direct result of the lumber industry's dynamism. Patterns of expansion varied, however. In Saginaw City, the phase of rapid development occurred between 1864 and 1870, at the conclusion of the Civil War, when the population increased by more than 110 percent. During this period, Bay City grew by only 46 percent. But the depression of the 1870s hit Saginaw City harder than Bay City: its population grew by only 8.8 percent between 1874 and 1880, whereas Bay City experienced its strongest growth of the nineteenth century in this period, growing by nearly 94 percent from 1870 to 1874 and nearly 98 percent from 1874 to 1880.

The depression that began in 1873 was difficult for the lumber sector. The overproduction at the beginning of the depression led to a dramatic fall in the price of lumber products. In fact,

TABLE 2.4

**Population of the Main Lumber Towns in the Saginaw Valley,
1860–1900**

	Saginaw*	East Saginaw	Bay City	West Bay City**
1860	4,704	3,000	1,583	—
1864	8,928	—	4,848	—
1870	18,811	13,225	7,064	—
1874	27,148	—	13,690	—
1880	29,541	19,016	27,040	6,397
1884	42,845	29,100	38,902	9,492
1890	46,322	—	40,730	12,981
1894	44,643	—	42,382	—
1900	42,345	—	40,747	13,119

Sources: McGaugh, "Settlement of Saginaw Basin," 124–25. Data for 1880, 1884, and 1890 are from Kilar, "Lumbertowns," 238, and includes East Saginaw and West Bay City. For the towns of East Saginaw and West Bay City, published state census data were used.

*In 1889, the towns of East Saginaw and Saginaw merged.

** West Bay City did not exist under that name until 1877, when the villages of Banks, Salzburg, and Wenona merged. In 1905 West Bay City merged with Bay City.

overproduction was a recurrent problem throughout the century. Lumber output, which had long been dependent on climatic conditions, was inherently unpredictable. The entrepreneurs could have coordinated their efforts in order to maintain an even level of production, but their strongly individualistic outlook and desire to make the highest profits possible meant that their discussions rarely produced any concrete results.

The effects of the economic depression began to be felt in the fall of 1873. As early as September, the entrepreneurs conferred to seek solutions. One response was to delay sending workers into the woods and to recall those who were already there.[95] The entrepreneurs also imposed a 12.5 percent wage cut: applied from November 1 on, it brought wages down to their pre–Civil War level.[96] The curtailment of logging activities in the winter of 1873–74 created considerable unemployment and caused wages to fall.[97]

The wage cut imposed by the entrepreneurs was the first of several declines in workers' wages in the 1870s. From an average of $2.30 in 1872, the sawmill workers' daily wage fell to $1.75 in 1874 and to $1.25 in 1877—a fall of nearly 50 percent in five years. In May 1877, the wages of a common laborer in the sawmills ranged from 90 cents to $1.25 a day.[98]

The workers' situation continued to deteriorate throughout the depression. The labor market remained crowded, and many of the unemployed were reduced to the state of vagabonds within a few weeks, wandering about in search of food and shelter and begging at the doors of hotels.[99] Under these conditions, some families were attracted to agriculture.[100] Many, however, preferred to leave the valley to seek work elsewhere.

The Decline of the Lumber Industry, 1880–1900

The first signs of recovery were visible in the fall of 1878, when production rose rapidly. This had a positive impact on employment: the average number of employees per sawmill, which had fluctuated between forty-nine and fifty-six during the depression, jumped to sixty-two in 1880. The recovery was weaker on the wage front, but near the close of the decade, wages climbed once more. In 1879, laborers in the sawmills were earning between $1.125 and $1.50 a day on average, while the daily wage of skilled workers ranged from $2 to $4.[101] Production, which had hovered around 590 million board feet during the depression, soared to a record of one billion board feet in 1882.[102] The depression had, however, eliminated over twenty sawmills; from eighty-three in 1870, their number had fallen to sixty-one in 1880.[103]

But the recovery was of short duration. Beginning in 1884, the lumber industry entered a progressive structural decline, which was no longer the result of an economic downturn but reflected the exhaustion of natural resources. Already in the early 1880s, there were signs that the glory days of the lumber industry were definitely behind it. Some entrepreneurs had begun to explore new forest lands. In 1881, the Lumberman's Gazette reported that

many entrepreneurs had gone to Duluth, Minnesota, to investi-
gate the quality of the timberlands there.[104] In 1882, an entrepreneur from East Saginaw purchased pinewoods on the Ontonagon
River in the Upper Peninsula.[105] The workers also realized that the
market for their labor had declined. Hundreds of camp workers left
the Saginaw Valley after the 1882–83 logging season with their
wages and their savings, bound for a place further west where they
could acquire a piece of land to settle on.[106] Many sawmills were
put up for sale; that of Henry W. Sage was not sold until February
1892.[107]

A new crisis of overproduction began in May 1884, causing a 30 percent drop in the price of pine.[108] It also killed off a
good number of sawmills and was responsible for considerable loss
of employment. Signs saying "NO MEN WANTED" were posted on
the doors of the lumber companies' main recruitment offices during the winter of 1884–85.[109] Wages plummeted. In the logging
camps, wages for the 1884–85 season averaged about twelve dollars a month, down from twenty-five to thirty dollars at the outset
of the 1880s.[110] The sawmill workers' wages also fell considerably,
and a large number of workers lost their jobs.

The Saginaw Valley Strike of 1885

Since the earliest days of the lumber industry in the valley, labor
relations had never posed a serious problem. Faced with employers
who possessed impressive means of defending their interests, the
workers had had difficulty organizing. The seasonal character of
the work had discouraged the development of solidarity and class
consciousness. The isolation in which the workers were confined
and their own individualism represented further obstacles to the
emergence of labor militancy.[111]

Under these circumstances, it is astonishing that there were
any strikes at all. Work stoppages demanding higher wages and a
shorter working day occurred in 1865 and 1870 in Saginaw City
and in 1872 in Bay City and Saginaw City.[112] These were sponta-
neous, unorganized strikes, limited in time and space and involv-
ing only a fraction of the workers. They produced no concrete

results.[113] But the strike that broke out in 1885 was a different matter.[114]

This strike by workers from the sawmills and saltworks lasted two months. It, like previous strikes, failed to win the workers' demands, but it was a turning point for the history of the region for two reasons: first, because it illustrated the unease that had characterized labor relations for some years, and second because it marked the beginning of the end for the lumber industry.

At the beginning of the sawmill season in the spring of 1885, the owners had let it be known that because of the fall in the price of wood, wages would be reduced by 12 percent to 25 percent.[115] This decision, which lowered the average wage from $1.98 to $1.77 a day, was more or less accepted by the workers. As compensation for the lost wages, however, they demanded that the working day be reduced from eleven to ten hours, and that they receive their pay regularly every two weeks. As things stood, nearly 50 percent of the sawmill workers were paid only once a month, which prevented them from planning their budget and obliged them to rely on credit while waiting for their pay. Finally, all the workers wanted to be paid in cash: nearly 20 percent were paid in "store's money," which could only be used in the company store. The negative response to these demands added to the workers' dissatisfaction.

Meanwhile, Thomas Barry presented a bill for the ten-hour day in the Michigan state legislature. Barry, a member of the Knights of Labor, had been elected to the legislature in 1884 on the Democrat-Whig ticket. His bill, which included all factories, workshops, sawmills, logging camps, mines, and other manufacturing activity,[116] was supported by the national movement for the ten-hour day and accepted by most members of the legislature.

The traditional interpretation of the strike that followed is that it grew out of a simple misunderstanding concerning when the new law would come into force.[117] Some newspapers had discussed the law without indicating when it would take effect, and the workers had believed the date to be July 1, 1885, whereas in reality it was September 15 or 18.[118] According to this interpre-

tation, this misunderstanding led the workers to strike in order
to force the entrepreneurs to respect the new legislation at the
beginning of July.

A 1976 study presents a different hypothesis.[119] The workers
knew from the start of the strike that the law would come into
force only in mid-September because they knew the legislator who
had proposed the bill—Thomas Barry even acted as their ad hoc
leader during the strike. And it was precisely because they knew
that the law would not take effect before September that they
went on strike in July. They knew that mid-September coincided
with the end of the wood-processing season, and that they would
have to wait until the beginning of the new season in the sawmills,
in spring 1886, to enjoy the shorter working day. According to this
interpretation, the principal motive for the strike was thus to be
able to benefit from the shorter working day right away.[120]

The strikers were of diverse ethnic origin. The arrival of thousands of immigrants from Canada and various European countries had greatly diversified the ethnic composition of the labor
force.[121] This could have caused problems of organization, logis-
tics, and communication, as it did in a number of strikes in the
United States in this period. This was not the case at all, however. A strong sense of cohesion led the workers to develop a
class consciousness. The entrepreneurs were never able to play
on the strikers' ethnic diversity to weaken their solidarity, which
was reinforced by the holding of daily meetings of all strikers and
supporters in Madison Park or at Lafayette Hall in Bay City.[122]
However, within a labor force in which native-born Americans
predominated, it was the workers of Polish and German origin
who spearheaded this strike in Bay City and they who were arrested when the police intervened.[123] And when the strike spread
to Saginaw City, it was the French Canadians who were the most
active.[124]

Table 2.5 illustrates the ethnic diversity of the labor force including the large number of French Canadians within it at the
beginning of the strike. Because they represented a large proportion of the group, their participation was a determining factor in

TABLE 2.5

Ethnic Origin of the Labor Force in the Sawmills and Saltworks of the Saginaw Valley on July 1, 1885, by Number and Percentage

Origin	Number	Percentage
United States	2,119	38.0
Quebec	1,330	23.9
Germany	1,121	20.1
Poland	584	10.5
Ireland	200	3.6
Sweden	67	1.2
Bohemia	15	0.3
Scotland	8	0.2
England	3	0.1
Unknown	107	2.1
Total	5,554	

Source: State of Michigan, *Third Annual Report of the Bureau of Labor and Industrial Statistics*, 125.

the outcome of the strike. But in several respects, their role was less than entirely beneficial. On the one hand, Lafayette Hall, which was built in the 1860s by the *Société de bienfaisance canadienne française Lafayette* of Bay City for its offices and community services, was one of the places where the strikers often met to plan their strategy.[125] The fact that this hall, clearly identified with the French Canadian community, was used for meetings reflects the active participation of the French Canadian contingent in the strike.

But their role was not confined to this contribution. On Wednesday, August 12, 1885, when support for the strike was beginning to ebb, the strikers disrupted the activities of two saltworks that had recommenced production on a sporadic basis in Bay City. A group of three hundred strikers armed with sticks had no difficulty bringing production to a halt in these factories. As they were leaving one factory, they encountered Sheriff Brennan and his deputy sheriffs, who had been called to the scene. The sheriff ordered the group to disperse, and when they refused, fired shots into the air. Some of the strikers had the distinct impression that the shots were aimed in their direction. They rushed at the forces of order and a fight ensued, which culminated in the arrest and imprisonment of the main strike leaders. Nine strikers were formally accused of incitement to riot. Five of them were of French Canadian origin: Peter Payment, Charles Lamaux, Fred Hamon, Theodore Shabaneaux, and Alex Gravel. [126]

This two-month strike ended in failure for the 5,550 workers who had paralyzed the valley's seventy-seven sawmills and the fifty-eight saltworks adjacent to the mills. [127] The work stoppage had allowed the entrepreneurs to sell off the backlog of stock that had accumulated on the docks, which caused the price of wood to rise. [128] On September 1, 1885, normal operations had resumed in all the sawmills and saltworks. [129] And in mid-September, most of the sawmills and saltworks reduced their wages and working hours. [130]

This strike had a significance that went beyond the mere desire for a shorter working day. It reflected the frustration experienced by workers faced with employers who constantly and exclusively sought to protect their own interests. We have seen that several years earlier some of these entrepreneurs had demonstrated their indifference to the fate of the valley, its population, and the resources they had once so prized by pulling out operations to go west. The strike also forced many families to leave the region. [131] Some heads of companies had indicated clearly that they would not rehire the strike leaders the following year. [132] But above all, the strike spelled the end of the "pine era" in the valley as paternalistic labor relations, long typical of the companies, were undermined.

The lumber industry remained active for a few more years. But after 1886, pine production was unstable and then entered a slow but progressive decline. [133] During its decline, many plans for the diversification of the valley's economy and urban centers were presented. On March 3, 1890, the political authorities of Saginaw and East Saginaw decided to merge in order to instill a new dynamism in the region. In 1891, the Saginaw Improvement Company was established. Its objective—to stimulate the economic development of the region by selling land for agricultural use at affordable prices—offered an indication of the region's new vocation.[134]

In Bay City, however, the entrepreneurs remained active in the lumber industry. A number of them imported logs from Canada or northern Michigan to use in their sawmills. The result of their persistence was that when the lumber industry finally ended once and for all, Bay City was ill prepared for the new economic challenges.[135]

During the same period that saw the development of the Michigan lumber industry, the exploitation of copper mines in the Keweenaw Peninsula also became an important factor in the state's industrial history.

THE DEVELOPMENT OF THE KEWEENAW PENINSULA, 1840–1914

No copper of any account had yet been obtained from any but the Pittsburg or Cliff mine, nor was any of consequence shipped from the Point, save as aforesaid, while I was interested there. Shareholders, who had raised their $10,000 to $50,000 in fond expectation of early returns, found in time that every cent, and generally more, had been expended in constructing a rude pier whereon to land their supplies, cutting a road thence to their location, building a few rude shanties, drawing up their tools, . . . another, and still another assessment being required . . . to sink a shaft on the vein far enough to determine whether they had any ore or metal to mine. By this time, their patience, or their faith . . . had generally failed, and they were ready to sell out for a song, or abandon the enterprise in despair or disgust. Such is, in essence, the history of most mining enterprises on Lake Superior.[136]

Such was the harsh opinion of the celebrated American journal-
ist Horace Greely concerning the mining situation in the Keweenaw Peninsula in 1868. Yet twenty years earlier, Greely had
been dazzled by the peninsula's mining potential. He had visited
the peninsula in 1847, and had been so impressed that he had
acquired mining shares and had even become an administrator
of the Pennsylvania Mining Company, which was active in the
Michigan mines. Like a number of other investors, Greely soon
realized that it was necessary to invest a great deal before the mining sector would yield any profits. But although some people had
lost thousands in a mining adventure, others were not discouraged
and continued to invest in the region.

It was in this context that the Keweenaw Peninsula, which
included the counties of Houghton, Ontonagon, and Keweenaw,
gradually developed. The exploitation of mineral resources became an engine of social and economic development, transforming an isolated area into one of America's key mining regions.

Initial Exploration and Prospecting, 1840–60

The Keweenaw Peninsula is located in the northwestern part of a
larger peninsula that forms the northernmost section of Michigan.
The Keweenaw Peninsula is an arm of land that reaches into the
center of Lake Superior. The area is rich in mineral and timber
resources, but it was above all its immense wealth of copper ores
that led to its development.

The mining potential of the Keweenaw Peninsula had been
known for a long time. Certain obstacles had to be overcome,
however, before systematic exploitation could begin. The first
was major: the region did not belong to the United States.[137]
The eastern part of the Upper Peninsula, from Mackinac to Sault
Sainte Marie, had been part of the territory of Michigan since
its organization in 1805. But the western part, where the mining resources were located, had always been a possession of the
Chippewa nation.

In addition, the Keweenaw Peninsula constituted a hostile —

and therefore unattractive—environment. Winters were harsh, while in summer it swarmed with a large variety of mosquitoes, including one, the "Keweenaw Eagle," whose name suggests the damage it could cause. The region was also very isolated. The nearest town, Green Bay, Wisconsin, was nearly 300 miles (556 km) to the south, and navigation on Lake Superior, which was impossible during the five winter months, was dangerous whenever the lake was windswept.[138] The peninsula's development thus awaited the emergence of a favorable set of circumstances.

In 1820, an expedition led by Henry R. Schoolcraft confirmed the existence of copper deposits in the region.[139] The ensuing negotiations with the Indians led to the signing in 1826 of the Fond du Lac Treaty, which authorized Americans to do prospecting on Amerindian lands.[140] Another obstacle was removed in 1837, when the western part of the peninsula was annexed—without Amerindian consent—to the territory of Michigan, which became a state at the same time.

Within the year, the governor of the new state of Michigan, Stevens T. Mason, named Douglas Houghton to the position of official state geologist. Houghton surveyed the whole of the state and subdivided the land in order to accelerate its development. In 1841, he confirmed the presence of important copper deposits in the region. However, he warned potential prospectors that the ore was imprisoned in the rock and could only be extracted by means of state-of-the-art techniques.[141] The American authorities rapidly undertook new negotiations with the Amerindian bands.[142] With the signing of the Treaty of La Pointe in 1842, the Americans acquired all lands west of the Chocolay River, including the copper territory. All necessary conditions were now in place for the profitable development of the region.

"Copper Fever," 1843–47

In 1843, the American government set up a mining office in the small town of Copper Harbor on the shores of Lake Superior, on the west side of the Keweenaw Peninsula. This office was responsible for issuing mining permits in the region.[143] In the summer of 1843, only a few prospectors had been drawn to Copper Harbor,[144] but by the following spring the news had spread and the Keweenaw Peninsula was overrun with hordes of amateur prospectors and speculators convinced that they would find the mother lode that would make them a fortune overnight. The whole region was in the grip of "copper fever."

Rapidly, areas of exploitation were staked out. The first area developed at the extreme northeastern point of the peninsula, where small villages like Copper Harbor, Eagle Harbor, and Eagle River had sprung up. The second covered the other extremity of the peninsula, to the southwest, where prospecting was done on the banks of the Ontonagon. A third mining area—the richest of the three—developed around Portage Lake.[145]

By 1845, 45 mining companies held prospecting permits. In October 1846, there were 102.[146] The Cliff Mine, near Copper Harbor, which was owned by the Pittsburgh and Boston Company, was the first in the region to begin production. Another outfit, the Quincy Mine Company, concentrated its activities near Portage Lake.[147] However, the financial burdens encountered by the mining companies often meant that they extracted little ore.[148] Even before beginning extraction, all trees had to be cut down before prospecting could begin. This was financially demanding in itself, and in some cases, was a wasted effort as the prospecting did not always bring positive results. Under these circumstances, the change in 1847 from a government policy of issuing prospecting permits to a policy of renting or selling mining lands slowed prospecting activity and put an end to the "copper fever" that had affected the region since 1843.[149]

This brief surge of enthusiasm had nonetheless helped to draw the attention of investors in the Northeast to the region's potential. It had also attracted workers to this isolated area, leading to the official establishment of Ontonagon and Houghton Counties in 1843.[150]

"Copper fever" gave way to prospecting and mining operations that were better organized, although for the time being just as uncertain of success. The success of the Cliff and Quincy mines, as well as the fact that shares of the region's mining companies were listed on the Boston Stock Exchange as of 1855, enabled capitalists in New York and Pittsburgh to monitor developments in mining activities and to invest in the region.[151] Similarly, entrepreneurs from further west, with experience in lead mining in Wisconsin and Illinois, invested in the Upper Peninsula.[152] Their arrival led to the opening of the new mines of Isle Royale, Portage, Montezuma, Albion, Shelden, Huron, and Dodge in the early 1850s. The result was that by 1854, there were twenty-nine mines in operation in Houghton County, with a work force of 1,135.[153] Yet the success of mining in the region remained highly uncertain: many companies invested, but few attained their objectives.[154] Between 1845 and 1865, more than three hundred companies were set up in the region, and $13,109,154 was invested. Out of all these companies, only three, of which the Cliff Mine was one, ever paid any dividends.[155]

The obstacles that companies had to overcome in order to earn profits on the peninsula were numerous. They had to deal with a densely wooded environment. A preliminary task before they could begin prospecting was always to clear away the trees; as a result, the development of the mining sector was closely intertwined with logging operations. Logging paved the way for mining. But this was not the lumber industry's only role. A large quantity of wood was required to construct the infrastructure for mining operations. Wood was used for the shaft house, the main building, which protected the entry to the pits, and for the walls that supported the underground galleries. The mining industry's need for wood thus led to the development of the lumber industry,[156] and the mining companies always had in their employ a number of carpenters who were responsible for building their infrastructure. In addition, the companies were obliged to develop the infrastructure for whole villages in order to persuade workers to settle in such an isolated region. Rapidly, small villages were created—a few log cabins to serve as rooming houses, a general store, and often a hospital to meet the minimum requirements of workers and their families.[157] Thus the lumber industry became a highly dynamic sector, developing a close relationship with the mining sector.

Work and Working Conditions in the Mining Industry

Miners worked in difficult conditions. The work was physically very demanding and dangerous and was carried out in a dark, humid, dusty environment. Miners usually worked in two- or three-man teams. Each team worked an average of ten hours a day, six days a week. The mine operated day and night, employing workers in two alternating shifts.[158] According to the terms of a contract signed with their employer, the amounts the miners were paid depended on the quantity of copper and rock they extracted.[159]

In the 1840s, a good miner could earn about thirty dollars a month, an unskilled surface worker between fifteen and twenty dollars, and a tradesman about forty dollars. By the 1850s, miners were earning thirty-four dollars on average, and surface workers twenty-six to twenty-eight dollars. During the Civil War, wages increased rapidly, with miners earning sixty-five dollars and more a month, and surface workers averaging fifty-five dollars.[160]

Before the Civil War, the great majority of mining operations were done by the workers themselves, without any machinery. Later, the steam engine was used: carts on rails, pulled by motorized wire rope, transported the rock to the surface, and steam-driven pumps extracted water from the mine.

The ore was extracted in several steps. The rock detached in blocks from the walls of the mine was brought out of the pits and taken to the "Rock House." This was where the surface workers took over. The large pieces of rock were placed on immense iron screens. Using hammers—and creating an infernal din—the workers crushed the rocks into small bits, which fell through the screen to a cart placed underneath. Once full, this cart was taken, along rails, to the stamp mill, which was generally situated on a body of water. In the stamp mill, the bits of rock were reduced to dust by means of steam hammers. At the conclusion of this operation, the copper was separated from the sand. The copper was washed, while the sand was disposed of, often by dumping it in the adjacent body of water. Finally, the copper was transported to markets by boat.

The Origin and Composition of the Population before the Civil War

From its very beginning, the mining industry changed the face of the region. Gradually, small villages grew up around each mine, as hundreds of men, women, and children were drawn to the new operations and the employment possibilities they represented.

Before 1850, the population of Keweenaw Peninsula was small and largely Amerindian. In 1860, there were about 1,100 residents.[161] The village of Ontonagon had a population of 389, while Houghton, to the north, already had 456. The township of L'Anse and the village of Eagle Harbor each had 126 residents.[162] Four years later, the peninsula's population had risen considerably, to 6,535–2,873 in Houghton County and 3,662 in Ontonagon County.[163]

This demographic growth is all the more remarkable in light of the peninsula's isolation at this time. For those who lived in the northeastern part of the continent, or for European immigrants arriving in Atlantic ports, the voyage to Michigan's Upper Peninsula was long and arduous.[164] The opening of the Sault Sainte Marie Canal in 1855 greatly facilitated access to the region. The canal made possible direct navigation, without portage, between Lakes Huron and Michigan in the direction of Lake Superior. Above all, it allowed larger cargo ships to enter Lake Superior and to keep the region more regularly supplied with merchandise of all sorts. The opening of the canal thus greatly reduced the region's isolation, cut the cost of transportation, and increased the potential profit margins of the mining industry.[165]

The Keweenaw Peninsula's dependence on the Great Lakes waterways also explains why the eastern part of the continent provided most of its labor force.[166] Many of the first miners on the peninsula had previously worked in silver, copper, and lead mines in Maine, Vermont, and other parts of the East.[167]

These workers were not enough to satisfy the labor demands

of the mining companies, which therefore had to rely on immigration. From the start of mining operations in the region, Cornish workers (from the mining district of Cornwall, England) were
closely associated with the work.[168] The Cornish, who were highly
experienced mine workers, formed the mainstay of the underground labor force throughout the peninsula.[169] Irish and German
immigrants, who were considered ideal by the political authorities
due to their rapid assimilation and farming backgrounds, also settled in the Upper Peninsula in the mid-1840s.[170]

The population of the Keweenaw Peninsula thus displayed
great ethnic diversity from early on in its industrial development. In 1850, it was estimated that five people out of seven in
Houghton County were foreign-born; in 1860, the estimate was
two out of three.[171] The list of workers employed at the Amyg-
daloid Mine in 1864 illustrates this diversity: of 393 workers, 175
were born in the United States, 76 in Ireland, 70 were from German states, 40 were English, 27 Canadian, and 5 Swiss.[172]

The mining industry had an unstable, seasonal demand for
labor. Until the Civil War, most of the workforce arrived in the
springtime with the first boats and left the region on the last boats
out before winter.[173] Later, when the pits for some of the mines
were nearly dug, work could be continued into the winter months,
especially work designed to strengthen the underground galleries
or to extend them in preparation for the following season. The
dearth of workers was one of the major problems of the first mine
operators. This problem was particularly marked in the 1850s,
when the first lumber companies were established and all the
employers vied for the same limited pool of workers.

Thus, on the eve of the Civil War, the copper region had
reached a turning point in its development. After twenty years,
it was nearing the end of its exploration and experimentation
phase. More and more mine operators were now convinced that
the peninsula possessed rich ore deposits. The region retained certain frontier characteristics, but in the course of the 1850s, it had
already begun to emerge from its isolation and establish communication with the outside world. The scene was thus set for a major

development process leading to the systematic exploitation of the region's enormous mining resources and to the social and economic transformation of the peninsula.

The Civil War and the Consolidation of the Mining Sector, 1860–1900

The Civil War greatly stimulated the development of the copper industry. The war industry's strong demand for copper and the inflation inherent in a wartime situation caused the price of copper to climb in the markets. This rise, in turn, acted as a catalyst, transforming a sector that had still been considered unstable by many investors only a few months earlier into a highly profitable one. Paradoxically, however, the increase in the price of copper had the effect of reducing output, as the companies could not count on a large enough workforce to meet demand.

In this context, the companies set up the Mining Emigrant Aid Association, whose objective was to recruit workers outside the country.[174] Special effort was made in the Scandinavian countries, whose citizens were considered good, experienced workers. The companies hired over four hundred Scandinavians in 1864 and 1865.[175] In November of 1865, the Quincy Mine Company agreed to pay the travel expenses of thirty-two French Canadians.[176] But few of the workers hired at this time by the mining companies remained in the district.[177] It was not until after the war that immigration to the region picked up, the dearth of workers ceased to be a problem, and production levels increased.[178]

The end of the Civil War inaugurated a period of extremely rapid growth in the region. It finally lost its frontier character and began a phase of spectacular social, economic, and demographic development.[179] This expansion was closely linked to the exploitation of new copper deposits near Portage Lake in Houghton County, placing this area in the forefront of the peninsula's mining development. The expansion was concentrated principally at two neighboring sites—the Calumet Mine and the Hecla Mine, which had both been discovered in 1859. These two companies merged in 1871, forming the Calumet and Hecla Consolidated Mining Company (C & H).[180]

The establishment of C & H constituted a watershed in the peninsula's development.[181] Within a few years, this company dominated copper production on the peninsula, was the largest employer in the region, and had a powerful influence on the so-cial, economic, and political development of Houghton County. C & H was not only the most productive mining company in Michigan, for a number of years, it was also the largest in the United States.

Ontonagon County experienced certain economic difficulties after the war. In 1870, there were ten mines in operation, but they were not running at full capacity.[182] Mining activity in Keweenaw County grew steadily but not spectacularly between 1860 and 1870.[183] The development of these areas was no match for that of Houghton County, which had eleven mines in operation in 1870, including C & H, and a total of 2,961 workers—269 on average per mine.[184]

The Introduction of New Technology

The increase in productivity was closely linked to the introduc-tion of new technology in the mines. Although the basic pro-cedures remained the same, the tooling and the processing and refining plants were constantly evolving. This said, it is astonish-ing that until the early 1880s, digging operations continued to be carried out by hand in most cases. Only about 1880 did some mine managers decide to introduce the (Rand) compressed air drill, which was handled by two workers.[185]

The main change with respect to surface work concerned the establishment of processing and refining plants. The Quincy Mine Company was the first, in 1859–60, to build an advanced stamp mill near the village of Hancock on the shores of Portage Lake.[186] The Calumet Mining Company followed suit in 1867, with a processing plant on the banks of Torch Lake. A small-capacity plant for the refining of copper had existed since 1860 at Hancock, but in 1876, the owners of the plant at Hancock and

TABLE 2.6

Copper Production of the Calumet and Hecla Consolidated Mining Company (C&H), the State of Michigan, and the United States, 1860–1910 (in Millions of Pounds)

	1860	1870	1880	1890	1900	1910
C & H	—	14	32	60	78	73
Michigan	12	26	51	100	142	220
All U.S. states	16	28	60	260	606	1,080

Source: Wax, "Calumet and Hecla Copper Mines," 30.

TABLE 2.7

Copper Production in the Lake Superior Region, 1845–1915 (in Long Tons)

Year	Number	Year	Number	Year	Number
1845	1	1873	13,433	1895	57,737
1847	23	1875	16,089	1897	64,854
1849	75	1877	14,422	1899	65,803
1851	87	1879	19,129	1901	69,516
1853	145	1881	24,363	1903	85,848
1855	6,992	1883	26,653	1905	102,874
1857	4,255	1885	32,209	1907	96,481
1859	3,985	1887	33,943	1909	105,513
1861	6,713	1889	39,364	1911	97,741
1863	5,797	1891	50,992	1913	58,412
1865	6,410	1893	50,260	1915	118,430
1870	10,992				

Source: State of Michigan, *Mines and Mineral Statistics,* (1899–1900), 143–45; State of Michigan, *Mines and Mineral Statistics* (1902–1903); State of Michigan, *Mines Handbook and Copper Handbook,* 1319–20.

Note: One long ton contains 2,240 pounds; a standard ton contains 2,000 pounds. The data for the years 1845–53 represent the output of the state of Michigan.

a Detroit copper smelting firm merged their assets, forming the Detroit and Lake Superior Copper Company. It handled most of the region's copper refining until 1887,[187] when C & H decided to build the Smelting Works, south of Lake Linden. The new plant was under the joint ownership of C & H and the Detroit and Lake

Superior Copper Company.[188] These new processing and refining plants created jobs, attracting new workers to the peninsula, and stimulated the development of infrastructure for villages.

Demographic Development

The region's demographic development mirrored its economic development in that it was impressive but uneven. As Table 2.8 shows, Houghton County experienced spectacular growth, whereas in Ontonagon and Keweenaw counties, the population stagnated and even, at times, declined.

The demographic growth of Houghton County meant the rapid growth of certain townships and villages. In Portage Township, for example, the population almost doubled in ten years, rising from 1,540 inhabitants in 1870 to 2,863 in 1880, of whom 50 percent lived in the village of Houghton. The population of the township of Hancock rose from 1,618 in 1860 to 2,987 in 1880, of whom 1,783 lived in the village of Hancock. In Calumet Township, whose villages of Red Jacket and Laurium were located near the mines and processing plants of C & H, the population increased from 3,182 in 1870 to 8,299 in 1880. Finally, the population of Schoolcraft Township rose from 669 to 2,645 between 1870 and 1880, with the village of Lake Linden accounting for 2,610 of that total.

This demographic increase was in large part the result of heavy immigration to the peninsula. The new immigrants were predominantly of Irish, English, Canadian (with French and English Canadians about equally represented), and Scandinavian origin.[189] There were few immigrants of other origins before the 1880s. The arrival of members of these groups favored the consolidation of ethnic communities.

The Work Force and Working Conditions after the War

The economic development described above should have required a larger workforce. It is surprising that until the mid-1880s, the number of workers did not increase all that much.[190] The recovery of the market after the war, the depression that affected the

TABLE 2.8

Population of the Counties of the Keweenaw Peninsula, 1860–1910

	1860	1870	1880	1890	1900	1910
Houghton	7,558	13,879	22,473	35,389	66,063	88,098
Keweenaw	—	4,205	4,270	2,894	3,217	7,156
Ontonagon	4,568	2,845	2,565	3,756	6,197	8,650
Total	12,126	20,929	29,308	42,039	75,477	103,904

Sources: U. S. Department of Interior, *Twelfth Census*, table 5, p. 211; U. S. Department of Commerce, *Thirteenth Census*; table 1, p. 915.

TABLE 2.9

Number of Workers in the Houghton County Copper Mines, 1887–1916

Year	Workers	Year	Workers	Year	Workers
1887	6,221	1897	8,726	1907	17,509
1888	6,310	1898	10,459	1908	17,224
1889	6,480	1899	13,051	1909	17,974
1890	7,310	1900	13,971	1910	16,250
1891	7,702	1901	13,498	1911	15,361
1892	7,640	1902	14,130	1912	15,554
1893	7,591	1903	13,629	1913	13,813
1894	7,343	1904	14,321	1914	12,954
1895	7,249	1905	15,355	1915	16,005
1896	8,170	1906	16,509	1916	16,520

Source: State of Michigan, *Annual Reports of the State Inspector of Houghton County* (1887–1916).

mining industry in the late 1870s, and the introduction of new technology in the 1870s and 1880s all influenced the number of workers the industry required between 1864 and 1885.

Wages and working conditions changed little before the mid-1880s.[191] Wages increased considerably during the Civil War, but fell somewhat between 1865 and 1872. After that, mining output accelerated, the companies hired as many workers as possible in order to maximize production, and the resulting labor shortage drove wages up by 30 percent on average between 1872 and 1873. Then, in the spring of 1873, overproduction caused the price of copper to fall. This fall, together with the arrival of large numbers of new immigrants and the introduction of new technology, reduced the companies' demand for labor, which put pressure on wages. By 1874, they had reached their lowest level since the beginning of the 1860s.[192] They remained at this level through the depression, until copper prices rose again in 1880, and mining activities picked up on the peninsula.[193]

With respect to general working conditions, the introduction of new technology had in no way improved work safety. Both underground and surface work continued to be carried out in dangerous conditions. The bottom of the mines remained unhealthy, humid, poorly ventilated and lit, and subject to unpredictable firedamp explosions, which could be fatal. On the surface, too, accidents were common. Being run over by heavy carts loaded with coal was a potential risk for serious injury.

Community Life and Paternalism

Before the war, the mining companies had had to create the infrastructure required for a resident working population, but after the war, their intervention became institutionalized, taking the form of various paternalistic measures designed to tie the workers' well-being closely to the success of the company and to keep them free from the temptations of unionism. In this domain, as in others, C & H was a leader, seeking to intervene in all aspects of the workers' lives.

In addition to housing, access to which they essentially controlled, the companies offered their workers a host of other services. The workers' houses used electricity produced by the company and were heated by coal offered at an advantageous price by the company. A garbage collection service established by the company maintained sanitation in the streets of the mining villages. If the workers or members of their family had health problems, they could count on finding a doctor nearby, and often a hospital, whose services were available to workers in exchange for a fee deducted from their wages. In 1877, C & H innovated by setting up an Employee's Aid Fund, which was in fact a sort of health, accident, and life insurance fund, whose costs were assumed jointly by the company and the workers.[194] Some companies went even further, organizing sporting clubs, activities for children, travel outside of the vacation season, ceremonies to celebrate the national holidays of the various ethnic groups, and libraries. Some companies that possessed enormous tracts of land either gave ethnic communities land on which to build a school or church or sold it to them at a good price.[195]

Thus from 1870 to 1890, the companies took measures with a view to controlling the workers' lives, both in the workplace and elsewhere.

> If you lived on company property you rented one of the twelve hundred company houses and paid only six to eight dollars a month in rent. You could buy your own house if you preferred, but only on rented land with penalizing clauses in your lease. You could buy land outright in Red Jacket or Laurium and build the house of your choice, but your independence amounted to little more than a gesture. Your home was heated with coal brought on company boats, you washed in water from company pumps, had your dinner under company-made electric light. Even your garbage was carried off in company wagons. The books you read were from the 16,000 volumes of the $50,000 company library. The company penetrated your most private life; more than likely, your wife would have your children at the company hospital.[196]

The companies also controlled political institutions by making financial contributions or simply by presenting their own candidates for elective positions.[197] The consolidation of these company towns and the type of control they represented were to have repercussions on relations between the city masters and their workers.

Labor Relations and Strikes

Under these circumstances, it is easy to understand that labor relations were rarely tense.[198] In fact, before 1872, there were no work stoppages of any importance in the mining district.[199] A series of strikes began on May 1, 1872 in the Portage Lake area, starting at C & H, the Quincy Mine Company, and the Franklin Mine Company and then spreading throughout the district. The workers sought a wage increase and an eight-hour day.[200] The strike lasted three weeks, ending in failure when an infantry company stationed in Detroit was sent to Houghton to restore order. The strike leaders were arrested, tried, and convicted.[201] The workers accepted the companies' initial wage offer of seventy dollars a month for a miner and sixty-five dollars for a surface worker, and they all returned to work.[202] Despite its failure, this strike served as a wake-up call to company administrators, who paid closer attention after this to workers' complaints, which could lead to new strikes or the formation of unions.

The financial depression that affected the country after 1873 had little effect on the labor market in the mining region. In towns such as Houghton or Hancock, the constant improvements to urban and road infrastructure created increasing demand for workers.[203] It was mainly in the final years of the depression—from 1877 to 1879—that its impact was felt in the region.[204] In June 1879, the rate of unemployment was high,[205] and many workers left for Leadville, a major mining center in Colorado.[206]

The Erosion of the Social Consensus, 1900–14

Near the end of the nineteenth century, changes in the general economic climate obliged the mining companies to openly defend their own interests, coming out against the interests of those they claimed to protect and undermining the social consensus that had generally obtained until then.

Beginning in the 1880s, competition heated up between the copper mining companies of the Keweenaw Peninsula and those emerging further west in the United States. Rich deposits had been discovered and mines had begun operating in Montana and Arizona, and the high productivity of these upstarts created strong competition for the Michigan mines.[207] Part of the problem was that these mines were beginning to show signs of exhaustion. There was still plenty of ore, but the depth at which operations now had to be carried out made them more difficult and more costly.[208] In response to this situation, the companies relied more heavily on new technology and reconsidered their participation in the socioeconomic and cultural life of the region.

For the miners, the most radical change with regard to production was the introduction of the one-man drill, which replaced the Rand drill in the early twentieth century. Lighter and more effective, the new drill could, as its name suggests, be handled by a single miner. As a result, the companies needed fewer workers, while their productivity increased. But above all, the introduction of this drill put an end to the system of remuneration by contract for teams of miners, and consequently to teamwork in the mines, with the partnership and solidarity that that implied.[209] Henceforth, it was to be "each man for himself."

The introduction of new technology did not contribute to the improvement of working conditions. Underground workers still risked life and limb. Indeed, the work may have become more dangerous, since it was now conducted further from the surface, and rock falls, air blasts, and cave-ins were more frequent.[210]

Changes in the Ethnic Composition of the Workforce and the End of Social Consensus

Given this context of rationalization, the region's spectacular demographic development in this period is surprising. The increase was phenomenal: from about 42,000 inhabitants in 1890 to 104,000 in 1910. During the same period, the population of Houghton County grew from about 36,000 to 88,000. Keweenaw and Ontonagon Counties experienced similar growth (see table 2.8).

This increase was largely the result of a new wave of immigration in the 1890s, of entirely different origin from earlier ones.[211] In fact, it was not until the late 1880s or early 1890s that the real process of ethnic diversification occurred on the peninsula. The newcomers, who were predominantly from southern and eastern Europe—Italy, Poland, Austria-Hungary, Croatia, and Slovenia—altered the ethnic composition of the region's workforce.[212]

The rationalization measures undertaken by the mining companies were accompanied by a reconsideration of their involvement in the community and the services they offered the population. With respect to housing, for example, the companies were completely overwhelmed by the demand from the thousands of new arrivals to the peninsula. For economic reasons, instead of building new residential projects, they left the housing of the newcomers to nearby villages such as Houghton, Hancock, Lake Linden, Calumet, and Red Jacket. This led to a reduction of their direct social control over the workers, in addition to depriving these workers of the personal advantages of living in low-rent company housing near the workplace.[213]

Beginning in 1905, the social climate in the region deteriorated considerably. Predictably, the introduction of new technology, the continued use of dangerous, decrepit equipment, and the growing gap between the wages of miners in the West and in Michigan led the workers to demand improvements in their situation. The major changes in the ethnic composition of the workforce and the companies' loss of social control over many of their workers also had a mobilizing effect on the workers, leading them to strike in support of their demands.

The first important strike was started on July 23, 1906 by the underground workers of the Quincy Mine Company. They demanded improved safety measures and a wage increase of 10 percent to reduce the gap between their wages and those paid in the mines of the West. The company was willing to increase wages by 5 percent but refused categorically to negotiate the other demands. On August 14, three weeks after the start of the strike, the strikers accepted the company's offer and returned to work. They had won only half of their wage-related goal and none of the rest.[214]

The Strike of 1913–14

The strike of 1913–14 was a turning point in the socioeconomic evolution of the mining district, both by virtue of its duration and of the large number of workers involved.[215] It lasted nine months, from July 23, 1913 to april 14, 1914, when the leaders of the Western Federation of Miners (WFM), to whom the workers had entrusted the organization of their strike, advised their members to return to work.[216]

At the beginning of July, at the request of the underground workers, a referendum had been held to determine strategy. Ninety-eight percent of the workers had voted for a negotiation meeting between their union and the directors of the mining companies. The workers had given their union a strike mandate, to be implemented if the companies refused the invitation.[217] On July 14, a letter was sent to the directors of all the mining companies, inviting them to a meeting and advising them that in the absence of a positive response on their part, the union would declare a strike. This letter went unanswered. On July 23, the WFM called for a work stoppage.

The workers had many demands, including higher wages, an eight-hour day, and a base wage rate, but the demands for the elimination of the one-man drill and the recognition of the WFM for bargaining purposes seem to have been the ones that elicited the strongest reaction on the part of the companies. They had always refused to negotiate with the WFM, because to do so implied recognizing its legitimacy, which they had absolutely no intention of doing.

Two days after the beginning of the strike, all mining operations in the district were paralyzed. The strike affected about twenty mines and nearly sixteen thousand workers, including those of the Quincy Mine Company and C&H and its branches.[218]

The first few days were marked by violent clashes between security agents protecting the mines and strikers seeking to control access to them. Tensions ran so high that the mine owners sought assistance from the National Guard, which arrived in the region on July 27. It was replaced in November by deputy sheriffs and by private detectives specially hired for the situation. Apart from these early incidents, the prevailing atmosphere was calm.

In August 1913, the strikers' solidarity began to deteriorate, and a large contingent of workers from C & H and its branches decided to return to work under the old conditions. This decision by the workers of the largest company on the peninsula had a powerful impact on the outcome of the strike.[219] In September, to hasten the return to normal operating levels, the companies hired strikebreakers from outside the district.[220]

On October 30, 1913, the mining companies announced that starting on January 1, 1914, the duration of the working day would be eight hours. They added that if the leaders of the WFM withdrew from the strike and left the region, they promised to rehire all the strikers without exception. However, the company administrators refused to even consider the workers' other demands.[221] The application of this measure at the beginning of January 1914 seriously undermined the strikers' morale and solidarity, and many returned to work. In April 1914, nine months after the start of the strike, the WFM recommended that its members end the strike and return to work. With the exception of the eight-hour day, the strikers had not succeeded in improving their working conditions.

This strike had a number of serious consequences. The refusal of the mining companies to negotiate most of the workers' demands and their resort to armed force and strikebreakers revealed to the workers and residents of the region that the companies' ultimate objective was to earn profits, without any particular concern for the conditions in which they did so.[222] This strike brought home to the population the class conflict between the workers and the entrepreneurs that the paternalistic policies of the mining companies had long obscured.

The changes that had been under way in the mining sector since the 1890s obliged the mining companies to reveal that their priority was profit. Faced with strong competition, they had introduced technology—particularly the one-man drill—that created grave problems for their workers. The same changes in the industry also led the companies to abandon social programs, paternalistic measures that had previously earned them the workers' respect and enabled them to exercise social control over their workforce. This reduced control occurred at a time when the increasing size and ethnic diversity of the workforce was also acting to undermine the conditions established before the 1890s that had made paternalism effective.

Another consequence of the strike was a major wave of departures from the workforce. Both during and after the strike, thousands of workers left the peninsula. In 1913 alone, nearly 2,500 left, many for Detroit and other midwestern industrial centers.[223] In addition, many of those who remained did not return to the mines after the strike, preferring to find work in other sectors.[224] These massive departures created problems for the companies which, beginning in late 1914, found themselves with full order books but without a labor force large enough to satisfy their clients.[225]

But the mining companies were not disadvantaged for long. Their victory enabled them to make far more extensive use of the one-man drill. By 1915, output exceeded the best years of the past, reaching nearly 120,000 long tons. Thus, one year after the strike, stability and calm had been restored. But the strike was never forgotten.

In the mid-nineteenth century, Michigan underwent an industrialization process based on the exploitation of its natural resources. In the Saginaw Valley the lumber industry prospered; the Keweenaw Peninsula owed its development to the exploitation of its mineral resources. In valley and peninsula alike, progress was modest before the Civil War. The war acted as a catalyst for the development of both regions, which embarked on a rapid process of growth leading to high levels of output in its aftermath.

In the late nineteenth and early twentieth centuries, both sectors experienced difficulties caused by competition from more recently developed regions. In both cases, major strikes profoundly altered the social dynamic, revealing clearly the nature of the relationship the entrepreneurs had maintained with their workers.

The outcome of these strikes destroyed a social consensus that had existed until then.

The development of these two regions attracted many immigrants. Among them, French Canadians played a significant role. Although they were never the largest immigrant group, they participated actively in all phases of the development of the valley and peninsula.

Chapter 3

French Canadian Migration to the Saginaw Valley, 1840–1900

The French Canadians made major contributions to each phase in the development of the Saginaw Valley. Among the regions where it was possible for them to emigrate, they rapidly identified the valley as an area where they could improve their living conditions.

Their experience in the valley may be divided into three distinct phases. The first, from 1840 to 1860, saw the arrival of the first migrants and the beginnings of community organization. The second, from 1860 to 1880, was characterized by the rapid acceleration of the flow of migration, the establishment of social institutions, and the consolidation of the communities. The final phase began in 1880 and concluded with the end of the century. It was marked by the decline of the lumber industry in the region, social tensions, the departure of many migrants, and the marginalization of the French Canadian communities.

The French Canadians before the Civil War, 1840–60

Until the Civil War, there were few French Canadians in the Saginaw Valley (see table 3.1).[1] In 1840, there were only 60, in 1850, 85, and in 1860, there were still only 401. Furthermore, given this slow increase, the rapid growth of the overall population of the valley in this period had the effect of reducing the relative representation of the French Canadian population, which fell from 6.7 percent in 1840 to 2.5 percent in 1860. This twenty-year period was nonetheless important, because it marked the beginning of French Canadian settlement in the region.

The first French Canadians in the region—the Campaus, Desnoyers, Peltiers, Prattes, Tremblays, and Trudells—who migrated from southeastern Michigan when the fur trade declined there, had established themselves as farmers in the 1830s. Those who followed in the 1840s also began farming and then bought their land, the only difference being that half of them came directly from Quebec. In 1850, three out of four French Canadian farmers in the valley owned their land.[2] This information confirms the hypothesis that French Canadian families who left Quebec for the Midwest in the mid-nineteenth century had a certain amount of money and were looking for fertile land at a good price, on which they could continue to live by agriculture.[3]

However, the French Canadians who arrived in the valley in the 1850s had different objectives; they were primarily interested in the new employment opportunities created by the lumber industry. The reason for this change was that those who had migrated westward in the 1840s in search of good-quality land had to move further west in the 1850s, generally to Illinois, because the land that interested them was no longer available in Michigan.[4] It is the westward movement of the agricultural frontier that explains the decline in the number of French Canadians working in agriculture in the decade 1850–60. Their decline in this sector was offset by their emergence in the service and skilled labor sectors that developed as the increase of the valley's urban population gave rise to various needs. In 1860, one household head in five was either a shipwright or a saloon owner—a traditional institution in lumbering towns.

The husband was the principal breadwinner in the family. Nonetheless, because of the lumber industry's growing need for labor, boys of fifteen and over who lived with their parents contributed a substantial amount to their family's earnings. On the eve of the Civil War, three boys out of four worked outside the

Counties of the Saginaw Valley and surrounding counties.
From *Atlas of Michigan*, edited by Lawrence M. Sommers, 1977.
Courtesy of Michigan State University Press.

home, either as laborers in the sawmills or in agriculture. Wives, and girls over the age of fifteen still living with their parents, did not contribute as wage earners. In families that took in boarders, however, the women handled this activity, which increased the household income. Only 4 percent of households ran boarding houses in this period.

Although the French Canadian population of the valley remained small, by 1850 it was already geographically concentrated: 60 percent of its members lived in the township of Hampton, which became part of the newly created Bay County in 1857. Another 30 percent lived in the township of Saginaw. But from 1860 until the end of the century, most French Canadian residents of Saginaw County settled in Saginaw City—which had nearly 25 percent of the county's French Canadians in 1860—or in East Saginaw, which had 20 percent.[5] A near majority of the French Canadians in Bay County lived in the township of Bangor, a lumbering center before the Civil War, but the number declined after the Civil War, when Bay City and West Bay City attracted most migrants.[6]

The first French Canadians who migrated to the valley before the Civil War did not remain there for long. Only five of the fourteen families present in 1840 were still there in 1850. In fact, nine households left the valley and ten arrived in this period. Of the ten that arrived, seven came from Canada, two from Michigan, and one from Maine. This strong mobility continued in the 1850s. Of seventeen households in Saginaw County in 1850, only five were present in 1860.[7] Overall, the rate of retention from 1840 to 1860 was 35 percent. The instability of the population reflects the fact that for most of these French Canadians, migration to the valley was part of a medium-term strategy. They came to improve their economic situation; once that had been accomplished, they planned to return to their point of departure. But if their initial aim of improving their situation could not be achieved in the place to which they had migrated, they migrated again—to a new destination. Thus, for many migrants in this period, the Saginaw

Valley was just a stopping point on their itinerary. The situation stabilized after the war.

Although migration from Quebec to the valley was the most direct route, it was not the only one followed by the migrants. During the 1850s, a number of families migrated by step or sequence, following a winding path. An examination of French Canadians in the valley in 1860 shows that nearly 6 percent of household heads had been born in the northeastern states,[8] particularly New York and Vermont, while 8 percent of household heads born in Canada had resided in one of the northeastern states before migrating to the valley. Two had spent time in Vermont, and three in New York. Thus, whether they were born there or were temporary residents, nearly 10 percent of French Canadian household heads in the valley in 1860 had resided for some time in the northeastern United States.[9] Analysis of the birthplaces and birth dates of their children indicates that most of these households left for the West during the 1850s, when the pinewood resources of the Northeast were beginning to show signs of depletion.

These data shed a certain light on the presence of French Canadians in the valley before the Civil War, on their economic integration into the valley, and on the migration routes they followed. Their initial gravitation toward agriculture and then, beginning in the 1850s, their employment in the lumber industry confirm the attractiveness of these sectors in the respective periods. The French Canadians initially came with the intention of settling on the valley's low-priced land. Later they were attracted by the possibility of finding jobs in the developing lumber industry. Before 1850, French Canadians who sought land knew they could find it in the valley. After 1850, other French Canadians, looking for jobs rather than land, knew that if they migrated to the valley, they could find work in the lumber industry.

Before the Civil War, French Canadians followed three types of itineraries to the valley. Some migrated directly from Quebec. Others, who lived in semipermanent communities in Vermont, Maine, and New York, shared the ambition of many American farmers to participate in the "great migration" from East to West in order to acquire better lands. In addition, their migration was associated with another, broader process: the movement of the timber frontier, which created a market for migrant labor as it edged westward first from Maine and then from New York to Michigan— and within Michigan, to the valley in particular. The dynamism of this market was stimulated by the hiring policies of entrepreneurs from the Northeast, which drew on the northeastern states for part of the workforce on the new timber frontier as that frontier gradually shifted to the West. In this general sense, the French Canadians contributed both to the movement of the agricultural frontier by settling on virgin lands and to the movement of the timber frontier by participating in the market for migrant labor, whose westward movement led them to the Saginaw Valley.

Community Organization in the Valley

Other immigrant groups who shared the same religious faith had accompanied the French Canadians in their migration to the valley. Irish, Dutch, and especially German workers were also drawn by the opportunities for employment the valley offered. The arrival of these Catholics and their concentration in the main urban and industrial centers generated a desire to establish institutional structures for Catholics, on whose basis a Catholic community life could grow up in the valley.

The fact that the French Canadians, like the other immigrant groups, had migrated to a frontier region helps explain their behavior once they arrived in the valley. Because this region had as yet no real social or cultural identity, the migrants enjoyed considerable latitude or autonomy—their young communities could develop in continuity with their traditional values, without being obliged to integrate into a dominant culture. This situation contributed to the maintenance of their French-speaking, Catholic cultural identity, allowing the French Canadians to put off until later the task of defining themselves in terms of their new social and cultural environment.

The arrival of Catholic immigrants in the 1840s and 1850s had considerably increased the number of Catholics in the region. Already in the winter of 1850–51, under the direction of Father Kinderens, who took up missionary duties in the region in 1850, construction of St. Joseph's, the region's first Catholic church, had begun in Lower Saginaw (Bay City). This modest church was built on land offered free of charge by the Saginaw Bay Land Company.[10]

Catholics were also active in Saginaw City. In 1852, after receiving irregular missionary visits since 1842, these Catholics acquired an abandoned cabinetmaker's workshop, which they made into a place of worship where mass was celebrated by visiting priests. The following year, the group bought a larger plot of land, to which the former workshop was moved.[11] In the wake of these efforts, the parish of St. Andrews was officially created in Saginaw City in 1862.[12]

However, very early on the Catholics complained to Monsignor Caspar Borgess about the irregularity of the services and demanded that a resident priest be assigned to the region. Monsignor Borgess agreed to their demand, appointing H. T. H. Schutzes to the position of resident pastor in 1852.[13] The Reverend Schutzes was of Dutch origin and could speak both French and English.[14] We do not know whether he was chosen for his linguistic abilities, but they were surely useful for communicating with all the region's Catholics. The Reverend Schutzes was to be a key player in the establishment of two important parishes in the valley, St. Joseph in Bay City and St. Andrew's in Saginaw.[15]

In 1855, the Reverend Schutzes decided to settle officially in Lower Saginaw and personally supervise the completion of work on the church, which had been under construction for some years. In Bay City, the number of Catholics had risen from about twenty families representing some one hundred people in 1852 to two thousand parishioners in 1856.[16] The community life of the region's Catholic population, and of its first French Canadians, was thus primarily centered in the towns of Saginaw City and Lower Saginaw.

THE ACCELERATION OF MIGRATION AND THE CONSOLIDATION OF THE COMMUNITIES, 1860–80

The migration of French Canadians increased greatly after the Civil War, when the lumber industry attained a high level of development and its demand for labor reached unprecedented levels. As table 3.1 shows, the number of French Canadians rose both absolutely and as a proportion of the population of the valley from the war until the mid-1890s. In 1860, there were 401 French Canadians in the valley—barely 2.5 percent of its population. Twenty years later, their ranks had grown to 7,331–7.5 percent of the valley's population.

The arrival of large numbers of migrants accelerated the linguistic and religious consolidation of the French Canadian community. Whenever there were enough French Canadians in a town, they established social institutions that brought them together and favored the development of a complex, dynamic community life.

Their community life was organized around two central bases. The first was the family. The family, which played an essential supporting role in the migration process itself, was also the locus of socialization—the place where the values of the host society were introduced and confronted the values of the migrants' original culture. This interaction gave rise to a modus vivendi: creating an ethnic identity in which the values useful for adaptation were reinforced and those that hindered it were marginalized, while certain cultural characteristics essential for the preservation of the migrants' identity were maintained. It was also for the well-being of family members—to maintain or improve their quality of life—that specific decisions were taken and strategies for adapting to changing conditions were developed.[17] Work, the second pivot of community life, was also a locus of socialization. Long hours in the workshop, sawmill, or shipyard in the company of workers of diverse origins were conducive to discussion, the establishment of close contacts, and the gradual social and economic integration of the workers.

TABLE 3.1
French Canadian Population of the Saginaw Valley, 1840–1900

	Bay County	Saginaw County	Total French Canadian Population	Total Population of Saginaw Valley	French Canadians (%)
1840	0.0	60	60	892	6.7
1850	0.0	85	85	2,609	3.2
1860	221	180	401	15,857	2.5
1870	1,346	1,076	2,422	54,997	4.4
1880	4,536	2,795	7,331	97,176	7.5
1884	6,913	—	—	51,221	13.4
1894	7,348	—	—	61,304	12.0
1900	7,135	3,189	10,324	143,600	7.1

Source: Enumeration schedules, U. S. Census, 1840–1900.

Note: Figures for the years 1884 and 1894 are based on the enumeration schedule for the state census of Bay County only. The census figures for Saginaw County for 1884 and 1894 were not available.

The rapid growth of the French Canadian population prompted the creation of the first community structures. Taking as their model the familiar institutions of Quebec society, the migrants created parishes, churches, parish schools, newspapers, and French Canadian societies. These institutions gradually permitted the emergence of structured communities, whose existence in turn attracted potential migrants. These communities, which had been fluid and multilingual before the Civil War, gradually stabilized as their populations grew. Out of these communities of workers, young people, and others there emerged clerical and lay leaders who acted as intermediaries, interpreting the needs of their members to the host society and the requirements of that society to the French Canadians.

Before the Civil War, as we have seen, the first Catholics of French Canadian origin had felt the need, in a Protestant world, to ensure the survival of their religious specificity by taking common action with other Catholics to create a broad parish structure.[18] After the war, the steady arrival of Catholic immigrants encouraged the creation of new mixed or multiethnic parishes in the valley, which included all Catholics regardless of language or origin and brought them under the authority of a single pastor.[19]

This situation soon became problematic for the French Canadians, whose numbers were rapidly growing. Most of them did not understand the English spoken by the priest of the Catholic parish, making it difficult for them to understand the teachings and creating a sense of exclusion. This led the French-speaking Catholics to ask the authorities to create a separate parish with a priest who could provide the services and instruction in the language they understood.

This is what happened in the mixed parish of St. Joseph in Bay City, when the French Canadians, whose population had reached 500 by 1870, exercised pressure in order to acquire their own parish. Lengthy negotiations were undertaken between the representatives of the parishioners and the Catholic diocesan authorities—Monsignor Lefebvre, of Belgian origin, died in 1868 and was replaced by Monsignor Borgess, of German origin and a pronounced admirer of America[20]—with the aim of determining if the parish of St. Joseph should be subdivided.

It is difficult to know in what climate the negotiations took place. Elsewhere, when this sort of procedure was carried out by French Canadians, it had often given rise to heated debate culminating in overt struggle between the parties involved. In Muskegon, a lumber town in western Michigan, analogous demands by French Canadians concerning Saint-Jean-Baptiste Parish had led to a crisis. Even more bad feeling and angry discussion had occurred in Detroit under similar circumstances.[21] Although in some cases the French Canadians obtained their separate parish as requested, in all instances the discussions caused deep divisions in the Catholic population. And if the bishop decided in favor of the French Canadians, then new tensions arose when it was time to divide the assets and debts of the original parish and to agree on the financial participation of the diocese in the construction of a new church.

After prolonged discussions, the French Canadians obtained their own parish in 1868, and St. Joseph Parish was divided in two. The English Catholic parish of St. James was created, placed under the direction of the Reverend Schutzes, who had been a missionary in the valley for many years. St. Joseph thus became the first parish of the French Canadians, the first "Little Canada" in the valley. In addition, the French Canadians succeeded in convincing the clerical authorities to appoint a French-speaking priest, the Reverend Girard of France, to the parish—a major accomplishment. [22]

The Reverend Girard remained with the parish until 1872. After that, the parish of St. Joseph, like the regional lumber industry, entered a period of crisis. Between 1872 and 1888, it saw ten priests come and go, three of whom were of French origin. Because of the unstable leadership and the marginalization of French as a language of communication in the parish, St. Joseph's ceased to enjoy the full support of the French-speaking population and lost credibility with the French Canadian parishioners during this difficult economic period. [23]

There were other difficulties besides the unstable leadership. In 1888, the parish of St. Joseph and the French Canadian community of Bay City were shaken by a major crisis growing out of the material and spiritual problems experienced by the parish in the recent past. The material problems had begun in 1880, when the Reverend Thibodeau invested a large sum for a new church to meet the needs of the French Canadian population, which had grown considerably during the 1870s, reaching 2,000 parishioners in 1880 and over 3,300 in 1884. [24] When work on the church was finished in 1888, the parish still owed nearly six thousand dollars. Given this financial situation, after the departure of Father Thibodeau—whether voluntary or otherwise remains unknown—the diocese had great difficulty finding a successor to serve in a parish paralyzed by debt and was threatened, barring a rapid financial recovery, by trusteeship. [25] However, the Reverend Roth, of the Congregation of Holy Ghost, accepted the challenge.

From 1889 to 1894, he took energetic measures, concerning which
we know nothing save that they succeeded, to restore financial
equilibrium to the parish.

But stability was not reestablished for long. New financial
problems developed, and this time they divided the parishioners.
In the early 1890s, the church, the rectory, and the parish school
all required urgent repairs. For reasons that remain unclear, the
parish was deeply divided with regard to these repairs. It seems
likely that certain parishioners, probably the ones most recently
arrived, refused to pay for repairs during a depression, whereas
other parishioners, probably longtime, permanent members of the
parish, well established in the community, were more inclined
to grant the priest's request. Relations between the two factions
worsened, until the Reverend Dangelzer, who had taken over
as parish priest in 1895, managed to calm the troubled waters.
In any case, the repairs were done, and the bill came to five
thousand dollars, which was entirely covered by the parishioners.
But already, lacking dynamic clerical leadership and faced with
declining membership rolls—the number had fallen from 3,013
in 1894 to 2,539 in 1900—St. Joseph's Parish, which had been
the pivot of the French Canadian community of Bay City, was
increasingly returning to its initial role as a Catholic parish open
to all linguistic minorities.[26]

In addition to St. Joseph's, the English Catholic parish of
St. James in Saginaw City, which was led until 1901 by a priest
of Dutch origin, the Reverend Van der Heyden, and St. Mary's
Parish, established in 1874 in East Saginaw, were also places
around which the French Canadians organized their community
life, although in these parishes they were a minority.[27]

Many parishes had parish schools. Daytime classes for children and some evening classes for adults were organized. In the
case of French Catholic parishes, schools under the direction
of the parish priest contributed to the cultural survival of the
group by transmitting the French language and Catholic religion. Schools were usually built soon after the church, and often
classes were held in the church basement in the meantime. In the

United States, the establishment of Catholic schools demanded considerable energy and sacrifice on the part of parishioners, because confessional schools received no financial support from the state.[28] Despite these obstacles, a number of parish schools were established—one as early as 1872, in St. Joseph's Parish in Bay City, with the Reverend Delbaire as principal. Courses were initially held in the Watson Block, which could accommodate nearly two hundred students. The following year, the school moved into premises more appropriate for a school.[29]

French-language newspapers also provided a framework for community life, although in a more regional way. These newspapers, whose objective was to ensure the survival of French Canadian cultural characteristics, sought to furnish the most direct connection between their French-speaking readers and their homeland. Migrants could stay in touch with Quebec and keep their traditions and values alive as long as they did not hinder the harmonious integration of other members of the community. Characterized by short lives and limited circulation,[30] such papers often kept their readers better informed about news in their home country than about the life of the community they ostensibly served.[31]

The newspapers in the valley were Catholic and conservative, advocating social peace and respect for authority. Their editorial content essentially reflected the concerns of the civil and religious elites of the community. They completely ignored the migrants' experiences and the economic development of the region. In most cases, the contents of the page devoted to the community were so vague and so far from the concerns of the actual community that one could not tell by reading it whether the paper was published in a midwestern lumber town or a New England factory town. News about community life was scarce. What little there was consisted of notices concerning the dates and location of meetings of the various French Canadian institutions (concerts or social gatherings). The papers also reported arrivals and departures of important members of the community and publicized activities in neighboring communities.[32] As an institution aiming to bolster the French Canadian community, the newspapers clearly did not fulfill their role. By their content and approach, some newspapers more closely resembled assimilation agents than promoters of community survival. The publishers often exerted pressure to bring the political and social behavior of the migrants more in line with the expectations of the host society or attempted to prove to the host society that the French Canadians were adapting well to life in the United States.

It was in Bay City—the town with the most French Canadians in the valley—that all the French Canadian newspapers were published. The first to appear was *Le Courrier*, which began publishing in 1878 and continued for nearly three years.[33] *Le Patriote* took over when it ceased, appearing for the first time in November 1882 with H. A. Pacaud as editor.[34] Publication was interrupted on several occasions for long periods and ceased altogether in 1904. The first issue of *Le Souvenir*—probably a rival of *Le Patriote*—came out in late April 1883, but this paper, which was edited by Célestin Boucher, lasted only three months. Finally, June 1888 saw the beginning of *L'Ouest français*, edited by Charles Guérin and Télésphore Saint-Pierre, which disappeared after eleven months of existence.[35] The fact that the majority of these publications started in the 1870s and 1880s underscores that these were the years of maximum dynamism for the French Canadians of the valley and for those of Bay City.

French Canadian societies were also set up during this period. These were at first essentially mutual aid societies, offering life or invalidity insurance for French Canadians. The societies sought to provide moral support to families and come to the financial aid of widows, the sick, and orphans.[36] In this period, this sort of institution was not common in the small villages of Quebec; in rural regions, it was the clergy who took care of families in difficulty. Such societies existed mainly in urban centers like Montreal.[37] Influenced by the ideology of *la survivance* (the survival of French Canada) the French Canadian societies in Michigan aspired to play a pivotal social role as community leaders by saluting the French roots of their members and by celebrating with great fan-

fare the national holiday of the French Canadians. The creation of
this type of institution was closely linked to the arrival of new migrants beginning in the mid-nineteenth century. For many French
Canadians, this revived their desire to stick together, to vow solidarity and to struggle for the survival of their French-speaking,
Catholic culture. These societies were generally established at the
point when the community had grown large enough to support
them and members had developed a feeling of belonging to the
community. It was generally the earliest immigrants who became
involved in the leadership of these societies, especially those who
had decided to settle permanently in the region.[38]

One of the first French Canadian organizations of this type
was founded in Detroit in the early 1850s. Second in size after the
Saint-Jean-Baptiste Society of the state of New York, which had
been created in 1850, this organization was set up by E. N. Lacroix,
who had also participated that same year in the launching of the
newspaper *Le Citoyen*, which survived for about a year in Detroit. With the help of François L'Espérance and Robert Rhéaume,
Lacroix founded this mutual aid society in February 1852. Its objective was to bring together all the French Canadians of Michigan and to ensure that they were able to exert an influence consistent with their numbers.[39] Progress was slow, however; by the
end of the year, the organization had barely twenty members. Its
leaders invited Daniel J. Campau, a prominent French Canadian
of Detroit, to take over the leadership in order to bestow it with
a new dynamism. Under Campau's leadership, the organization
officially took the name of the Lafayette Society, after the French
general who had been popular in the United States and a close
friend of President Washington. With the new leader at the helm,
progress was so rapid that in 1857 the society decided to commem-
orate with pomp the hundredth anniversary of Lafayette's birth
by organizing celebrations with parades in the streets of Detroit.
This decision to invoke the memory of a French military leader
much appreciated by the Americans and to show that the French
Canadians wanted to be accepted by the American population, as
Lafayette had been, was a strategic one.[40]

In April of the same year, the leaders of the Lafayette Society officially incorporated the organization. Their objectives were to "stimulate and maintain favorable attitudes on the part of French citizens living in Detroit and other French-speaking people and to unite these people by acts and duties of mutual charity."[41]

The society's sphere of influence broadened rapidly, especially in the urban regions, where the French Canadian population was largest. By 1866, the Saginaw Valley had about one hundred members—enough to necessitate the appointment of special officers to represent them in Detroit. Louis Guérin of East Saginaw and Charles Rivet of Bay City were designated. The number of members increased so rapidly that by 1869 a branch of the Lafayette Society was set up in Bay City and construction began on Lafayette Hall to the society's offices.[42] The annual celebration of the birth of Lafayette spread from Detroit to the streets of Bay City.[43]

Other French Canadian societies also appeared in the valley. A chapter of the Union Saint-Jean-Baptiste was formed in Bay City, and the Saint-Jean-Baptiste Association of Michigan was established in West Bay City.[44] Founded in Detroit in 1864, this association recruited only French Canadians and sought to abstain from all political debates, which tended to divide communities more than they united them. Instead, the association offered its members an opportunity "to socialize and to cooperate in the task of raising the religious, intellectual, social and moral level of the French race of the State of Michigan." Its aim was to encourage the creation of Saint-Jean-Baptiste societies in every county of the state.[45] Highly patriotic, it organized the Saint-Jean-Baptiste celebrations every June 24.[46]

The founding of these institutions contributed to the emergence in these industrial and increasingly multiethnic towns of dynamic French Catholic neighborhoods with a thriving community life. Businesses, hotels, and saloons appeared, and a class of businessmen, tradesmen, and professionals grew up which, owing its existence to this compatriot market, endeavored to meet its needs. However, the French Canadian societies were to be rocked by an internal crisis that would disturb the communities of the valley.

The Annexationist Movement

The French Canadian communities of Michigan and their main organizations were the protagonists of a political debate that began in Canada in the late 1860s, one that raised explicitly the question of that country's future. The debate focused on the annexation of Canada by the United States, an idea proposed by Médéric Lanctot, a Montreal reformer.[47] The annexationists held that since the British conquest the French Canadians had been deprived of basic liberties by a colonial regime that refused them their full rights. The only solution was for Canada to obtain its political independence from the British Empire and become a part of a country that had made freedom a right so basic it was protected by the Constitution.

Invited to speak to the Club démocratique français (French Democratic Club) of Detroit in 1868, Lanctot presented his annexationist political thesis. His speech went over well; the members decided then and there to set up an organization, which they called the *Association de l'indépendance pacifique du Canada*, and proceeded to elect the new organization's officers.[48]

With this support, Lanctot left Detroit for New England, where he gave a number of lectures on the subject. He also participated in the convention of French Canadians in the United States, which was held in October 1868 in Springfield, Massachusetts, where he sought—unsuccessfully—to influence the discussion along the lines of his doctrine. Returning to Detroit, Lanctot succeeded in obtaining the support of all the French Canadian societies of Detroit.[49] At the annual assembly of the *Association Saint-Jean-Baptiste de l'état du Michigan* in September 1869, Lanctot was nominated, with others, to represent the society at the next convention in Detroit.

This fifth convention of French Canadians in the United States, held on October 13, 1869, was attended by representatives

from thirteen French Canadian societies in the United States.[50]
The resolutions committee was dominated by Médéric Lanctot
and L. H. Fréchette, a member of the Saint-Jean-Baptiste Society
of Chicago, who managed to include among the resolutions to be
adopted a vote on Lanctot's annexationist proposal. The wording
of the proposal was as follows:

> Considering that the French Canadians who have emigrated
> to the United States were forced to leave their homeland by
> the shamefully corrupt and cruelly arbitrary administration
> which has constantly oppressed Canada since its conquest
> by England; considering that as long as the colonial regime
> exists in Canada, the expatriate Canadians will not be able to
> return home, because the regime, by its very nature, deprives
> them of bread and liberty, which they find in abundance in
> the United States; considering that the independence of
> Canada and its annexation to the United States are the only
> way for French Canadians expatriated in the United States
> to enjoy the advantages they have here, and that as a result
> they cannot return to their homeland unless it becomes free
> and is annexed to the American Union; [be it] resolved that
> we, French Canadians, accept no other solution as being
> reasonable and favorable to the happiness of our homeland
> and the end of our expatriation, than Canada's independence
> from the British mother country, and the annexation of our
> country by the American Union.[51]

The resolutions committee also proposed that a general commission for the independence of Canada and its annexation to the
United States be formed, with its headquarters in Detroit, that a
newspaper be created to spread the ideas of the annexationists,
that the next convention be held in Montreal, and that it be a
continental convention—with French Canadians from all over
America. All the resolutions proposed by the committee were
adopted, by twelve votes to seven.[52]

The adoption of this resolution was a turning point for the French Canadians of Michigan. The vote demonstrated clearly that there was a division between the organizations of the Detroit region, which were favorable to the idea of annexation, and the other organizations of the French Canadians in Michigan.[53] Encouraged by his victory, in November 1869, Médéric Lanctot published in Detroit the first issue of L'impartial, in which he expounded the annexationist doctrine.[54]

However, the annexationist movement soon ran out of steam. L'impartial was published for only five weeks. After that, Lanctot publicly repudiated his Catholic faith and created the Anti-Roman Advocate, a Protestant newspaper. This second newspaper lasted only five months. Lanctot returned to Canada where, in addition to reembracing his original religion, he revised his political positions considerably, thus undermining support for the annexationist movement he had spearheaded. The planned Montreal convention was never held, and the annexationist movement faded away.[55]

Notwithstanding its ephemeral nature, the annexationist movement succeeded in creating a major division among the leaders of the French Canadian societies, between those operating out of Detroit, the heart of Michigan's French-language community, and those in other centers within the state. It is easy to understand that in Detroit, where people of French Canadian origin had been present for longer, where the use of French was declining, and where a large proportion of the French Canadians were permanently settled and their social integration was well under way, the idea of annexation did not encounter strong opposition or present a threat their way of life. Elsewhere in the state, however, and especially in the valley, the majority of French Canadians still intended to remain in Michigan for only a limited period and then return to Canada. Gradually, the interests of the French Canadians of Detroit had taken them in a different direction from those in the rest of the state, who wanted to maintain their cultural specificity and who opposed the annexation of

their French-speaking, Catholic country to the English, Protestant United States. This episode sowed confusion in the ranks of
the elites who sought to perpetuate the cultural characteristics of
the immigrants. The annexation of Canada, as advocated by the
annexationists of Michigan, would have condemned the French
Canadians, sooner or later, to assimilation.[56]

After this convention, nothing was ever the same for the
French Canadians of Michigan. This episode had a profoundly
divisive effect on the French Canadian societies, as it completely
eliminated any hope that they might all be united within one
state federation, and thus reduced the chances of maintaining
French Catholic characteristics in that state. The Association
Saint-Jean-Baptiste, whose delegates had voted overwhelmingly
for annexation, survived for another two years, until 1872. The
Lafayette Society of Detroit, which had likewise supported Lanctot's ideas, remained active but decided, from 1871 on, not to send
delegates to national conventions anymore. Only the Saint-Jean-
Baptiste Society of Wayne County joined the Michigan Union of
Saint-Jean-Baptiste Societies.[57] But the union went bankrupt in
1879, which forced the Wayne County Saint-Jean-Baptiste Society to take care of its members by itself. The annexationist movement not only disrupted the societies; above all, it undermined the
credibility of their leaders in the eyes of the French Canadians.

THE MIGRATION IN THE 1870S AND COMMUNITY LIFE

These institutional storms were, however, not enough to slow the
influx of French Canadians, who migrated in greater numbers to
the valley after the Civil War, despite the fact that the 1870s
were marked by a strike in the lumber industry (in July 1872) and
a major economic depression between 1873 and 1879. In fact,
the figures show that from 1870 to 1880, the French Canadians
increased more rapidly than the overall population of the valley.
In Saginaw County, their ranks swelled by nearly 160 percent

during this decade, whereas the total population rose by only 51 percent. In Bay County, the phenomenon was even more extreme: the French Canadian population increased by 240 percent, while the county population as a whole rose by 140 percent.

These data suggest two things. On the one hand, the socioeconomic integration of the French Canadians was so advanced in the 1870s that an economic depression, notwithstanding the factory closings and wage reductions that marked it, did not make them leave the region. For newcomers, there were compatriots with experience of living and working in the region to help them integrate rapidly in this unstable period. On the other hand, the data also suggest that the migratory process of the French Canadians had reached the phase of chain migration—that the valley was no longer attractive exclusively because of the employment possibilities it represented, but also because of the ethnic solidarity that had developed; new arrivals could expect to receive material and emotional support from friends and relatives who were already settled and who could help them achieve socioeconomic integration.

Migration into the region accelerated for many reasons. First of all, job openings increased greatly with the consolidation of the lumber industry. At the same time, a more developed community infrastructure was a factor, as were improved transportation routes between the heartland of Quebec and Michigan. Since 1860, the Grand Trunk Railroad Company had linked central Quebec with Sarnia, Ontario, from which passengers could take the St. Clair River ferry to Port Huron, Michigan. From there they had direct access to the valley.[58]

Migrants arriving in the valley in this period came increasingly from Quebec and less frequently from other parts of Michigan or from the Northeast (see table 3.2).[59] In 1860, 82 percent of household heads were born in Quebec, 12 percent were born in Michigan, and about 6 percent were born in the Northeast. Ten years later, the situation had changed: 94 percent were from Quebec, 4 percent from Michigan, and 2 percent from the Northeast.[60]

TABLE 3.2A

Place of Birth of French Canadians in the Saginaw Valley,
1850–1900 (by percentage)

	Year				
Place of birth	*1850*	*1860*	*1870*	*1880*	*1900*
Michigan	47.1	12.3	3.9	6.4	13.1
French Canada	47.1	82.2	94.1	88.8	80.9
Northeastern U.S.	5.8	5.5	2.0	4.8	6.0

TABLE 3.2B

Socioeconomic Profile of French Canadians in the Saginaw
Valley, 1850–1900 (by percentage)

	Year				
Economic sectors	*1850*	*1860*	*1870*	*1880*	*1900*
Agriculture	52.9	36.9	5.81	2.0	23.7
Sawmill and saltworks	5.8	35.5	58.8	52.0	31.3
Skilled labor and crafts	0.0	17.8	13.7	20.0	11.6
Service	0.0	0.0	13.7	8.0	11.6
Manufacturing Labor (unspecified)	35.2	0.0	0.0	0.0	9.5
Other	7.1	9.8	8.0	8.0	12.3

Source: Enumeration schedules, U. S. Federal Censuses, 1850–1900.

Even though migration was now more direct, some French Canadians made a number of stops in the Northeast on their way to the valley.[61] This was the case, for example, of Georges Lavigne, who was born in Quebec in 1814.[62] Georges and his wife migrated to the United States; in 1852, they had a child in New York State.[63] In 1856, the Lavigne family was in Michigan, where another child was born. Two more children were born in Michigan, in 1862 and 1867. In 1870, the Lavignes were living in Saginaw County, where Georges worked as a laborer in the lumber industry.

Other migrant families followed the same itinerary. A case in point is that of Jos Mallette, born in 1831. In the early 1850s, Jos married a Canadian and, in 1852, still in Canada, the couple had their first child. But the following year, their second child was born in New York State, as were the next three children, in 1856, 1859, and 1861. After the beginning of the Civil War in the United States, the Mallette family returned to Canada, where the next child was born in 1863. But the family returned to the United States in 1867, as soon as conditions there seemed more stable. This time, they went to Michigan, where two more children were born, in 1867 and 1869. In 1870, Jos was working as a shipwright and he and his wife and eight children were living in Saginaw City.

These examples show how complex the migration process was, the remarkable mobility of the migrants, and the many steps that marked their itineraries. In the cases cited, the state of New York constituted a way station in the migration toward the valley.

From 1860 to 1880, the new French Canadians who arrived in the valley settled mainly in the industrial towns, where the chances of finding work had improved greatly. Over 50 percent of all the French Canadians in Saginaw County during this period lived in Saginaw City and East Saginaw, the two main industrial towns. The situation was similar in Bay County: the French Canadians were concentrated in the most important industrial areas—Bay City and the township of Bangor—which together accounted for nearly 75 percent of the county's French Canadians. In 1880, 30 percent of the French Canadians in the county resided in West Bay City, a town formed in 1877 when the villages of Banks, Salzburg, and Wenona merged.[64]

The occupational profile of the French Canadians in the valley, which changed rapidly in the 1850s, stabilized during the 1860–80 period, when the majority of household heads were drawn to work in the sawmills and the related sector of salt production. Although some household heads worked as laborers in the sawmills, a large percentage (particularly in the sawmills of Saginaw County) already held well-paid positions of responsibility, such as supervisor, or were skilled workers—mill carpenters, planers, or sawyers.[65] This diversity in the economic integration of the French Canadians shows that despite their recent arrival on the labor market, many of them had been able to take advantage of their skills to rapidly obtain positions of responsibility in the sawmills.

About 14 percent of household heads held jobs in the service sector in 1870, but only 8 percent did so in 1880. They worked primarily as hotel owners, saloon keepers, and liquor merchants. Their presence in the latter occupation is surprising. Previous research has not accustomed us to associate French Canadians with the sale of spirits. This is no doubt related to the fact that it did not correspond to the value of temperance that the clerical elite sought to inculcate in parishioners. The strong presence of French Canadians in this field of activity may be connected to their experience in various lumber towns in Canada and the United States, where they may have come to the realization that being a saloon owner, contrary to the admonitions of their parish priest, did not necessarily entail buying a "ticket to hell," and that despite the considerable initial investment and the expensive license required by the authorities, it could be a very lucrative line of work.

In addition, the owner of a saloon held a special social status in the community because the saloon was a social and recreational center and a place where important information was exchanged, particularly regarding the job market. Saloon owners often served as intermediaries between workers seeking jobs and employers seeking workers. In this way, not only did they provide a service for people who frequented their saloon, but they also ensured that their establishment would become a necessary stopping place for those looking for work. The presence of French Canadian saloon owners—generally immigrants who were respected and influential in the community—facilitated the economic integration of new migrants in the region. Saloon keepers like Edmond Voyer, thirty-five, of Saginaw City, or Edouard Francis, thirty, of East Saginaw, were called on to play this important, reassuring role for French Canadian migrants.[66]

Approximately 14 percent of household heads in 1870 and 20 percent in 1880 were craftsmen or skilled workers, employed as shoemakers, bricklayers, or shipwrights in the shipbuilding yards of Saginaw County. The agricultural sector, which was already in decline in 1860, accounted for only 6 percent of household heads in 1870 but for considerably more ten years later: 12 percent were farmers in 1880.

The changes in the occupational profile of the French Canadians between 1870 and 1880 are closely related to the economic depression that lasted from 1873 to 1879. The facts that in 1880 fewer boys of fifteen and older were working, that the percentage of households taking in paying boarders had fallen, that the number of household heads working in agriculture and as craftsmen had risen while that of household heads engaged in the lumber industry had fallen slightly all reflect the impact of the depression on the job market in the lumber industry (see table 3.3).

People devised new strategies to get through the depression. Some families left the valley and returned, either temporarily or permanently, to their home country. Thus, for example, Joseph Paquette, a carpenter born in Canada in 1834, spent the 1860s and early 1870s in Michigan and returned to Canada between 1873 and 1876 with his wife and their children, all born in Michigan. Then, when the effects of the depression had abated, the family came back and settled in East Saginaw in 1880, with two more children born during their stay in Canada.[67]

But the great majority opted for other solutions. Some chose agriculture, which, as we have seen, was the occupation of 12 percent of household heads in 1880. Other relied on a more active participation by all members of their family. During the depression, girls aged fifteen and older contributed significantly to their family income by their earnings from work outside the home. In 1880, 23 percent of them were employed in this way, whereas ten years earlier, the contribution of girls in this age group was nil.

The practice of taking in boarders became much more common in this period. Between 20 percent and 25 percent of households relied on this type of activity to boost their income.[68] The data show a fairly clear correlation between household composition and the decision to accept paying boarders. They show that 80 percent of the households with boarders had children under the age of fifteen. It was households with young children, who could not work outside the home and who required supervision by their mothers at home, that tended to take in boarders. Household composition and the age of children thus influenced the choice of strategies employed by families to improve their living conditions.

The jobs generated by the development of the lumber industry after the Civil War fostered such a strong sense of confidence in the immigrant population that some household heads expressed the desire to settle permanently with their families in the United States and to obtain their American citizenship in order to be able to participate fully in political life. During this period of consolidation, nearly a third of household heads applied for and obtained American citizenship.[69]

Like becoming a citizen, acquiring property marked a decisive step in the evolution of a household. Although it was often a way to invest savings, it also illustrates eloquently the migrants' desire to settle more permanently. Generally—as I have observed elsewhere[70]—buying land confirmed the migrants' resolve to put an end to the quest that had often led them from place to place before finally settling down. But during this period, the analysis of the data, notwithstanding their fragmentary nature,[71] is surprising (compared to the situation in New England), because it shows that in 1870 nearly 35 percent of household heads owned landed property worth between $400 and $1,500. This propensity of the French Canadians to become owners of their homes, together with a high rate of naturalization, confirms the fact that very early on, an appreciable number of French Canadians decided to put down roots in the United States.

The 1872 Strike in the Lumber Industry

Curiously, the short strike in July 1872 stirred up more feeling in the French Canadian community of Bay City than in the valley as a whole. At the beginning of the strike, the workers created a labor organization that many of the French Canadians joined. Their participation in it rapidly became a source of tension in

"Little Canada." Bay City's Catholic clerical elite condemned the strike and the labor organization, describing the organization as pagan and heretical because it required that its members swear allegiance.[72] In his Sunday sermon, the newly appointed parish priest, Gilbert Girard, also strongly condemned the French Canadian workers who had taken part in the establishment of this organization and who were participating in the strike.[73]

The active contribution of the French Canadians in this labor conflict is surprising. Previous research on the French Canadians in the United States has not depicted them as being involved at such an early date in labor conflicts.[74] In fact, they were generally hired as strikebreakers during labor conflicts. There are examples of French Canadians participating in strikes in New England. But the great majority of such strikes occurred in the twentieth century, in towns with firmly established French Canadian communities: for example in Lawrence, Massachusetts, in 1912, and in Manchester, New Hampshire, in 1922.

In the valley, where the migration process was still recent, participation in this strike is even more surprising, especially since it seems to have been considerable, judging from the reactions it provoked among clerical leaders. One explanation may be that the French Canadians' lifestyle and work culture, together with the weakness and instability of their clerical and lay leaders, soon freed them from a certain social isolation—perhaps sooner than was the case with their compatriots elsewhere—and enabled them to integrate more rapidly into the socioeconomic life of the host society. They were thus better placed to understand the main economic issues and to defend more promptly their own interests.

THE DECLINE OF THE LUMBER INDUSTRY AND THE IMMIGRANT COMMUNITIES, 1880–1900

The period that began in 1880 and ended at the end of the century was characterized by instability in the lumber industry and the weakening of the region's French Canadian communities. With

the end of the economic depression of the 1870s, the labor market recovered a measure of stability. However, before long—in
1884—the lumber industry entered a new period of instability,
which was followed by the strike of 1885. The depression of 1893
to 1897 confirmed the decline of the industry and of the communities that depended on it.

For the French Canadian communities, this was thus a period
of great turmoil. Although the population increased considerably
between 1880 and 1884, rising from 7,331 to 10,700 inhabitants,[75]
it stagnated from 1884 to 1894 and fell gradually to 10,324 inhabitants[76]—just over 7 percent of the total population of the
valley—during the last half of the 1890s[77] (see table 3.1).

The decline of the lumber industry and the closing of one
sawmill after another eliminated many jobs, which were not replaced at the same rhythm by the concomitant development
of new economic sectors.[78] The French Canadians experienced
many additional problems that contributed to the economic de-
stabilization of their own communities. The French Canadian
merchants were strongly affected by the decline of the lumber
industry. Wage cuts and job losses that reduced the buying power
of their clientele jeopardized their businesses. This situation was
particularly difficult in Bay City, where much of the French Canadian population lived. Some merchants placed messages in the
Bay City newspaper *Le Patriote* to advise their clientele that due
to financial difficulties they were closing their stores, inviting cus-
tomers to take advantage of prices slashed for liquidation before
the official closing date.[79]

Business was apparently so bad in Bay City's Little Canada
that several shopkeepers did not hesitate to appeal to their cus-
tomers' nationalist sentiments. In the pages of *Le Patriote,* a number of messages urged French Canadians to remember their ethnic origin and "buy *Canadien.*" Carrier, the Bay City pharmacist,
published the following advertisement in 1884: "If you have pre-
scriptions to be filled, bear in mind that the *Canadiens'* drugstore is
on Water Street, and that it is owned by H. Carrier."[80] During the
1880s, and especially in 1884, some French Canadian storeowners

declared bankruptcy, while others had no choice but to sell their business. This was the case of Joseph Fortin, who was obliged to sell his grocery, located on Woodside Street in Bay City's Little Canada, in August 1884.[81]

Despite the decline of the lumber industry, some institutions, such as the Lafayette Society in Bay City, sought to maintain a certain dynamism. In the early 1880s, the Lafayette Society continued to organize balls, banquets, and concerts in Lafayette Hall. However, these activities concerned the French Canadian elite rather than the community as a whole.[82] The Lafayette Society also openly affirmed its attachment to American society and its American patriotism. Every July, it held a ball in honor of Independence Day and participated in the parade organized by the municipal authorities through the streets of Bay City.[83] By contrast, its celebration of June 24, Quebec's traditional holiday, was decidedly low key.[84] This behavior accurately reflected the role that the Lafayette Society—like many others—aspired to play in the lives of its members: it aimed to foster the integration of the community it served into the host society, which it held in high esteem. The Saint-Jean-Baptiste Society of West Bay City, although present in the Fourth of July festivities, also celebrated—apparently in keeping with its regular practice—the French Canadian holiday in June 1885 by organizing a banquet at Sainte-Marie Church in West Bay City.

Among the French Canadian societies, the Saint-Jean-Baptiste societies, whose nationalist and patriotic origins are well known, took the most pains to perpetuate the traditions of French Canada, to maintain an active relationship with Quebec, and to celebrate holidays associated with Quebec.[85] Thus, for example, it invited all the American Saint-Jean-Baptiste societies to a gathering in Montreal in June of 1884. More than three hundred societies, including a number from New England and the Midwest, accepted the invitation.[86]

Despite its efforts, the Lafayette Society ran into problems. In August 1884, it underwent a "reorganization" whose causes, like its effects, remain obscure. In the obituary notice published in

Le Patriote on July 31, 1884 for Alexandre Laroche of Bay City, a devoted member of the society, the resolutions adopted by a meeting of the Société de bienfaisance Lafayette on August 3, 1884 indicated that a reorganization had been carried out. These resolutions were signed by J. P. Le Roux, Régis Boutyette, and Zotique Aubry, the members of the executive committee. Of the three, only Zotique Aubry was part of the executive elected at the annual elections in March 1884. The fact that the composition of the executive committee was not the same as that elected five months earlier suggests that there were changes in the leadership of the society. The causes are unknown. But at the same time a new mutual aid society was established in Bay City, whose members held regular meetings in Madison Hall, on the corner of Madison and First Streets.[87] This coincidence suggests instability in the leadership of the Lafayette Society, which may have taken the form of resignations or at least of tensions among the members of the board of directors, which led to the creation of a new mutual aid society.

During the 1880s, the French Canadians of Bay City were increasingly wooed by political parties and participated actively in the political life of their community. Both the political organizations and the French-language newspapers of the region sought their support. In the period leading up to the November 4, 1884 elections, during which the population elected the representative from the Tenth District to the state legislature, the publishers of the French-language newspapers *Le Patriote* and *Le Courrier* clearly indicated that they supported the Democrat Spencer O. Fisher, who was the mayor of West Bay City, and that they hoped that Americans citizens of French Canadian origin would vote for the same candidate.[88]

However, the French Canadians of Bay City did not participate in the electoral process merely as voters. Several also ran as candidates for positions in the municipal administration. In the April 1884 municipal elections in Bay City, four out of twenty-one positions were won by candidates of French Canadian origin. In the Fifth District, whose population was primarily German American but where French Canadians accounted for 15 percent of the population, a French Canadian, A. O. Perrot, was elected sheriff. In the Sixth District, where Polish Americans formed the majority and French Canadians comprised only about 5 percent of the population, William Trombley was elected to the position of town councillor and J. Ruelle to that of supervisor. Similarly, in the Seventh District, in which Germans predominated and where French Canadians represented only 7 percent of the population, Louis Bouchard was elected supervisor.[89]

These changes in the valley between 1880 and 1900 are reflected in the decline in the percentage of household heads who had been born in Quebec: 94 percent in 1870, 89 percent in 1880, and by the end of the century, only 81 percent. By contrast, more and more household heads had been born in Michigan. In 1870, only 4 percent were from Michigan, in 1880, 6 percent, and by 1900, the figure had reached 13 percent. The percentage of French Canadians born in the northeastern United States also rose in this period: it was 2 percent in 1870, 5 percent in 1880 and 6 percent in 1900.[90] The considerable increase in the proportion of Michigan natives bears witness to a certain stabilization of the population of the communities as well as the consolidation of the second generation.

A new phenomenon emerged in this period. Whereas previously, household heads who had been born or had lived in the Northeast before migrating to Michigan had come mainly from New York, Maine, and Vermont, now some new arrivals had spent time in the manufacturing states of New England—New Hampshire, Massachusetts, and Rhode Island—before coming to the valley. Guy Martin offers one example. Born in Canada in 1844, he married a Canadian, and the couple had a child in Canada in 1863. In 1882, they migrated to the United States and had another child the same year, in New Hampshire. In 1894 and 1896, two children were born in Michigan, and in 1900, this family was living in Bay County, where Guy Martin worked as a laborer.[91]

The case of Henri Bourdon also illustrates the new trend in East-West migration. Bourdon was born in 1852 in Canada. He and his Canadian wife emigrated to the United States in 1878. In 1880, they had a child in Rhode Island, after which they moved to Michigan, where four more children were born between 1889 and 1899. In 1900, the Bourdons were living in West Bay City, and Henri Bourdon was employed as a carpenter.

The migratory trend these cases illustrate began about 1890 and linked certain manufacturing states of the Northeast more closely with the Saginaw Valley. It seems likely that the economic depression of the 1890s, together with the difficulties the New England cotton manufacturing industry faced as a result of competition from the southern cotton industry, prompted some French Canadians to leave the Northeast for the West. Some probably came to the valley in hopes of finding inexpensive land or more stable employment in the manufacturing sector. If this hypothesis proves correct, it will confirm once again the existence, in one form or another, of a migratory triangle that linked (unequally and according to their respective economic situations and organizational models) Quebec, the American industrial Northeast, and Michigan.[92]

The occupational profile of the French Canadians also changed. Already, the proportion of French Canadians who were active in the lumber industry had fallen, in the wake of the depression, from 59 percent in 1870 to 52 percent in 1880. This decline continued during the two remaining decades of the nineteenth century; by 1900 only 31 percent of household heads worked in lumber. Skilled labor was also affected by the depression. From 20 percent of household heads in 1880, this area of activity declined to 12 percent in 1900. The French Canadians became slightly more active in the service industries in this period; from 8 percent of household heads in 1880, this sector rose to nearly 12 percent in 1900, still mainly consisting of saloon and hotel owners. One sign that industry was experiencing difficult times was that agriculture, which the French Canadians had long neglected, now became more attractive; 12 percent of household heads were farmers in

TABLE 3.3

Socioeconomic Indicators in French Canadian Households in the Saginaw Valley, 1870–1900, (by percentage)

	1870	1880	1900
Wives working (outside the home)	2.1	1.6	1.2
Boys 15 and older working	93.0	70.0	83.3
Boys under 15 working	7.7	5.4	2.5
Girls 15 and older working	0.0	22.6	26.1
Girls under 15 working	0.0	0.0	0.0
Households renting to boarders	25.5	20.0	5.5
Naturalized citizens	31.8	—	60.0
Property owners	34.6	—	63.5

1880, and nearly 24 percent in 1900 (see table 3.2). After the region's economic leaders proposed conditions favorable to economic renewal, a number of manufacturing industries were established. In 1900, box factories, foundries, stone mills, and sugar refineries employed about 10 percent of household heads.

Under these circumstances, taking in boarders was no longer a viable strategy to fall back on, because the decline of industrial activities reduced the number of temporary jobs and in consequence, the number of boarders. In 1880, 20 percent of households had relied on this strategy to boost their incomes; in 1900, less than 6 percent did so (see table 3.3).

Child labor was also affected by the changing conditions. In 1880, 70 percent of boys aged fifteen and older worked outside the home, mainly in the lumber industry. In 1900, the percentage had risen to 83 percent, but the areas of employment were much more diversified and also more precarious, ranging from corner groceries to box manufacturing, and including bricklaying and the fire brigade. It was no longer possible for boys to find work in the lumber industry.

In this context of change, the great majority of the French Canadians who were still living in the valley had chosen to settle permanently in the United States. In 1900, 60 percent of household heads born in Quebec had American citizenship or were in the process of obtaining it.[93] About 64 percent of those who re-mained in the region reported that they owned land, and 50 per-cent of these landowners had already paid off their mortgage.[94]

The economic restructuring of the valley at the end of the nineteenth century thus required some major adjustments on the part of the working-class families who had previously depended on the lumber industry. The French Canadians were able to adapt to the new conditions. Although the phenomenon is impossible to measure precisely, the initial effect of this economic transition had been to cause French Canadians to leave. Some returned to Quebec, while others probably followed the industry, once again, toward the new timber frontier, which was now located further west.

Among the households that had decided to stay in the val-ley and whose heads had acquired American citizenship, many turned to agriculture. Near the end of the century, it became eas-ier to buy land again, because logging was finished in the region and the land was available for agriculture and sold at an afford-able price. Although agriculture constituted a risky activity after the disappearance of many logging camps, which had provided an important market for agricultural production, many French Canadians doubtless saw the possibility of working their own land and of being self-employed—not dependent on the fluctuations of the job market—as an attractive option. This behavior is all the more probable in that the development of the lumber industry had passed through the same phases everywhere, and it always ended in a return to agriculture. In this sense, the behavior of the French Canadians was based on their previous work experience in this area and their awareness of the typical evolution of the lumber industry and of the cycles of the labor market. They took advantage of the employment possibilities offered by the lumber industry during its glory years to economize—and indeed some of them had accumulated savings—in order to be able to buy land in the region when, as they expected it would, the lumber industry declined. Other French Canadians, probably those who were al-ready active in industry, found work in the manufacturing sector, which was gradually developing in the region and which required few specific skills.

By the beginning of the twentieth century, these communities, which had once been so dynamic, began to disappear. Without the lumber industry, which had drawn the French Canadians to the region, these communities could no longer attract newcomers, and gradually they lost the French Catholic characteristics that had distinguished them. Today, only the names on certain street signs and tombstones recall the passing presence in the region of thousands of French Canadians.

The French Canadian presence in the Saginaw Valley during the nineteenth century was the result of a movement that had several geographic origins and several causes. Initially, people of French Canadian origin living in communities in southeastern Michigan in the early nineteenth century were among the first to come to the region, setting in motion a modest process of settlement and development in the valley.

At about the same time, a migratory movement of a different nature and animated by other concerns took shape in the valley. By the 1840s, the deplorable state of Quebec's economy, together with the disappearance of survival strategies developed within the North Atlantic economy, had obliged many French Canadians to rethink their future and opt for migration to Michigan.

In migrating to the Saginaw Valley, the French Canadians were behaving in a manner perfectly consistent with the cultures of movement and work they had developed over decades. The Saginaw Valley represented a familiar territory. The economic sectors that were developing there were in all respects compatible with the various objectives of the French Canadians. The valley had fertile, inexpensive land; it also had abundant timber resources whose industrial exploitation, which was about to begin, would require a large and experienced workforce. The French Canadians were ready to fill the need.

The few French Canadians in the valley before the Civil War had not all arrived there by the same itinerary. While direct migration from Quebec to the valley intensified in the course of the century, it was supplemented by a steady secondary stream of migrants from the semipermanent French Canadian communities that had grown up in the relatively recent past in lumbering and agricultural areas of the northeastern states. On the one hand, just like American farmers in the Northeast, many French Canadians participated in the great East-West migration, which in some cases led to the valley. On the other hand, their arrival in the valley was also part of another process: that of the regular, progressive westward movement of the lumber frontier. This displacement created a northern migratory labor market, in which the French Canadians had participated since the very beginning of the nineteenth century and which had transformed them into migrant workers forever following the lumber frontier. The movement of the main logging activities to the valley in the period 1850 to 1860 had thus prompted a similar movement by a part of this French Canadian workforce from the Northeast to the Saginaw Valley. In these two models, migration to the Northeast of the United States seems to have been a transitory phase in the migratory continuum leading westward.

After the Civil War, the rapid development of the lumber industry in the valley led the French Canadians to rely heavily on migration, with the result that agriculture, the main focus until then, no longer ranked among their priorities. This migratory trend, although more direct, did not link Quebec exclusively with the valley. Some French Canadians who spent time in the northeastern states, especially New York, and who were affected by the decline of the lumber industry in that region, followed the industry when it moved westward, and some of those migrants ended up in the valley—the new lumber frontier. In this sense, whether they had previously resided in Quebec or in the northeastern states, the French Canadians of the valley participated in a migratory process that may be described as triangular, linking Quebec, the northeastern states, and the Saginaw Valley.

Overall, two factors are essential for an understanding of the many facets of the migration experience and the socioeconomic integration of the French Canadians in the Saginaw Valley. The first concerns the culture of movement that characterized the French Canadians, which simultaneously oriented the migratory movement, reassured the migrants regarding their movement, and enabled them to rapidly feel at ease in the Great Lakes area. The second factor is the culture of lumber-related work acquired by the French Canadians in the course of their experiences in this line of activity throughout the continent. These two factors influenced all aspects of the French Canadian migration to the valley and the behavior of the migrants, with regard both to the host society and to the unique institutions they created within it.

As soon as they arrived in the valley, the French Canadians sought to create familiar social institutions. First in the 1850s, but primarily in the 1860s and 1870s, several Catholic parishes were established. All were initially multiethnic, but some, when the number of parishioners had reached a certain level, became specifically French Canadian parishes. Often, in close association with these parishes there developed private parish schools, newspapers, and mutual aid societies—all structures whose initial objective was to create a framework for the members of the community and to give them a sense of belonging and safety.

However, these institutions soon experienced phases of turbulence resulting in internal divisions, the undermining of their leaders' credibility, and a weakened ability to provide reassurance and stability. Thus the emergence of the annexationist political movement in the late 1860s destabilized the French Canadian societies of Michigan. This ultimately ephemeral movement perturbed all the French Canadian organizations in the state, obliging them to take a stand on this issue and subsequently creating profound differences between the Detroit societies and those located elsewhere in Michigan. This movement also sowed confusion within the latter institutions, which sought to ensure *la survivance* (French Canadian survival). Organizations that had until then pursued a common objective of uniting all the French Canadians of the state found themselves at the conclusion of the annexationist crisis isolated from each other, divided and weakened.

Beyond these deep divisions, other pivotal French Canadian institutions also experienced periods of instability and internal tensions. Thus, for example, in St. Joseph's Parish in Bay City, the largest French Canadian parish in the valley, the parishioners faced constant changes in the parish leadership from 1872 to the end of the century. Some of the priests did not seem attuned to the needs of French Catholics, and the parishioners had to make the effort to become familiar with one new spiritual leader after another, lessening their sense of religious stability. In addition to these spiritual problems, temporal and financial difficulties demanded sacrifices on the part of the parishioners and created tensions within the whole community.

The valley's French-language newspapers also experienced instability. Although never characterized by a high degree of longevity, some of them tried to provide guidance and reassurance to the community they served, advocating *la survivance* but also taking an interest in the social, economic, and political evolution of the context in which thousands of French Canadians lived. But in the valley, the French Canadian newspapers always gave the impression of being detached from the community whose development they should have been following and illuminating through their commentary. Although they were not the main cause of the community's instability, their lack of involvement contributed to it.

In addition to these religious and institutional problems there were major economic changes. During the last quarter of the nineteenth century, economic instability was chronic in the valley. The French Canadians had to deal with the depression of the 1870s, the lumber industry's difficulties in the 1880s, the strike of 1885, and the progressive decline of the lumber industry.

Given this unstable climate, the characteristics of the French Canadians' migration, and the nature of their socioeconomic integration into the valley, it is possible that their cultures of work and of movement and the ease with which they integrated into a world they already knew fairly well contributed somewhat to tensions and divisions—first among their institutional elites, and then between parishioners and the clerical elite. Perhaps the

French Canadians, self-assured by their long experience of working and living in lumbering communities, did not feel a need
(to the degree their clerical leaders would have liked) for protection by sheltering institutions that recommended isolation from
English Protestant and industrial society as the only sure way to
preserve their French Canadian Catholic identity. This very dynamic, which marked the evolution of the region's French Canadian communities, weakened their institutional leadership further, compromising its authority and allowing French Canadians
considerable latitude. Less and less attuned to the traditional argu-
ments of their elites, they became increasingly open to American
society.

The deepening gulf between a waffling, incoherent leadership
and individuals seeking greater autonomy had a major impact on
the behavior of the French Canadians. The conflict dulled the
"ethnic" consciousness that their leaders sought to foster among
the migrants—and that would have tied them more closely to
those leaders. This distance also hastened the emergence of a class
consciousness that found expression in the desire to improve the
living conditions of the family and in the use of specific means to
achieve this objective.

It is from this perspective that certain aspects of the French
Canadians' behavior can best be understood, particularly their
participation in the strikes of 1872 and 1885, their tendency to
obtain their American citizenship in short order, their active role
as both voters and candidates for elected office in the local administration, and their desire to become homeowners as soon as
they were able. These behaviors, which the French Canadians displayed after living in the valley for only a few years, show that they
realized very early that their interests and those of their families
went beyond the simple maintenance of their cultural specificity
and required greater commitment to the improvement of all areas
of their lives.

In economic terms, the considerable growth of the French
Canadian population during the depression of the 1870s reflects
the confidence of the valley's inhabitants and those who joined

them in this period. They were able to cope with unstable industrial conditions, with which their culture of work had clearly familiarized them. The diversity of the jobs the French Canadians held in 1870, barely a decade after migration began in earnest, illustrates the ease and rapidity with which they managed to integrate into the economic life of the valley. They worked in all sectors of the economy. Although they were concentrated in the lumber industry, some held jobs in shipyards or on the railroads, or worked as craftsmen, skilled workers, or laborers. Their role as liquor merchants also grew out of their work experience in the lumber towns of the East Coast. They were well aware that this type of activity, although condemned by the clergy, was lucrative, and that it also enabled them to offer newcomers guidance and support in their integration into the labor market. Also, in a context where traditional institutions experienced periods of instability, the French Canadian saloon keeper and his establishment quite likely came to play an even more indispensable role in the community. Above all, in this fluctuating climate, they could count on family solidarity to help them handle difficulties that they saw as temporary and not requiring dramatic decisions. The family remained the only institution that was reliable, versatile, and resourceful—capable of adapting to the requirements of the industry and its cycles on the basis of its own needs.

This culture of work and of movement explains why, when the lumber industry declined in the valley, the French Canadians showed no signs of panic. Instead, they developed new strategies based on the options available. Some returned to Canada, whose economy was performing better by the beginning of the twentieth century; others preferred to remain in the valley and to adapt to the emerging manufacturing structure. Still others had acquired affordable land, and others decided to follow the lumber industry to the next lumber frontier.

Within this broad migratory process, the French Canadians showed themselves neither passive nor victims of circumstance. In every phase of their lives in the valley, they drew strength from their culture of work and their lifestyle, which facilitated their socioeconomic integration and made them more dynamic and enterprising. Their behavior consistently expressed their self-confidence and their ability to shape their future. They made informed choices based on their knowledge and specific needs, and this enabled them to retain a sense of continuity between the past and the present.[95] Their behavior was remarkable enough to signal a special relationship between them and the surrounding society, a relationship based on self-confidence founded on knowledge and experience.

The French Canadian communities in the region, without any real leadership, eventually disintegrated, having lost over time their specific cultural characteristics and their reason for existing. Nonetheless, the experience of the French Canadians in the valley underscores not only the complexity of the migratory process that led them over vast reaches of the continent but also the pivotal role played by their culture of work and their values, which guided them in the many choices they faced in seeking to improve their living conditions.

Chapter 4

French Canadian Migration to
the Keweenaw Peninsula, 1840–1914

French Canadians participated in the successive phases of development of the Keweenaw Peninsula, just as they did in the Saginaw Valley. It is remarkable, however, that they should be attracted to the mining operations that were starting up in the region in the nineteenth century, since in Quebec at this time there was very little mining activity. As we shall see, these migrants understood that the peninsula offered numerous opportunities for those who wished to improve their circumstances.

In a remarkable echo of the French Canadian experience in the Saginaw Valley, their experience on the peninsula may also be divided into three distinct phases. The first, from 1840 to 1860, was marked by the arrival of the first migrants and the beginnings of community organization. The second phase, from 1860 to 1900, saw an acceleration of migratory movement, the establishment of social institutions, and the consolidation of the communities. The last phase, from the last years of the nineteenth century until the start of the First World War, was characterized by the erosion of social consensus, the strike of 1913–14, the departure of many migrants, and the decline of French Canadian communities in the region.

THE FRENCH CANADIANS BEFORE THE CIVIL WAR, 1840–60

Before the Civil War, there were few French Canadians on the peninsula.[1] In 1850, there were 71, representing less that 7 percent of the total population of the region. By 1860, their number had risen to 703, still only 5 percent of the total population (see table 4.1).[2] These statistics are startling because they show that French Canadians, although in admittedly negligible numbers, were already present in this isolated region at such an early period in the development of mining.

We know very little about these first French Canadian arrivals, though we do know where they came from. Among all heads of households living there in 1850, two out of three were born in Quebec, while one in four was born in Michigan and one in eight was from Wisconsin, the neighboring state. But this diversity of place of origin rapidly changed. From the early 1850s until the 1870s, Quebec was the birthplace of nine out of ten heads of households on the peninsula. It was not until the 1880s that

TABLE 4.1

French Canadian Population in the Counties of the Keweenaw Peninsula, 1850–1910

Year	Houghton	Keweenaw*	Ontonagon	Total	Total population of the Region	French Canadians (%)
1850	36	—	35	71	1,097	6.5
1860	377	—	326	13	802	5.1
1870	1,290	271	249	1,810	20,929	8.6
1880	3,061	351	250	3,662	29,308	12.5
1900	7,840	326	638	8,804	75,477	11.6
1910	6,348	275	474	7,097	103,904	6.8

Source: Enumeration schedules, U. S. census for the counties of Houghton, Keweenaw and Ontonagon, 1850–1910.

*In 1861, this county was created from a part of Houghton County.

a certain diversity of birthplaces reappeared, becoming more pronounced in the 1890s and the 1900s (see table 4.2).

The closer connection between the peninsula and Quebec
that becomes evident in the 1850s may be explained by the
marked improvement in transportation routes. It should be noted

TABLE 4.2A
**Place of Birth of French Canadians on the Keweenaw
Peninsula, 1850–1910 (by percentage)**

Place of Birth	Year					
	1850	1860	1870	1880	1900	1910
Canada	62.5	96.7	98.5	92.8	85.1	74.2
Michigan	25.0	1.1	1.1	4.3	10.2	22.7
Wisconsin	12.5	1.1	0.0	1.4	1.7	0.8
Maine	0.0	1.1	0.4	0.0	0.3	0.0
Minnesota	0.0	0.0	0.7	0.3	0.0	0.0
Other	0.0	0.0	0.7	2.4	2.2	0.0

TABLE 4.2B
**Socioeconomic Profile of French Canadians on the Keweenaw
Peninsula, 1850–1910 (by percentage)**

Economic sector	Year					
	1850	1860	1870	1880	1900	1910
Agriculture	0.0	6.8	8.7	5.0	7.5	12.0
Mining	0.0	17.0	16.7	25.9	29.2	44.0
Lumber	0.0	23.8	13.8	9.3	13.2	5.8
Fishing	37.5	0.0	1.8	1.45	0.0	0.9
Skilled labor	12.5	6.8	1.4	0.7	2.0	4.8
Service	0.0	15.9	6.2	5.1	11.8	9.3
Labor	31.2	20.4	41.5	47.5	25.8	4.8
Transportation	0.0	2.2	1.1	0.0	1.0	3.4
Canal work	0.0	0.0	4.0	0.0	0.0	0.0
Home	0.0	0.0	0.0	3.6	0.0	2.2
Other occupations	6.2	0.0	3.3	1.4	1.0	5.3
Unspecified	12.8	6.81	1.3	0.0	8.5	6.6

COUNTIES OF THE KEWEENAW PENINSULA.
From *Atlas of Michigan*, edited by Lawrence M. Sommers, 1977.
Courtesy of Michigan State University Press.

that before this time, the St. Lawrence River had been the principal transportation route linking the two regions. The Ontario and St. Lawrence Steam Boat Company sailed between Quebec City and Buffalo, New York, with stops at Montreal, Lachine, Cascades, Les Cèdres, and Coteau du Lac.[3] From Buffalo it was possible to reach Detroit, although not very rapidly, and there board a boat headed for the Upper Peninsula of Michigan.

But after 1860, French Canadians, like their compatriots heading for the Saginaw Valley, could take the Grand Trunk Railway, which ran through Quebec to Sarnia, Ontario. From there it was easy to reach Michigan and board a boat sailing north. Migrants could also ride the Great Western Railway, taking them directly to Detroit, from which point they could also reach the Upper Peninsula by boat. But of all the innovations of the 1850s, the opening of the Sault Sainte Marie Canal in 1855, which provided access to the heart of the mining region of the peninsula, did the most to attract new immigrants into the region.

This direct route was not the only one taken by French Canadian migrants, however. Some chose less conventional itineraries, relying on their skill at moving around the continent. This was the case of Olivier Laplante, born in Canada in 1826. Olivier and his Canadian wife left for the United States, and their first child was born in New York in 1846. Their next three children were also born in this state, in 1849, 1851, and 1853. Sometime between 1853 and 1856, the family left New York for Michigan, where another child was born in 1856. In 1860, the Laplante household resided in the township of Portage, in Houghton County, where the father worked as a laborer.

The case of the Nadeau family is similar. The father, Auguste, was born in Canada in 1831 and married a Canadian. The couple had their first child in Canada in 1855. The family left Canada for New York between 1855 and 1857; the second child was born there in 1857 and a third in 1858. Between 1858 and 1860, the family moved to Houghton County, where Auguste was working as a laborer in 1860.

While the itineraries of some migrants included stops in the eastern part of the continent, those of others included stops in the West. This was the case for the Lantonneau family. Edouard Lantonneau, the head of the household, was born in Canada in 1815. He married a Canadian, and they had their first child in Wisconsin in 1836. This birth was followed by two more in Wisconsin, in 1839 and 1843. The family then moved to Michigan, where another child was born in 1847. In 1850, Edouard was a fisherman in Houghton County.

Another example illustrating mobility is the Lamarre family. The father, Antoine, was born in Canada in 1800. He married a

Canadian in the 1820s, and the couple had a child in Wisconsin in 1826 and another in 1830. The Lamarre family moved to Michigan, where they were living in the village of Ontonagon in 1850, where Antoine worked as a laborer.

These are just a few of the known itineraries followed by these migrants. The data show that many Canadian-born heads of households living on the peninsula had previously lived in New York and Wisconsin. In New York, the decline in logging activities probably forced some migrants to leave, while in Wisconsin it was the end of the fur trade that obliged many families to pull up stakes and move to the peninsula, where mining operations were getting under way.

Between 1840 and 1860, the concentration of the French Canadian population followed the development of mining activities. At the start of the Civil War, the township of Portage, which included the village of Houghton, had attracted over 45 percent of the whole French Canadian contingent in Houghton County, while the township of Hancock—which included the village of the same name—directly across the Portage River from the village of Houghton, was in second position, with 22 percent of the French Canadians. The township of L'Anse, which ten years earlier had contained 90 percent of French Canadian heads of households, now had only 18 percent.

This concentration in the township of Portage was related not only to mining activities but to the fact that a Catholic parish, St. Ignatus of Loyola, had been created in the village of Houghton in 1858. Ministering to the spiritual needs of the growing Catholic population of the region, this parish—the first of its kind on the Keweenaw Peninsula—embraced all Irish, German, and French Canadian Catholics.[4]

The socioeconomic profile of the French Canadian population changed during this period. In 1850, fishing supported nearly 40 percent of the French Canadian families on the peninsula, while the occupation of laborer supported 31 percent of heads of households. But in 1860, several years after the real beginning of the mining industry, the range of occupations was much broader.

Fishing had disappeared as a sector of employment, while occupations in the lumber industry—including lumberjack and lumber contractor[5]—supported one family out of 4, followed by the occupations of laborer (20 percent of heads of households)[6] and miner (17 percent), and then by service sector jobs (16 percent) and agricultural work (7 percent).

To understand these changes, one must bear in mind that mining development was unstable before 1850 and that many of the French Canadians living in the region at that time came from former trading posts around the Great Lakes. Some of these had become small, isolated villages where fishing was the principal activity. It was not until the 1850s that the mining sector began to develop and stimulated the influx of Canadian-born French Canadians who were looking for employment opportunities. Mining activities were not the only ones, however, to interest the French Canadians. As we have seen earlier, lumber work and prospecting often went hand in hand during the initial phase of mining development. The need for laborers in the timber sector explains why the peninsula attracted so many loggers at this time, an occupation in which the French Canadians had vast experience. From 1860 on, reflecting the rapid demographic development of the region, hotels and saloons began to appear, and many were run by French Canadians.

THE ACCELERATION OF MIGRATION AND THE ESTABLISHMENT OF COMMUNITIES, 1860–1900

The French Canadian presence increased significantly in the region after 1860. During the turbulent period of the Civil War, a labor shortage on the peninsula provided opportunities for French Canadians. In June 1863, the *Portage Lake and Mining Gazette* (*PLMG*), a weekly published in Houghton and dedicated to the interests of miners, signaled to its readers the arrival of a steamship bringing 250 Canadian workers. They were accompanied by a recruiting agent, Euchariste Brûlé, specially hired by the Mining

Emigrant Aid Society. Brûlé, who had lived in the Lake Superior region since 1847, was originally from Saint-Barthélemy in the county of Berthier in Quebec and had been hired by the mining companies to recruit labor in Canada.[7] The new arrivals, described as young and short but possessing great physical strength, had been attracted by the high wages paid in the region, about double the rate being offered in Canada.[8]

However, the arrival of these French Canadians was not of great help in solving the problem of the labor shortage during the war. In March 1864, the *PLMG* put the arrival of these Canadians in perspective and deplored the fact that most of them—who lacked experience in the mining sector—had already left the region. The newspaper pointed out that those who had stayed worked mainly in logging, a type of work in which they excelled and whose production was in demand by mining companies for their exploration activities.[9] The paper also noted that in 1863, these French Canadians had obtained government contracts to supply lumber to the builders of the Mineral Range State Road, a state-funded road that was to be built in the region that year to facilitate transportation among the mining centers. Those who had been granted these contracts included Charles Gariépy, Jean-Baptiste Jolicoeur, Paul Perreault, and John Fournier.[10]

Other French Canadians doubtless moved into the region during the war. But many more of them went there after the hostilities had ceased. The second half of the 1860s coincided with the beginning of a more harmonious and stable period in the development of the mining industry, now concentrated more heavily on the Keweenaw Peninsula. This encouraged migration to the region, revitalized existing communities, and fostered the establishment of new ones.

At the end of the war, mining activities became concentrated in Houghton County. It was in the region of Portage Lake that the richest copper deposits were discovered, and it was also in this county—where the operations of the Quincy Mine Company were already located—that the activities of C & H were principally undertaken. From this time, Houghton County largely dominated the mining activities of the entire Keweenaw Peninsula.

The French Canadian population, which had been distributed about equally between the two counties before the war, also followed this tendency toward concentration in Houghton County. Mining development had led to the construction of several processing plants and stimulated work on urban infrastructure projects, canals, and bridges, creating numerous opportunities for migrants to find work. These processing activities, often carried out at a distance from the actual mining sites, favored the outlying development of small hamlets, some of which welcomed a growing number of French Canadians.

It has been noted that before the war, French Canadians were mainly located in the established villages of Houghton and Hancock. While Houghton already had its Catholic parish (St. Ignatus of Loyola), the village of Hancock, on the other side of Portage Lake, had no Catholic parish until the founding of Ste. Anne's Parish in 1861. It served as a gathering place for Catholics, many of whom were French Canadian, for many years.[11]

In addition to these two villages, small hamlets that had been isolated and sparsely populated underwent substantial changes under the influence of the surrounding mining developments. Among these were Lake Linden, located in the township of Schoolcraft, and the village of Calumet in Calumet Township. The rise of these two villages was closely tied to the presence of C & H, whose ore-processing plant created employment and attracted a considerable number of families.

The Village of Lake Linden and Its Community Life

The origins of Lake Linden go back to 1851.[12] The names of several French Canadians figure among its first inhabitants. The brothers Peter and Joseph Robesco, Joseph Grégoire, Euchariste Brûlé, and J. B. Tonpont were among the pioneers who settled near the lake and began to develop a small hamlet there.[13] But significant development did not begin until 1867, when C & H built a stamp mill there. This factory rapidly attracted a good number of migrants, to the point where the tiny hamlet was reorganized as a village in 1868.[14]

The construction of the factory was not the only reason for the rapid demographic development of Lake Linden. In 1867, Joseph Grégoire teamed up with two other recently arrived French Canadians—a pharmacist named Louis Deschamps and J. Normandin—to build a sawmill in the village. The mill, which they named Joseph Gregory and Company, would greatly benefit from the impressive resources of pine available in the region.[15]

Joseph Grégoire was born in Saint-Valentin in Quebec and arrived in the Lake Superior region in 1854. For several years he traveled the region, going as far as Duluth, Minnesota.[16] He worked as a lumberjack at first, and later obtained logging contracts for various mining companies, eventually becoming a successful entrepreneur. Grégoire and several associates undertook to establish the village of Portland in Minnesota, but when the project failed, he lost his entire fortune. As a result, in 1859, Grégoire decided to settle in the Portage Lake region, which was then seeing the start of a concentration of mining activities that promised to be profitable for lumber entrepreneurs. He soon landed contracts to supply lumber to certain mining companies and signed others with municipal authorities for the construction of urban infrastructure. Business was so good that in 1860 Grégoire acquired new timber lands in the region.

In 1867, with the help of associates whom he bought out in 1872, Grégoire built a sawmill equipped with the latest technology, at a cost of close to fifteen thousand dollars. His sawmill, which had a production capacity of five million board feet,[17] acted as a veritable magnet for French Canadians, as Grégoire let it be known that he would employ only his compatriots.[18] This announcement helped make Lake Linden a "Little Canada," with the highest concentration of French Canadians on the peninsula.[19] Grégoire quickly became a popular figure, and his social and financial participation in numerous community and religious causes led his fellow Canadians to nickname him the "Father of the Lake Superior Canadians."[20]

The large influx of French Canadians to Linden Lake was highly significant, especially at the political level. In the first elections held in 1866 to fill positions in the newly created township of Schoolcraft, Joseph Grégoire was elected to the office of clerk, a post he held for some fifteen years.[21] On this same ballot, Prosper Robert was elected treasurer, Norbert Sarrasin and Célestin Rémilliard were elected road commissioners, Léandre Marcotte was elected justice of the peace, and David Picard took one of the positions of township constable. In all, 50 percent of the fourteen electoral positions were won by French Canadians. The presence of candidates of French Canadian origin and their electoral victories reflect not only their demographic importance in the township but also their desire to integrate into the social and political life of the community by obtaining American citizenship.[22]

Practical considerations prompted the French Canadians of Lake Linden to create a parish in their immediate region. Those who had settled there at the end of the 1860s and wanted to attend mass had to travel several kilometers to the nearest Catholic parish, that of Sacred Heart in the neighboring village of Calumet.[23] In 1871, the Catholics of Lake Linden, on the strength of their numbers, presented a request to the diocese to create a Catholic parish in their village. As soon as authorization was obtained, the parishioners set about building a church, the construction of which was directed and financed in part by Joseph Grégoire. The diocese appointed the Reverend Francis Héliard, a forty-three-year-old Francophone, to lead the parish, which was given the name of St. Joseph.[24]

The construction costs of the church were evidently higher than expected, since in October of 1874 a special fair was organized by the parish to raise funds to help reimburse its debt.[25] It is not known whether the objective was met. The organization of fairs was a tradition, as every year—sometimes several times a year—such an event was organized and widely publicized in the newspapers, to provide financial support for the parishes.[26] It was at one of these fairs in November of 1874 that Joseph Grégoire was honored by the prominent citizens of Lake Linden, who presented him with the "cane of honor" in recognition of his "exceptional contribution" to the community life of Lake Linden and to the development of the French Canadian community.[27]

Given the increasing numbers of parishioners, the religious authorities decided to enlarge the church in 1876, and this work was funded by Joseph Grégoire.[28] Six years later, this place of worship had become too small, and the parish found itself with two options: to enlarge the church again or to build a new one. The second, more expensive, option was chosen, and it was decided that the old church would serve as a chapel.[29]

The project was carried out under the leadership of the Reverend Mesnard, who had taken over from the Reverend Héliard in 1881. Under his administration (1881–93), the parish of St. Joseph witnessed astounding development. The number of French Canadians in the township of Schoolcraft increased considerably, rising from 1,306 in 1880 to 2,178 in 1900. The number of parishioners of German and Irish origin also rose rapidly, to the point where the authorities of the diocese decided to appoint two assistants for the Reverend Mesnard. Also, in February 1888, the diocese agreed to subdivide St. Joseph Parish and create a new parish for the Irish and German congregations.[30]

The community of Lake Linden also went through some dark periods. According to the religious authorities themselves, the parish of St. Joseph was disturbed by the strikes that occurred in the region, including the one at C & H in 1872, although we do not know the exact consequences of these disturbances.[31] Additionally, the sawmill owned by Grégoire, an important employer of French Canadians, was twice destroyed by fire during the 1870s. The first fire, which occurred in June 1875, completely razed the building.[32] Grégoire built a makeshift, temporary sawmill in order to meet his commitments to supply lumber to the mining companies, among them C & H. The following year, in August 1876, another fire broke out, and the sawmill, which had been rebuilt at a cost of thirty thousand dollars, was completely destroyed. Grégoire was insured for only about a third of its value. Nevertheless, he rebuilt his sawmill yet again. This disaster had been so spectacular that its repercussions were felt as far away as the Saginaw Valley. The *Lumberman's Gazette* in that region reported on the misfortunes that assailed Grégoire and especially on the great financial losses he faced.[33] The sawmill that he built after the fire of 1876 made him one of the biggest lumber producers in the region, employing eighty workers.[34]

Fires had not finished wreaking havoc in Linden Lake. In May 1887, the whole village was devastated by a disastrous fire that destroyed over 260 houses.[35] The entire business sector of the town was affected. Losses were estimated at nearly 3 million dollars. One person died and 300 families were left homeless. This fire deeply disturbed the community. And although it inspired a spirit of solidarity and mutual assistance among the victims, it also caused many inhabitants to move away.

St. Joseph Parish quickly got back on its feet and attracted migrants once again. After the division of 1888, the parish went through two further subdivisions. The parish of St. Francis of Assisi was created in 1892 at Dollar Bay, south of Lake Linden on the shore of Portage Lake. It ministered to migrants of Slavic, German, Italian, and French Canadian origins. The parish of St. Cecilia was founded in 1893 in Hubbell, a small village located near Lake Linden on the shore of Torch Lake, where C & H had built a stamp mill. French Canadians formed the majority of its population.[36]

The demographic growth of the community also stimulated the founding of parish schools in Lake Linden.[37] In 1867, a public school was built. Two others followed. The first was another public school, while the second was built by C & H. The latter was destroyed by fire in 1881 and rebuilt by the company the same year at a cost of fifteen thousand dollars. The company rented it to the school board for a nominal fee.[38]

It was not until 1881 that French Canadians could receive instruction in their own language, when Adeline Garneau opened a school in the parish of St. Joseph. Seventy students attended classes in the first year. In 1882, 135 students were enrolled.[39] The number of French Canadian school children increased rapidly in Lake Linden, and in 1886 a new school, the Académie Ste. Anne, opened its doors. It was first run by the Soeurs de Sainte Croix (Sisters of Holy Cross), a Francophone religious community originating in Notre Dame, Illinois. They continued to run the school until 1889, when secular leaders temporarily took over. From 1893 to 1895, the administration of the Académie was handed over to the Soeurs des Saints Noms de Jésus et de Marie (Sisters of the Holy Names of Jesus and Mary), whose mother house was in Montreal. After another year of secular administration, the Sisters of St. Joseph, from Concordia, Kansas, were given responsibility for the institution.[40]

French Canadian associations serving as mutual insurance companies were also set up on the peninsula. In many cases, these associations also took on the mission of promoting patriotism, galvanizing national sentiment among their members, and celebrating their origins by organizing festivities to mark the national holiday.[41] It is not surprising that in 1879, Lake Linden was the birthplace of the first Saint-Jean-Baptiste Society on the Keweenaw Peninsula. Other chapters of this society were founded in the region in the mid-1880s, notably at Calumet in 1885 and in the towns of Houghton and Hancock in 1886.[42]

The annexationist movement of 1869–70 does not seem to have had any significant effects on the French Canadians of the peninsula, as the French Canadian associations were not yet strongly organized at this time. Nevertheless, the movement did have some repercussions. The Société Saint-Jean-Baptiste of Houghton—which was absent from the Detroit convention— seems to have experienced serious problems in 1871, which led to its dissolution. An article published in April 1871 in the *PLMG* confirmed that the Saint-Jean-Baptiste Society of Houghton had been dissolved by the decision of several members, who then generously helped themselves to the treasury of the society.[43] This article caused such a stir that the following week in the same newspaper, a spokesman for the Houghton Saint-Jean-Baptiste Society insisted on explaining the reasons for the dissolution. According to the spokesman, the society had recently found itself with members who did not share its ideology and who were no longer disposed to respect the conditions of membership. The society had not wanted to cause a scandal by expulsing the rebel members and had opted for dissolution, pure and simple. Nothing was said about the use of funds.[44]

In October 1885, the first convention of French Canadians of Upper Michigan was held, although its exact location is unknown. Delegates from the Saint-Jean-Baptiste Societies of Marquette, Lake Linden, Calumet, Ishpeming, and Republic were present. At this convention it was unanimously agreed to create an association of all the French Canadian societies in Upper Michigan. It was first of all resolved that all the French Canadian societies of Upper Michigan would join to form a regional union. It was also resolved that a central union should be created to bring together all the French Canadian societies of the state, with the ultimate goal of creating a federal union of all such societies in the United States and those in Canada, to be led by the mother society, the Saint-Jean-Baptiste Society of Montreal.[45] A provisional constitution was adopted to create a central association for mutual aid and it was agreed that all societies present would now belong to that association. There seemed to be a consensus among participants at this 1885 convention that a larger unifying structure should be created to strengthen the organization.

A second convention was therefore held in Lake Linden in 1886 and the same societies attended. A third assembly was held in Ishpeming in 1887, when a deep disagreement emerged among the delegates. The exact nature of this dispute is not known, but according to Télésphore Saint-Pierre, "the jealousy existing between the officers of two or three of the societies was the ruin of the mutual aid association and the idea of conventions was thus abandoned."[46]

Problems also dogged the development of the Saint-Jean-Baptiste Association of the State of Michigan. In 1885, the officers of this association had proposed uniting all the French Canadian societies of the state under one central administration. According to Saint-Pierre, "wherever the idea of a federation was debated, it received a most favorable reception." However, "when it came to applying the idea, it once again proved impossible to please all of those who posed as leaders of the societies."[47] The problem of the French Canadian institutions seems to have been that, in spite of the often-expressed need to be able to count on a larger organization, none of the existing societies had either the prestige or the leadership required to take the initiative of establishing a national and charitable union.[48]

This dissension illustrates the difficulties these leaders experienced in the 1880s and their inability to put the interests of their members above their personal interests. The problems reveal a lack of leadership at the national level and a reluctance on the part of certain local leaders to give up some of their powers over their immediate community and cede them to a central organization with the aim of keeping alive the cultural characteristics of all the French Canadians in Michigan.

The leaders of Lake Linden also founded French-language newspapers to keep French Canadians informed of events in their own community and in their homeland. These publications helped meet the needs of French speakers for information, as well as their need to maintain contact with their place of origin. It is revealing to note that the first newspaper published by the French Canadians on the Keweenaw Peninsula was bilingual. This paper, *Le franc pionnier*, was a weekly first published in Lake Linden on April 26, 1875.[49] Jos. A. Rooney and François-Xavier Thibault, the latter from Montreal, were partners in founding the paper.[50] Rooney was responsible for the English section, while Thibault supervised the French section of a newspaper whose motto was "in union there is strength." Was this joint venture of English and French speakers a sign of amicable and egalitarian relations between the two groups or simply a demographic-linguistic fact of Lake Linden that the founders wished to respect? Whichever it was, the association was short-lived, as the newspaper ceased publication in December of the same year.[51]

It was not until the end of the 1880s that the first newspaper published entirely in French was founded in the Keweenaw Peninsula. This was *L'Union franco-américaine*, published in Lake Linden in 1889 by a joint stock company led by Télésphore Saint-Pierre.[52] In 1891, J. E. Rochon was the managing editor and F. O. Mayotte was the manager. The paper reported on the French Canadian centers of the Upper Peninsula and on Quebec. It also ran advertisements, such as the one for a pilgrimage to Sainte-Anne-de-Beaupré, giving the price of tickets and the train schedules from Lake Linden to Sainte-Anne. The trip was priced at twenty-five dollars.[53] *L'Union franco-américaine* had a short life, disappearing in 1891.[54]

Even though the enterprises quickly disappeared from the scene, these attempts to found newspapers are evidence of a will to inform the population and maintain contact between the migrant population and their point of origin. The fact that both papers were founded and published in Lake Linden confirms the central position of this village in the French Canadian landscape of the peninsula.

The proliferation of organizations and institutions rapidly led to a concentration of French Canadians, which created an interesting potential market. Thus many French Canadian merchants followed this demographic movement and settled in the region. Others seized on the opportunity to become shopkeepers, looking to benefit from the ethnic sentiments of their fellow citizens by catering to a large and captive market.

In this respect, the village of Lake Linden was a paradise for merchants. Besides Grégoire, who quickly established himself at the center of the economic and political elite of the peninsula, a host of small merchants and tradesmen set up small shops and boarding houses, refurbished hotels or built workshops to provide services, giving rise to a mercantile, French-speaking middle class that was well attuned to the needs of its target clientele. These stores were joined by a number of saloons run by French Canadians in Lake Linden, notably that of Norbert Fortier, which was well attended in the 1870s. In 1879, Lake Linden had ten saloons to serve a population of 2,610 inhabitants.[55] Other entrepreneurs became proprietors of renowned hotels, such as Paul Perreault, who owned the popular Lake Linden Hotel, built in 1888.[56]

Lake Linden rapidly developed a framework of social institutions that could consolidate and nourish community life and support arriving migrants, enabling them to adapt to their new environment and giving them the tools to shape their futures.

The Village of Calumet and Its Community Life

The village of Calumet, seven kilometers from Lake Linden, was the second most important village for the French Canadians. It was founded in 1866 and its development was closely linked to the activities of C & H, to such an extent that Calumet became a company town.[57] However, its development was less spectacular than that of Lake Linden and its French Canadian community less dominant. From its very beginning, Calumet was a cosmopolitan, multiethnic town, home to French Canadians, Irish, and Germans. From the end of the 1880s, these were joined by Poles, Finns, Slovenes, and Croats. Nevertheless, the French Canadians were able to quickly establish supportive social institutions that favored the arrival of new migrants.

In 1867, when the place was still a mining camp, the Reverend Edward Jacker arrived in Calumet to minister to the Catholics of the region.[58] Its first Catholic parish, Sacred Heart, was created in 1868 to meet the needs of Irish, German, and French Canadian Catholics.[59] The first church was erected in 1869. The Reverend Jacker remained there until October 1873, when he left for Mackinac and was replaced by the Reverend Eis.[60]

The number of French Canadians in the township of Calumet had increased continuously. As table 4.3 clearly shows, by 1870 the French Canadians had become an important segment of the community, accounting for almost 10 percent of the total population. Later on, although the absolute size of the population rose considerably until the end of the century, the French Canadians declined slightly as a proportion of the town's population. They were numerous enough at the beginning of the 1870s for

Eugène Vacher to establish a French-language class.[61] In 1884, they obtained a subdivision of the Sacred Heart Parish to create the French Canadian parish of St. Louis, located in Red Jacket, a village in Calumet Township, while Sacred Heart remained the parish of the Irish and German Catholics.[62]

Besides the Saint-Jean-Baptiste Society, the French Canadians of Calumet could count on special social organizations such as the Lafayette Court no. 26 and the Foresters of America. The founding date of these is not known, nor are their objectives, but they were in operation in 1896 and sought to help French Canadians in difficulty.[63]

The festival of Saint-Jean-Baptiste was celebrated in Calumet on a regular basis. During that of 1891, E. S. Lanctôt, president of the local Saint-Jean-Baptiste Society, emphasized in a speech that the festival had been especially successful that year, in spite of the fact that some observers had remarked that patriotism was not what it had once been and that assimilation was on the rise. Lanctôt concluded his speech by warmly thanking the members of the other ethnic communities of the region who had actively participated in the French Canadian holiday. C & H did not miss the chance to collaborate in this 1891 celebration and graciously agreed to make its train and passenger cars available to the French Canadians of Lake Linden so that they could travel to Calumet for the occasion.[64]

THE MIGRATION, 1860–1900

From 1860 to 1900, the French Canadian population of the peninsula increased considerably, doubling almost every decade. It rose from 703 inhabitants to 1,710 in 1870, then to 3,662 in 1880, and reached 8,804 inhabitants in 1900 — nearly 12 percent of the total population of the peninsula (see table 4.1).[65]

Apart from the short strike of 1872 and the financial depression of the 1870s, no other events hindered the development of the region. In fact, even these events seem to have had few significant consequences for the peninsula and even less impact on the French Canadians. Like that of the Saginaw Valley, the French Canadian population of the peninsula made a great leap during this decade, rising from 1,710 to 3,662 inhabitants—an increase of over 100 percent, while the total population of the peninsula increased by only 40 percent. This increase offers evidence of the region's attractiveness for French Canadians, and the ease and confidence with which they now made their way to the peninsula, regardless of the socioeconomic climate that prevailed there. Beyond the migratory networks linking Quebec with the peninsula, the presence of organized communities and protected employment sectors contributed to the flow of migration.

During this period, the great majority of French Canadians settled in Houghton County, while the counties of Keweenaw (newly created) and Ontonagon were home to only a small fraction of the French Canadian contingent. In fact, from 1860 to 1900, Houghton County always retained over 75 percent of the French Canadians on the peninsula, and in 1900 it even counted 90 percent of all those in the region.

Within Houghton County, the French Canadians were concentrated mainly in the township of Portage (which included the village of Houghton) and the township of Hancock (which included the village of the same name). But as we have seen, the village of Lake Linden quickly expanded. In 1870, the township of Schoolcraft, which included the village of Lake Linden, already had more than a quarter of all the French Canadians of Houghton County, and these represented almost 50 percent of the total population of the township.

Gradually, as mining developed between 1860 and 1900, the French Canadians moved away from the medium-sized towns such as Houghton and Hancock and formed more concentrated settlements in the outlying villages such as Lake Linden and Calumet. While there were good employment opportunities in Houghton and Hancock, the outlying villages had the advantage of organizational structures and cultural institutions suited to protecting the cultural identities of migrants in what was still a frontier area, where the dominant culture was not yet clearly defined and where migrants could participate in its definition. In fact, by moving into smaller communities, the French Canadians were giving themselves a better chance of controlling their own futures.

Nevertheless, at the end of this period, new concentrations of French Canadians sprang up, such as the parish of Chassell in Houghton County, which was created in 1890. By 1900, 45 percent of Chassell's parishioners were of French Canadian origin. Another was the township of Torch Lake, which included the village of Hubbell—an extension of Lake Linden—where 23 percent of the total population was French Canadian. On the whole, the new French Canadian communities created between 1870 and 1900 were the result of a demographic overflow from the village of Lake Linden.

From 1860 to 1900, the majority of the French Canadian population of the region was from Quebec. During these forty years, nine out of ten heads of French Canadian households were born in Quebec (see table 4.2). It was not until the end of the nineteenth century that more than 10 percent of these heads of households were born in Michigan, reflecting the rise of the second generation. The diversity of birthplaces of heads of households is astonishing in this period. They include not only the western states (Wisconsin, Minnesota), but also the industrial states of New England (Massachusetts, New Hampshire), which had never before been listed as places of origin.

Although it was increasingly possible to migrate directly from Quebec to the peninsula, stops in the West continued to feature in the itineraries of those heading to the Keweenaw Peninsula. This was the case of Joseph Galipeau, born in Canada in 1848, who married a Canadian. The couple had a first child in Canada in 1867. By the following year, they had left Canada; a second child was born in Illinois in 1868. They stayed only a short time there, and two years later the household was living in the township of Calumet, where Joseph was working as a cooper.

Others had taken routes that included stops in both the Northeast the Midwest. For example, Frank Drapeau, born in Canada in

1822, married a Canadian and left with her for New York, where their first child was born in 1857. It was in Minnesota, however, that their second child was born in 1859. They then left for Michigan, where three more children were born in 1863, 1868, and 1869. In 1870, this family was living in Houghton County, where Frank was working as a teamster.

Economic depressions in the destination country often stimulate a return to the country of origin. The itinerary of the Pagé family is eloquent in this regard. Born in Canada in 1822, Constant Pagé married a Canadian. The household soon left Quebec and one of their children was born in Maine in 1857. Affected by the economic crisis of 1857, the couple returned to Canada, where another child was born in 1860. But the family soon headed for Ohio, where two more children were born in 1863 and 1866. In 1870, the Pagé household was living in the township of Schoolcraft, Houghton County, and Constant was working on the construction of the Portage Canal.

The depression of 1893–97 affected the behavior of French Canadians on the peninsula as it did that of their compatriots living elsewhere in the United States. It forced them to revise their plans and migrate to more prosperous regions. This was the case of the Fontaine family. Eugene Fontaine, a Canadian born in 1866, married a Canadian in 1890. They had their first child in Canada in 1891. After this birth, the family left for Vermont, where their second child was born in 1892. Possibly affected by the depression, the family came back to Canada, where another child was born in 1895. After the depression, the family migrated again, this time to Michigan, where another child was born in 1899. In 1900, the Fontaine family was living in the township of Franklin in Houghton County, where Eugene was a surface worker in a stamp mill.

In addition to this east-west movement, a regional migratory movement was also discernible. Many French Canadians who had lived in the Great Lakes region migrated to the Keweenaw Peninsula at the end of the nineteenth century. This tendency may mean that while certain regions were having serious economic problems, the peninsula seemed relatively stable. This is suggested by the movements of the Quenneville family. Paul Quenneville was born in 1871 in Canada. He married a Canadian and migrated with her to the United States in 1890. He headed to the West, and in 1893 a first child was born in Wisconsin. Two others were born in the same state in 1895 and 1897. The Quenneville family moved to Michigan, where another child was born in 1899. In 1900, the family was living in Ontonagon County, where Paul worked as a trammer.

Alfred Biron followed a similar path. Born in Canada in 1868, Biron married a Canadian and migrated to the United States with her in 1889. They went to Illinois, where their first three children were born in 1894, 1895, and 1898. The couple left Illinois for Michigan, where another child was born in 1899. In 1900, the Biron family was living in Keweenaw County, where Alfred worked as a laborer.

Some migrants also shuttled back and forth between the Midwest states. This is the impression given by the family of Jos Champagne, a Canadian born in 1857 who married a compatriot. After their first child was born in Canada in 1879, the Champagne family migrated to the United States in 1881, probably to Michigan, as a child was born there in 1884. The family then left Michigan for Wisconsin, where their next five children were born: in 1889, 1892, 1893, 1895, and 1897. In 1900, the Champagne family was living in the township of Greenland, in Ontonagon County, where Jos worked as a laborer.

This was also the case of Henri Lemieux, born in Wisconsin in 1862, who married in the same state. A first child of the marriage was born in Wisconsin in 1891. The family migrated to Michigan, as the couple had children there in 1893, 1894, and 1895. The Lemieux family returned to Wisconsin, where a child was born in 1897, and then returned to Michigan again, where another child was born in 1899. In 1900, the Lemieux family was living in Ontonagon County, where Henri was a sawyer in a shingle factory.

Considering these itineraries, it is difficult to describe one migratory model. However, the emergence of new routes should be noted. In the 1890s, these included sojourns in the manufacturing states of New England. This situation may be linked to the decline of industrial centers toward the end of the nineteenth century and the relative stability found in the Keweenaw Peninsula.

On the whole, it may be said that the mining industry held limited appeal for French Canadian heads of households between 1860 and 1900. Such had also been the case during the preceding period. From 1860 to 1900, there had never been more than 30 percent of French Canadian heads of households working in jobs directly related to mining. Yet jobs such as common laborer,[66] sawmill worker, lumber contractor, or lumberjack always drew between 40 percent and 50 percent of these men. On average, the service sector provided work for 10 percent of heads of households, while agriculture attracted 7 percent of them.[67]

The occupational profile of heads of households reveals great diversity. The French Canadians worked in a number of sectors, although no one sector clearly dominated. Overall, while they did not refuse work in the mining sector, they much preferred work in areas peripheral to the mining sector, such as forestry and services, in which the migrants seem to have had more work experience.[68]

But toward the end of the nineteenth century, as the mining industry matured, its lumber requirements decreased and the peripheral sectors had less need of workers. This meant that more and more French Canadians were obliged to work in the mining sector—a good number of whom were of the second generation—until nearly 30 percent of heads of households were employed there. At this time, only 13 percent were working in the lumber sector, mostly as lumberjacks and very few as sawmill workers. The service sector employed 12 percent of them, while agriculture supported 7 percent.

Although the mining sector was not particularly attractive to the heads of households, it seems that their sons regarded it more favorably. From 1870 to 1900, it is estimated that 75 percent of boys fifteen years of age and older, still living with their parents and working outside the home, were employed in the mining sector. Most were common laborers (51 percent), while 22 percent were surface workers. In 1900, sons of that age contributed even more to the family income, by working in the mining, agricultural, or service sectors. Very few, however, worked in the lumber sector.

Wives did not work outside the home. But their contribution to the family income lay elsewhere. They looked after the tasks associated with lodging boarders. During this period, taking in boarders continued to be a strategy employed by some 30 percent of households, although by 1900 that percentage had fallen to 12 percent.

During this period, the French Canadians not only accelerated their rate of migration but gradually moved out of the large centers like Houghton and Hancock and concentrated their settlement in smaller villages. Before 1870, French Canadians were not very numerous in the region, and for the most part they integrated into the community structures established by their fellow citizens. After 1870, the rapid improvement of the labor market and living conditions on the peninsula accelerated migration, and the new arrivals exerted pressure on the authorities of the diocese to create ethnic parishes. As we have seen, of all these ethnic communities, Lake Linden and Calumet were the most important to emerge, as a result of the migratory influx of French Canadians who deeply influenced all facets of the social, economic, and political life of these villages.

THE EROSION OF SOCIAL CONSENSUS, 1900–14

Toward the end of the 1890s, the introduction of new technology, together with the mining companies' attitude to their workers, modified the socioeconomic climate of the region and raised questions about the relatively harmonious social relations that had characterized the region until that time. These changes inevitably affected the French Canadian communities, already shaken and weakened by internal disputes.

In this new context, the communities lived through more difficult times. After experiencing a constant increase in their numbers for a half-century, the French Canadians saw their population decline remarkably in the first decade of the twentieth century,[69]—from 8,804 to 7,097—which reduced their relative weight on the peninsula from 12 percent in 1900 to less than 7 percent in 1910. In that year, there were 1,707 fewer French Canadians than in 1900, and of that number, 1,492, or 87 percent, had lived in Houghton County. This county, which had benefited most from the migration, was the one that lost most in the decline.[70] This shrinkage of the population, on the order of 20 percent, was all the more significant considering that the overall population of the peninsula increased by nearly 40 percent. The number of French Canadians had fallen in all three counties: by 20 percent in Houghton, by 15 percent in Keweenaw, and by 25 percent in Ontonagon (see table 4.1). Houghton County remained by far the one with the most French Canadians, with 90 percent of their numbers. For the first time in the period under observation, it did not follow the general demographic tendency of the region. All the communities, even the "Little Canada" of Lake Linden and the village of Calumet, saw their populations dwindle.

These losses were related to the increasingly strained social climate that pervaded the region following the reorganization of work and the introduction of new technology, especially the one-man drill. At the turn of the century, when mining companies were beginning to restructure their operations, the *Copper Country Evening News* was already reporting that many groups of French Canadians had returned to Canada and that others had left for more promising regions, such as Butte, Montana, where they could find support among a small community of their compatriots.[71]

The source of social instability was not merely external to these communities. At the turn of the century, certain parishes were faced with financial difficulties in which some of their religious leaders lost their credibility, and parishioners lost the proud self-assurance they had once possessed.

The parish of St. Joseph in Lake Linden, the French Canadian mother parish, the one to whom all others turned in times of difficulties, was in the throes of religious instability and serious financial problems.[72] Father Mesnard, who had been head of the parish for thirteen years, was transferred in 1895 to the parish of Escanaba, in the Lower Peninsula of Michigan. He was replaced by the Reverend Michel Letellier. The latter held the position for only a few days before the Reverend F. S. Marceau took over; he remained head of the parish until April 1896. The Reverend J. A. Sauriol, who had been the assistant to the Reverend Marceau since November 1895, then occupied the post until May 1896. The Reverend Paul Datin succeeded him and was pastor of St. Joseph until February 1897, when the Reverend M. T. Dugan became interim pastor until May 1897. He was then replaced by the Reverend Edouard P. Borduas, who assumed leadership of the parish from May 1897 to September 1905. In an interval of two years, the parish had been led by no fewer that six priests, with no satisfactory explanation of the reasons for these departures.

This instability was combined with a lack of consensus among the parishioners and a lack of leadership on the part of the parish priest. During the administration of the Reverend Borduas (1897–1905), there was talk of building a new church. This proposal did not meet with the approval of all parishioners and created serious rifts within the community, resulting in the project being shelved, which deeply irritated the Reverend Borduas.[73] However, important renovations were carried out.

In 1905, the Reverend Napoléon J. Raymond succeeded the Reverend Borduas. The latter had left the parish in a very bad state financially. The church council was nearly twenty-two thousand dollars in debt. The exact cause of this debt is not known, but the recent work on the church may have accounted for some of it. The Reverend Raymond, within a period of three and one-half years, successfully erased this debt through tight management and by demanding a sustained financial effort on the part of his parishioners.[74] Under his guidance, a special renovation fund was even created for future work, to which each parishioner was obliged to contribute. In 1912, the Reverend Raymond undertook major restoration work on the church, changing its facade and solidifying its original foundation. This work, which transformed the building remarkably, was finished by the end of the year. Relations between pastor and parishioners soured, going from collaboration to confrontation, as parishioners were increasingly unhappy with the financial consequences they incurred because of decisions made by their parish priest.

The village of Lake Linden—perhaps more than other villages in the region—felt the impact of the difficulties experienced by some of the mining companies, especially C & H, the most important employer of French Canadians. The total population of Lake Linden started to fall in the 1880s, a decline related to the fire of 1887 that forced some residents to move elsewhere. Its population that year was 2,610. By 1890, it had dropped to 1,862. But in 1900, it had risen again to 4,197 inhabitants. This increase was short-lived, however. The parish lost more parishioners and in 1910 was down to 2,325. The French Canadian population followed the same trend. It stood at 1,306 in 1880. It had risen to 2,178 by 1900 and then—after two subdivisions in 1892 and 1893—fell to 1,446 inhabitants in 1910 (see table 4.3).[75]

From 1900 to 1910, the picture of French Canadians' places of origin changed significantly. During the nineteenth century, Quebec had been the birthplace of nearly nine out of ten heads of households. This proportion had begun to decline in 1900, however, and by 1910 fewer than 75 percent of heads of households were from Quebec. Moreover, almost a quarter of heads of households in 1910 were born in Michigan. These data clearly reflect the decline of migration from Quebec and the emergence of the second generation of French Canadians born in Michigan. They also illustrate that the region had become considerably less attractive to French Canadians living in other parts of the United States.

In spite of this fall in numbers, the French Canadians remained concentrated in the same regions they had occupied during the nineteenth century. The township of Schoolcraft still contained 23 percent of all the French Canadians in the county, but they now represented only 35 percent of the total population of

TABLE 4.3
French Canadian Population of the Townships of Lake Linden
and Calumet, Houghton County, 1870–1900

	Lake Linden		Calumet	
Year	French Canadians (%)	Total population	French Canadians (%)	Total population
1870	333 (49.7)	669	298 (9.4)	3,182
1880	1,306 (49.4)	2,645	567 (6.8)	8,299
1900	2,178 (51.9)	4,197	1,736 (6.7)	25,991

the township, where they had always accounted for at least 50 percent in the nineteenth century. As for the township of Calumet, it had only 6 percent of all the French Canadians in the county, and they represented only 3 percent of the population of the township, a third of what they had been in 1900. All the strongholds of the French Canadians were in decline in 1910.

In this context, the occupational profile changed considerably. In 1910, the mining sector supported 44 percent of all heads of households (almost half of whom were surface workers)—the highest percentage ever. The lumber sector now attracted only 6 percent and the service sector 9 percent. However, agriculture had become more appealing. Whereas it had accounted for only 8 percent of heads of households in 1900, it supported 12 percent in 1910. The data show that as the first generation gave way to the second, the mining sector (especially surface work) became a more attractive option, while there was less work in the lumber sector once mining development leveled off and the agricultural sector came to represent a certain degree of stability.

A significant number of French Canadians left the peninsula at the end of the nineteenth century and during the first decade of the twentieth. But those who stayed had taken the decision to remain there for good. In some communities, like Lake Linden, it was well known that the French Canadians quickly adopted American nationality. In 1900, 55 percent of all heads of households had obtained their American citizenship and 17 percent had taken steps to apply for it (see table 4.4). In 1910, 63 percent of all heads of French Canadian households were naturalized Americans and 17 percent had applied for American citizenship. In 1900, as in 1910, around 40 percent of heads of households owned the house they lived in and almost 50 percent were tenants.

After the husband, sons aged fifteen years and older contributed the most to the family income. In the first decade of the twentieth century, almost 90 percent of all youths of that age were working, principally in the mining sector. Daughters fifteen years of age and older also contributed—30 percent worked as clerks in commercial establishments, domestics, or seamstresses. Only 11 percent of households rented rooms to boarders in 1910. The contribution of the wife to family income was thus limited to domestic work and the care of boarders. Only 1 percent of wives worked outside the home, mainly as domestics.

Although the number of French Canadians was in decline, another French newspaper appeared in the Lake Linden region—*Le Courrier du Michigan*, founded in 1912 under the direction of Eudore Mayrand. It is not known whether it was published on a regular basis. However, reflecting the loss of vitality of the French Canadian community in the region—and perhaps the direction many of its members took at the beginning of the twentieth century—Mayrand decided to move his newspaper to Detroit in 1919. It was the last French newspaper to be published on the Keweenaw Peninsula.[76]

The French Canadian communities were seriously affected by the strike at C & H in 1913–14. A strike that paralyzed the most important employer of the region necessarily had many repercussions. However, not much is known about the role that French Canadians played in the events. We know that some of them participated actively. The workers' committee of the WFM delivered a famous letter to the mine directors on July 14, 1913, summoning them to negotiate with the workers' representative. The letter was signed by four workers of French Canadian origin. In addition to the name of William Williams, the letter bore

TABLE 4.4
Socioeconomic Indicators in French Canadian Households on
the Keweenaw Peninsula, 1870–1910, by percentage

	1870	1880	1900	1910
Wives working (outside the home)	0.0	0.0	1.0	1.0
Boys 15 and older working	77.1	80.0	87.0	90.0
Boys under 15 working	4.7	4.5	1.2	0.5
Girls 15 and older working	0.0	10.0	30.0	25.0
Girls under 15 working	0.0	0.0	0.0	1.0
Households renting to boarders	27.3	30.0	12.0	11.0
Naturalized citizens	—	—	72.0	80.0
Property owners	—	—	40.0	42.0

the names of Little (Petit), James Rowe (Roy), James Paull, and Anton Pechauer (Pécheur)—all representatives of the committee of the local union of the WFM.[77] Apart from these individuals, it seems that few French Canadians took an active part in the strike.[78]

This labor dispute had been several years in the making. From the time the companies became aware of the competition arriving in the mining sector and the changes they would need to make in the paternalistic policies that had, until then, guaranteed social peace, they knew that a serious confrontation was brewing. If the companies knew it, the workers suspected it as well. Therefore, a good number of French Canadians began to leave the region well before the strike to avoid the coming confrontation. Some of them returned to Canada, where the economic situation had improved somewhat since the beginning of the century. Others headed west to the mining town of Butte, Montana, where a French Canadian community was already established, wages were good, economic activities were just beginning, and miners and loggers were in high demand.

C & H maintained its mining activities in the region until the 1960s. This continued presence of the principal employer of the region helped to keep alive French Canadian communities that depended on this company. Nevertheless, from the 1920s on, the gradual decline of French Canadian migration to the peninsula progressively weakened the communities, diluting their identity as they melted into the English-speaking American landscape.

The beginning of mining development on the peninsula during the 1840s attracted French Canadians living in various regions of the continent. While the majority of these migrants were born in Canada, many were native to the Great Lakes region, mainly from former trading posts such as Mackinac and Sault Sainte Marie, at the extremity of the peninsula, or from posts in Wisconsin that had fallen into decline. These first French Canadians participated very little in the principal activity of the region. Rather, they ensured their families' survival by working as fishermen, probably for the American Fur Company.

In fact, the French Canadians were not attracted to the min- ing activities per se, but rather to the growing employment op- portunities peripheral to its development and to the potential market being created around the sector. Some of them settled as farmers in the region, reflecting the desire of those arriving with sufficient capital to take advantage of available land and of the startup of mining activities that were generating a small—but expanding—market. Also, the close relationship of the mining industry with logging activities encouraged other French Cana- dians experienced in this field to move to the region. Once the first communities were established, the migratory movement ac- celerated. One fact that deserves attention is that a remarkable diversity prevailed in the ways the French Canadians integrated economically before the Civil War.

The end of the Civil War began a thriving period for the French Canadians in the creation, development, and consolida- tion of their communities. It saw a rapid and significant leap in the size of the migrant population, which grew more rapidly between 1870 and 1880 than the overall population of the peninsula. This migration was the result of a more stable, harmonious develop- ment than that which had characterized the region before the Civil War. But it was also increasingly linked to the existence of communities organized around institutions—parishes, churches, schools, newspapers, ethnic societies, economic elites—that supported and reassured new arrivals. Communities such as Lake Linden and Calumet were created by French Canadians who had been able to assert themselves numerically and politically and to consolidate institutions in order to maintain their ethnic-religious identity and exercise self-determination. They were thus able, in a very short time, to create an overall environment with which they could identify, with a clerical elite and a dynamic commercial class. This situation helped to reinforce the model of direct migration, although other unusual itineraries continued to be followed, from both east and west, leading French Canadians from various locations to take up residence on the peninsula.

If the French Canadians tended to avoid the mining sector—especially the area of underground work—they also tended to withdraw from the larger centers, such as Houghton and Hancock, to live in frontier zones in small isolated hamlets, hastily set up by the mining companies, where the chances of establishing an independent community were greater. These communities developed on the margins of the social and economic centers of the region, reinforcing the socioeconomic isolation of the French Canadians and enabling them to retain their own identity.

The mining industry greatly affected the type of contributions family members could make to the family income. The salaries offered by the mining sector were better than those offered in the East, especially if the paternalistic policies of the companies are taken into account. The poverty so often found in the manufacturing centers of New England had no counterpart in the socioeconomic conditions of the workers on the peninsula. The wages of a husband, often supplemented by those of a young son and the extra income provided by taking in boarders, was enough to assure a satisfactory living for a family.

The migratory models that brought French Canadians to the peninsula during this period were as varied as they were uncommon. While the practice of migrating directly from Quebec to the peninsula grew stronger over time, many migrants followed more

peripatetic routes on their way to the same destination. Certain of
the northeastern American states—especially New York—were
important transit points during the period from 1860 to 1900.
The Midwest also, notably Wisconsin, served as a stop on the migratory route before migrants found their way to the peninsula.
Furthermore, these migrants did not hesitate to make temporary
returns to Canada if they had reason to do so. Another point that
should not be forgotten is the decline of the logging industry in
the Saginaw Valley and its effect on the movement of French
Canadians toward the peninsula. At the first signs of depletion
of resources, some entrepreneurs in the valley had acquired timber lands in Ontonagon County and had transferred their logging
activities there, thus favoring the movement of lumber workers
to the peninsula (see chapter 3). Also not to be underestimated
is the slowdown of manufacturing activities in New England in
the 1890s, which played a role in sending new French Canadian
migrants to the peninsula. All these scenarios demonstrate the
high degree of mobility of French Canadians on the continent,
as well as their knowledge of the available labor markets and the
ease with which they could move about.

The peninsula underwent profound changes at the turn of the
century. A new economic situation obliged companies to mod-
ify their approach to labor relations and social relations in general. It forced them to actions that cast a harsher light on their
true objectives and caused a rapid deterioration in working conditions overall. The French Canadians seem to have foreseen this
deterioration. While their numbers, in terms of percentage, had
risen more rapidly than those of the general population during the
1870s, the opposite situation was the case during the first decade
of the twentieth century. They stopped coming to the peninsula
and their numbers declined while the total population continued
to grow. It seems the French Canadians read the situation differently than did their fellow citizens. This fall in migration was
accompanied by return migration to Canada, where the economy
had picked up since the beginning of the twentieth century, as

well as migration to the West, where the new mining frontier was located.

But this falling off of interest in the region was not related only to its socioeconomic instability. Some of the French Canadian communities were wracked by internal dissent. The long-standing problem of uniting French Canadian organizations into a single federation became an even more urgent issue in the 1880s, with the result that these societies ended up more divided than they had been before. In some parishes, consensus was ever more difficult to reach and to maintain. Parishioners had begun to show signs of irritation and dissatisfaction with the decisions taken by their religious leaders. It was a sign of the times that even the religious leadership in the "Little Canada" of Lake Linden was questioned.

This state of affairs destabilized the communities. It was not unrelated to the departures of some inhabitants and the diminished attractiveness of these communities for potential new arrivals. When acrimonious social tensions erupted in the early twentieth century, especially during the strike of 1913–14, some French Canadians—mainly those who had never firmly intended to settle there and who were neither homeowners nor American citizens—left the region.

After the strike, which marked the end of an era in the social development of the region, the French Canadian communities lingered on for some time. But without the replenishment of new settlers, their institutions gradually declined and disappeared, leaving behind communities that still evoke the once-vibrant presence of French Canadians in the region but that have now lost their former identity.

For many French Canadians, their experience in the mining sector of the Keweenaw Peninsula was only one of many stops in their itinerary through the continent before they moved on to new regions.

Conclusion

The French Canadians made a significant contribution to the socioeconomic development of the Saginaw Valley and the Keweenaw Peninsula. From the early period of colonization to the dawn of the twentieth century, they participated actively in this development, first as pioneers and farmers, later as loggers and miners.

An analysis of the migratory process of the French Canadians has revealed an exceptional transcontinental geographic mobility that runs counter to the "image of a static society that prevailed until recently in a good deal of the North American historiography of rural Quebec in the nineteenth century."[1]

While their contribution to the development of the two regions is remarkable, the nature of their participation in various labor markets presents some differences that are worthy of note. The French Canadian presence in the Saginaw Valley and the Keweenaw Peninsula was modest before the Civil War. In 1860, the valley was home to four hundred French Canadians, and the peninsula to about seven hundred. For the most part, the first French Canadian migrants, already present in the broad region of the Great Lakes, had once worked in the fur trade and were unemployed after its decline in the 1830s. Consequently, the new development starting up in various regions of the state in the 1840s was of vital interest to them. In the Saginaw Valley, easy access to fertile land at affordable prices was the main attraction for migrants before the Civil War, while on the peninsula the attraction was the demand for unskilled labor to build the initial infrastructures for prospecting and mining.

After the end of the Civil War, the economic context of both regions changed, and along with it their needs for labor, bringing greater numbers of French Canadians to the area. In 1900, the valley had a population of over ten thousand French Canadians, while the peninsula had almost nine thousand. The forestry and mining sectors were the main poles of attraction for the migrants until the end of the period examined here. The decline of the lumber industry, which began during the 1880s, together with the strike of 1885, slowed migration to the valley. French Canadian Catholic communities, deprived of new members, collapsed toward the end of the nineteenth century. Their counterparts on the peninsula survived for a longer period, but the changes affecting the mining industry at the end of the nineteenth century, in conjunction with the social tensions arising in the early years of the twentieth—including the strike of 1913–14—took a toll on those communities and they also declined. In spite of similarities in the development and migratory currents of the two regions, this study has shown that the migratory models for each differed significantly and that the behavior of the migrants also varied according to the economic structure of each area and the nature of their labor markets.

In the valley, migratory models took different forms in different periods. Before 1840, the French Canadian presence was mainly the result of migration from southeast Michigan, while after 1850, migration from Quebec became the dominant model. However, we have seen that other models of migration developed alongside these ones, with points of departure in the semipermanent centers in New England, where French Canadian loggers and agricultural laborers were out of work due to the cessation of lumbering activities and the mechanization of agricultural production. Faced with this new situation in the Northeast, many French Canadian households decided to follow the timber frontier westward. Some of these households, having passed through Maine, New York, and Pennsylvania, reached the new timber frontier, which was by then in Michigan, during the 1850s. Some French Canadians residing in the Northeast wished to maintain their connection with agriculture and sought to take advantage of fertile lands available in the West.

Apart from the predominant model of migration, French Canadians relied on two other migratory models. On the one hand, they participated in the "great migration" from the East to the West, looking for better-quality land. On the other hand, the continuous advance of the timber frontier drained a significant portion of the labor pool from east to west, creating a migratory market in the lumber industry—with which French Canadians had always been closely associated—that drew migration toward Michigan, mainly to the Saginaw Valley. When resources began to be depleted again, starting in the 1880s, the timber frontier moved west once again, drawing with it a portion of the French Canadian population to Wisconsin and Minnesota.

For the Keweenaw Peninsula, migratory models are more dif-ficult to define. Nevertheless, it is possible to state that before 1850 the French Canadians living in this region came mainly from small communities formerly associated with the fur trade in the broad region of the Great Lakes. After 1850, especially with the opening of the Sault Sainte Marie Canal, French Canadians, like many other migrants, could reach the Keweenaw Peninsula more easily, although a detour through Detroit was always necessary. It is possible that French Canadians, looking for land or jobs in the forestry sector, learned in Detroit that employment was available in the Upper Peninsula and then decided to go there. However, the steady development of mining, less affected than other indus-trial sectors by economic downturns at the end of the nineteenth century, may have provided the conditions whereby, besides the model linking Quebec to the peninsula, another, more tentative model developed. This model involved migrants from several of the continent's western frontier regions, including Ontario, Wis-consin, Minnesota, Ohio, and Illinois.

From the 1870s on, strong migratory networks were estab-lished both in the valley and on the peninsula. In spite of a less favorable economic situation in that decade, the migration of

French Canadians to these two regions continued unabated, to such an extent that the French Canadian population increased proportionately much more rapidly than the general population.[2]

In the case of the Saginaw Valley, this study has shown that the French Canadians' culture of mobility, together with their familiarity with the lumber industry, gave them a self-assurance that influenced all aspects of their socioeconomic and political behavior. A good knowledge of the territory, acquired in the fur trade, coupled with long-standing work experience in the forestry sector and constant participation in the migratory market of the North American lumber industry enabled them to feel sure of themselves and to integrate more easily—not only into the labor market but also into its particular sociopolitical environment.

This attitude greatly influenced the nature of their relations with all members of the community and their role in society. For one thing, parishioners began to openly criticize the lack of direction of their religious elite, which reinforced more independent behavior on their part. The example of the parish of St. Joseph in Bay City is telling in this regard. The most important French Canadian parish in the valley was plagued by recurring financial problems, and the insensitivity shown by certain parish priests to the particular needs of French-speaking Catholics gave rise, in the 1870s and 1880s, to strong reactions among parishioners. The local elite also acted in ways that demotivated French Canadians in their struggle to maintain their particular characteristics. This was the case regarding the annexationist movement; short-lived though it was, it confronted all French Canadian organizations in the state and forced them to take a position on the leadership they ought to provide. This questioning led to a deep division between the French Canadian societies of Detroit and those in the rest of Michigan and eventually undermined the credibility of these institutions.

The gulf thus created between a wavering elite and parishioners well integrated and confident in their new living environment doubtless made the parishioners less receptive to the traditional message of survival propounded by their elite, which advocated isolation from English Protestant society as the only sure way to maintain their own identity. The effect of this situation was to water down the "ethnic awareness" of the migrants and to foster a more pronounced awareness of their first interest, the improvement of their living conditions.

It is in this light that we must examine certain unique aspects of the behaviors of the French Canadians only a few years after their settlement in the valley. Their participation in the labor conflicts of 1872 and 1885 marks a distinct change from the attitude of their predecessors during the strikes in the New England manufacturing sector earlier in the century.[3] Likewise, their strong propensity to become naturalized citizens and to participate actively in the political process, both as electors and as candidates for elected office, contrasts markedly with the tendencies always observed in their compatriots in the Northeast.[4] These behaviors show that these French Canadians had a keener awareness of their own interests and those of their families, an awareness that translated into active measures to improve their material lives.

By contrast, they display the same uniformity of behavior as French Canadian migrants elsewhere in their reliance on family solidarity to cope with the changing nature of the labor market. The contribution of older sons to the family income, the renting of rooms to boarders, and even the work of older daughters were strategies adopted by families to meet their own needs and adapt to change.[5]

The work culture of French Canadians also came to the fore during the decline of logging operations—a decline that was predictable for those familiar with the sector. Relying on their knowledge of the environment, they developed new strategies. While some returned to the homeland, some adapted to the new conditions by settling on land or integrating into the developing manufacturing sector, and others followed the logging industry to its new frontier farther west.

The development of the mining sector led the French Canadians of the Keweenaw Peninsula to react differently than their compatriots in the Saginaw Valley. Although mining was the principal activity of the region, the French Canadians, who had little experience in this area, did not integrate into it immediately, but worked initially at peripheral occupations in the lumber and service sectors.

The French Canadians very early on sought to move away from the larger mining towns such as Houghton and Hancock, preferring to settle in small isolated villages created by the mining companies, where there was greater opportunity to build an autonomous community. This isolation, however, did not prevent them from being politically and socially active, especially in the villages of Lake Linden and Calumet, where some became candidates for elected office.

In the 1890s, the French Canadians seem to have taken into serious consideration the profound economic changes affecting the region, as migration to the peninsula diminished while the population of the region continued to grow. The social tensions arising in the 1890s within certain French Canadian communities, especially in the very stable community of Lake Linden, should also be borne in mind. These factors caused many French Canadians to leave the region. Some returned to Canada, responding to the improvement in economic conditions there at the beginning of the twentieth century, while others moved further west or settled in Detroit.

An analysis of the characteristics of migration to Michigan shows some important differences compared with migration to New England. On one hand, the distinct economic structures prevailing in the two regions in the nineteenth century presented migrants with different challenges. In New England, French Canadians integrated mainly into the labor market in the manufacturing sector, in which they had little experience and were obliged to acquire skills rapidly.[6] Furthermore, the labor needs of the manufacturing industries did not always coincide with the needs of families, since the factories relied primarily on the low-paid work of women and children, while the men, whose labor commanded higher wages, were often relegated to marginal sectors.[7] In Michigan, by contrast, the French Canadians were very familiar with the labor market in the lumber sector. And although they had little experience in the mining sector, it resembled the lumber sector in that it essentially required the labor of adult men and, to a lesser extent, that of boys over fifteen years of age. Few women, and even fewer married women, were required.

In light of these facts, the labor needs in Michigan were more in keeping with the traditional responsibilities expected of members of a French Canadian family. In New England, French Canadian households no doubt found the labor market disorienting at first.[8] It challenged traditional family roles and the hierarchy of power within the family. This would have constituted a socially disruptive factor, even if it was a factor to which families could adapt. The needs of the labor markets in the lumber and mining sectors were better suited to the organization of the household and the roles traditionally assigned to each of its members.

It is also important to remember that the first French Canadians to go to the Saginaw Valley and the Keweenaw Peninsula were heading out to a frontier zone, where the sociocultural characteristics were not completely established, a social model was still being defined, and migrants had more freedom to express, maintain, and even assert their cultural identities. In New England, by contrast, French Canadians found themselves in urban centers with well-established social environments, where there was little opportunity to express or maintain their difference, pressure to integrate was strong, and they were dependent on their religious elite and primary social institutions to isolate themselves and protect their own particular identity.

In this context, we can understand more clearly the differences between the behavior of the migrants in the Saginaw Valley and that of the French Canadians in New England. The self-assurance demonstrated by the migrants in the valley enabled them to distance themselves sooner from the influence of the religious elite, as they had less need of its protection to ensure their survival. In fact, this situation allowed French Canadians to better integrate into their new environment—socially, politically, and economically.

This socioeconomic situation may explain why the French Canadians in New England, in spite of certain tensions with their religious elite, accepted more easily its message of survival.[9] They were more closely bound to the Church, considering it essential for their survival as French-speaking Catholics. This may also explain why the French Canadians of New England, following the recommendations of the religious elite, were late in becoming involved in labor disputes, except as strikebreakers. In fact, with a few minor exceptions, the French Canadians of New England did not openly question their clerical leadership until the beginning of the twentieth century, culminating in the *sentinelliste* crisis of the 1920s regarding their opposition to the marginalization of French in parochial institutions proposed by the Irish clerical elite.[10] And it was not until the beginning of the twentieth century that they really began to become involved in labor conflicts.[11]

This study has uncovered elements of a possible migratory triangle linking Quebec, New England, and Michigan. While the constant westward shift of the timber frontier connected the three regions, the depression in the manufacturing industries of the Northeast during the 1890s also encouraged, though to a lesser extent, the migration of French Canadians from New England to Michigan. Considering differences of economic structure and the effects of economic crises on these structures, it is quite probable that a period of instability would not have the same effect everywhere. This difference may explain the movement of part of the labor force in a sector affected by the depression to another sector that was less affected by the depression or that had a labor market more compatible with family organization. The existence of such a migratory triangle remains, however, a hypothesis that further research, based on more detailed sources and an appropriate methodology, may define more clearly, revealing the full continental dimension of the phenomenon.

Finally, this study has focused especially on the challenges faced by French Canadians, showing that they were rarely the powerless victims of a shifting economic context, but that they always, with varying degrees of success, attempted to adapt by using their life and work experience and their sense of family solidarity to the best of their ability.

Notes

Introduction

1. U.S. Census Office, *Eleventh Census*, 1:clxxx. The American federal census defines the Northeast as the north Atlantic states: all six New England states (Maine, Vermont, Massachusetts, Connecticut, Rhode Island, and New Hampshire) as well as New York and Pennsylvania. It defines the Midwest as the north central states: Illinois, Indiana, Michigan, Ohio, Minnesota, and Wisconsin.

Chapter 1

1. *Rapport du comité spécial* (1849), 51.
2. Armstrong, *Structure and Change*, 52.
3. Ibid., 57.
4. Trudel, *Initiation à la Nouvelle-France*, 15.
5. Ouellet, *Histoire économique et sociale du Québec*, 1:273.
6. Armstrong, *Structure and Change*, 60.
7. Vicero, "Immigration of French Canadians to New England," 47.
8. See Little, *Nationalism, Capitalism, and Colonization*, particularly chapters 1 and 2.
9. Roby, *Les Franco-Américains de la Nouvelle-Angleterre*.
10. Armstrong, *Structure and Change*, 62–63.
11. Vicero, "Immigration of French Canadians to New England," 50.
12. Ibid., 59.
13. Ibid., 62.
14. Ibid., 62 and 66. This problem was particularly acute in the Montreal area and the Richelieu valley.
15. Roby, *Les Franco-Américains de la Nouvelle-Angleterre*, 15.
16. McCallum, *Unequal Beginnings*, 43.
17. Armstrong, *Structure and Change*, 22.

18. Ibid., 80.
19. Vicero, "Immigration of French Canadians to New England," 39.
20. Armstrong, Structure and Change, 79.
21. Roby, Les Franco-Américains de la Nouvelle-Angleterre, 17.
22. McCallum, Unequal Beginnings, 44.
23. Vicero, "Immigration of French Canadians to New England," 44.
24. One should note that the French Canadian mobility during the New France era has received attention from numerous scholars. See Mathieu, Therrien-Fortier, and Lessard, "Mobilité et sédentarité."
25. Morissonneau, La terre promise, 47.
26. Morissonneau, "Mobilité et identité québécoise," 30.
27. Greer, Peasant, Lord, and Merchant, 179.
28. Innis, The Fur Trade in Canada, 57.
29. Benoit Brouillette, in Lanctôt, Les Canadiens français.
30. Brouillette, La pénétration du continent américain, 37, 47.
31. Ibid., 79.
32. Greer, Peasant, Lord, and Merchant, 183.
33. Brouillette, in Lanctôt, Les Canadiens français. 154.
34. Morissonneau, La terre promise, 56.
35. Dunbar, Michigan, 172.
36. Brouillette, in Lanctôt, Les Canadiens français, 162–63.
37. Ibid., 163.
38. Armstrong, Structure and Change, 116.
39. Auger, "La grande mouvance et la route du Bois," 47. The imposition of a blockade by France against Great Britain in 1806–7, which had the effect of closing all ports of the Baltic region, was the catalyst in the process of exploitation of Canadian lumber. This situation enticed American entrepreneurs to Canada.
40. Lower, The North American Assault, 36.
41. Ibid., 189.
42. Lapointe, "L'Outaouais," 80.
43. The valley produced more than 50 percent of all cut wood in terms of value of production throughout the nineteenth century. See Séguin and Hardy, Forêt et société en Mauricie, 7.
44. Ouellet, Histoire économique et sociale du Québec, 1:242.
45. Tulchinsky, La rivière et la forêt, 4.
46. Ibid. The study of Séguin and Hardy (Forêt et société en Mauricie) confirmed that most of the workers attracted by lumber activities were between twenty-six and thirty-five years old, young married men or bachelors.
47. McCalla, "Forest Products and Upper Canada Development," 184.
48. See Reid, The Upper Ottawa Valley.
49. McCalla, "Forest Products and Upper Canada Development," 185.

50. The improvement of canals between Canada and the United States in the 1820s and 1830s facilitated the penetration of Canadian products.

51. Tulchinsky, *La rivière et la forêt*, 9; Reid, *The Upper Ottawa Valley*, lxx.

52. Rameau de Saint-Père, *La France aux colonies*, 121–22.

53. Lower, *The North American Assault*, 88.

54. The production dropped from 375 million board feet in 1841 to 250 million in 1842, the lowest level since 1826 (Armstrong, *Structure and Change*, 114, 121).

55. See Reid, *The Upper Ottawa Valley*, lix; Lower, *The North American Assault*, 88.

56. Armstrong, *Structure and Change*, 114.

57. Ouellet, *Histoire économique et sociale du Québec*, 1:475.

58. Lower, *The North American Assault*, 92.

59. Entrepreneurs like Levi Young of Maine, O. H. Ingram, A. H. Baldwin, Harris Bronson, a Mr. Perley, and a Mr. Pattlee of New York, and E. B. Eddy were part of the process.

60. *Rapport du comité spécial* (1849), 84–85.

61. "Going to the States is part of a survival strategy as going to the pineries cutting wood in the forest of the province of Quebec" (Roby, *Les Franco-Américains de la Nouvelle-Angleterre*, 54).

62. The gold rush in California at the end of 1840s attracted a number of French Canadians looking for wealth and adventure. See the novel of Desrosiers, *Nord-Sud*.

63. Roby, *Les Franco-Américains de la Nouvelle-Angleterre*, 19.

64. Vicero, "Immigration of French Canadians to New England," 90–94. In 1831, the French colony of Waterville, Maine, had 150 persons (Roby, *Les Franco-Américains de la Nouvelle-Angleterre*, 19). These little colonies were the beginning of a building process that lead to the creation of more stable communities like St. Joseph of Burlington.

65. We know that French Canadians went to the United States as early as the Revolution era. Others went after the rebellions of 1837–38 seeking refuge, the motivation at this time being mainly political, not economic.

66. Steer, *Lumber Production*, 11.

67. Smith, *A History of Lumbering in Maine*, 12.

68. Testimony of John Heath, from L'Isle Verte, Quebec, to the committee of 1857 investigating emigration to the United States (*Rapport du comité spécial* (1857), 82).

69. Roby, *Les Franco-Américains de la Nouvelle-Angleterre*, 14.

70. Ouellet, *Histoire économique et sociale du Québec*, 1:349.

71. Hansen and Brebner, *The Mingling of the Canadian and American Peoples*, 135.

72. Rameau de Saint-Père, *La France aux colonies*, 172.

73. Faucher, "L'émigration des Canadiens français au XIXe siècle," 304; Hansen and Brebner, *The Mingling of the Canadian and American Peoples*, 105.

74. Hansen and Brebner, *The Mingling of the Canadian and American Peoples*, 130.

75. Roby, *Les Franco-Américains de la Nouvelle-Angleterre*, 19.

76. Hansen and Brebner, *The Mingling of the Canadian and American Peoples*, 129; McQuillan, "French Canadian Communities," 101.

77. *Rapport du comité spécial* (1849), 37 and 45.

78. *Rapport du comité spécial* (1857), 5.

79. McQuillan, "French Canadian Communities," 102.

80. Trudel, *Chiniquy*, 125.

81. Vicero, "Immigration of French Canadians to New England," 108–9, citing Rameau de Saint-Père.

82. Rameau de Saint-Père, *La France aux colonies*, 173.

83. Hansen and Brebner, *The Mingling of the Canadian and American Peoples*, 132.

84. Roby, *Les Franco-Américains de la Nouvelle-Angleterre*, 22.

85. McQuillan, "French Canadian Communities," 103.

86. Armstrong, *Structure and Change*, 163–64.

87. See Lalonde, "L'intelligentsia du Québec"; Silver, "French Canada and the Prairie Frontier."

88. Faucher, "L'émigration des Canadiens français au XIXe siècle," 317.

89. McQuillan, "French Canadian Communities," 99.

90. Rameau de Saint-Père, *La France aux colonies*, 17; *Rapport du comité spécial* (1857), 5.

91. McQuillan, "French Canadian Communities," 99. Rameau de Saint-Père estimated that seven thousand French Canadians lived in Michigan in 1851 (*La France aux colonies*, 173).

CHAPTER 2

1. The Saginaw Valley includes Saginaw County, created in 1822 and Bay County, detached from Saginaw and created in 1857.

2. Benson, "Logs and Lumber," 97.

3. Ibid., 7.

4. Ibid., 10.

5. Ibid., 97; Kilar, "The Lumbertowns," 20.

6. Kilar, "The Lumbertowns," 17.

7. U.S. Census Office, *Eleventh Census*, vol. 1, part 1, table 4, p. 26.

8. Foehl and Hargreaves, *The Story of Logging the White Pine*, 3; McGaugh, "The Settlement of Saginaw Basin," 39–40.

9. Sweet, "Brief History of Saginaw County," 486.

10. Ibid.; Kilar, "The Lumbertowns," 35. Named Sagana in 1822, it afterward became Saginaw, which means "gathering place" in an Amerindian language (possibly Chippewa). See McGaugh, "The Settlement of Saginaw Basin," 1.

11. Miller, "The Saginaw Valley," 268. As I suggested, several French Canadians were working for the American Fur Co., which was looking for experienced workers to open new markets. According to Albert Miller, Louis Campau left Saginaw City in 1826 and his brother, Antoine Campau, was responsible for the fur trade post.

12. McGaugh, "The Settlement of Saginaw Basin," 40–41; Kilar, "The Lumbertowns," 39.

13. Partridge, "Bay County History."

14. The county of the same name had been created two years before.

15. Partridge, "Bay County History," 317; Kilar, "The Lumbertowns," 50.

16. Kilar, "The Lumbertowns," 50; St. Joseph Parish, Diamond Jubilee, 11.

17. Partridge,"Bay County History," 317–18 and 330–32; Kilar, "The Lumbertowns," 49–50.

18. Kilar, "The Lumbertowns," 41.

19. Miller, "The Saginaw Valley," 240. Millington bought them from Samuel W. Dexter who got them in 1835 for eleven thousand dollars.

20. Kilar, "The Lumbertowns," 44.

21. Ibid., 55.

22. Ibid., 18.

23. Mills, History of Saginaw County, 1:395.

24. Arndt, The Bay County Story, 105. The William brothers asked their uncle of Detroit, Harvey William, who knew how to build a sawmill, to help them. He used the engine of the first steamboat that sailed on the Great Lakes, Walk on the Water, to activate the sawmill.

25. The Industries of Saginaw, 12; Benson, "Logs and Lumber," 98.

26. Leach, "Paul Bunyan's Land," 78; Partridge, "Bay County History," 320.

27. Mills, History of Saginaw County, 1:394. In 1833, in St. Clair County, Francis P. Browning was the owner of a newly built and well-equipped sawmill that produced ten thousand board feet in twelve hours (Benson, "Logs and Lumber," 62).

28. Benson, "Logs and Lumber," 140. Miller sold his sawmill to James McCormick and his son James J. in 1841 (Arndt, The Bay County Story, 107).

29. A few miles away, south of East Saginaw, William Gallagher and his brother, both speculators, bought land in 1853 that they named Salina. Three years later, the village of Florence was founded, comprised of only two streets, on which were a sawmill, a saltworks manufacture, and several saloons (Kilar, "The Lumbertowns," 47–48). Florence became part of Carrolton in 1866.

30. Ibid., 57–59.
31. Ibid., 57.
32. Benson, "Logs and Lumber," 88.
33. Ibid., 100.
34. Maybee, *Michigan's White Pine Era*, 12; Jensen, *Lumber and Labor*, 8.
35. Engberg, "Labor in the Lake States Lumber Industry," 11.
36. According to Steer, the value of lumber production in New York State, for example, decreased between 1850 and 1860, going from $13 million to $9.7 million, showing that activity continued even when production fell (*Lumber Production*, 11).
37. Kilar, "The Lumbertowns," 56.
38. Benson, "Logs and Lumber," 99; Mills, *History of Saginaw County*, 2:396.
39. Kilar, "The Lumbertowns," 19.
40. Dunbar, *Michigan*, 296.
41. Benson, "Logs and Lumber," 98.
42. Wood, *A History of Lumbering in Maine*, 226. The ad was published January 10, 1854.
43. Dunbar, *Michigan*, 404–5.
44. Wood, *A History of Lumbering in Maine*, 227. See especially Chapter 12, dealing with the migration of lumber entrepreneurs from Maine to the West and to the Saginaw Valley. See also Mills, *History of Saginaw County*, 2:72 and 415.
45. Mills, *History of Saginaw County*, 2:1 and 25; Sweet, "Brief History of Saginaw County," 498.
46. Hotchkiss, *History of the Lumber and Forest Industry of the Northwest*, biographical notes pp. 103–50.
47. Kilar, "The Lumbertowns," 55; Arndt, *The Bay County Story*, 116.
48. Hotchkiss, *History of the Lumber and Forest Industry of the Northwest*, 139.
49. Ibid., 100. These data do not include lumberjacks, who were subject to migration according to the regional needs of the work market.
50. Ibid., 230.
51. Mills, *History of Saginaw County*, 1:397.
52. Ibid., 1:259.
53. The population by township in 1850 was: Saginaw City, 917; North Hampton, 122; Hampton, 546; Bridgeport, 374; Buena Vista, 251; Taymouth, 58; and Tittabawassee, 341 (Benson, "Logs and Lumber," 260).
54. Ibid.
55. Engberg "Labor in the Lake States Lumber Industry," 42. The westward migration of the lumber workers was stimulated by entrepreneurs, who preferred dealing with experienced workers to open new lands.
56. Wood, *A History of Lumbering in Maine*, 234.

57. Danford, "The Social and Economic Effects of Lumbering on Michigan," 348.

58. Jensen, *Lumber and Labor*, 33; Dunbar, *Michigan*, 397.

59. Jensen, *Lumber and Labor*, 21; Benson, "Logs and Lumber," 260.

60. Benson, "Logs and Lumber," 260.

61. Jensen, *Lumber and Labor*, 21.

62. Engberg, "Who Were the Lumberjacks?" 239; Quinlan, "Lumbering in Michigan," 40.

63. Engberg, "Lumber and Labor in the Lake States," 153; Benson, "Logs and Lumber," 261.

64. Benson, "Logs and Lumber," 263.

65. Ibid., 119. This was true in Michigan until 1876 with the coming of the railroad, which extended the log-driving season beyond winter.

66. Ibid., 318.

67. Ibid., 264.

68. Kilar, "The Lumbertowns," 26; Maybee, *Michigan's White Pine Era*, 34. The Tittabawassee Co. ran until 1864.

69. Kilar, "The Lumbertowns," 26.

70. Ibid., 240.

71. Maybee, *Michigan's White Pine Era*, 21.

72. Ibid., 19.

73. Ibid., 29.

74. Engberg, "Labor in the Lake States Lumber Industry," 113.

75. Ibid., 141. The workers often wanted to know the name of the cook before working for a company.

76. Engberg, "Labor in the Lake States Lumber Industry," 360.

77. Quinlan,"Lumbering in Michigan," 40; Maybee, *Michigan's White Pine Era*, 19. The monthly average wage in the 1854–55 season was seventeen dollars. See Benson, "Logs and Lumber," 275.

78. Maybee, *Michigan's White Pine Era*, 21.

79. Engberg, "Labor in the Lake States Lumber Industry," 359. This practice disappeared at the end of the nineteenth century under workers' pressure.

80. Vander Hill and Warner, *A Michigan Reader*, 48.

81. Quinlan, "Lumbering in Michigan," 40.

82. Engberg, "Labor in the Lake States Lumber Industry," 351.

83. Ibid., 359–60.

84. Brinks, "The Effects of the Civil War in 1861 on Michigan Lumbering and Mining Industries."

85. *Tariff on Lumber*, East Saginaw, 1870, p. 4., states that during the cutting season of 1869, 7,685 workers were employed.

86. Jensen, *Lumber and Labor*, 57. Workers who had urgent need of money or

had to leave town could cash their checks before the date on the check in certain stores. But the merchants took 10 to 30 percent off for this service (Mills, *History of Saginaw County*, 2:407). Beginning in 1880, time checks became the reason for strikes and several companies decided to change the method of paying wages.

87. Maybee, *Michigan's White Pine Era*, 18.

88. Ibid., 37.

89. Quinlan, "Lumbering in Michigan," 39.

90. Engberg, "Labor in the Lake States Lumber Industry," 78.

91. Vander Hill and Warner, *A Michigan Reader*, 48. In 1860, the average wage was $1.125 and in 1870, it was $1.52.

92. Ibid., 254.

93. Ibid., 257–58.

94. Salt manufactures had been complementary to sawmills since 1859–60. The low-quality wood was used to heat water boilers in order to produce salt.

95. *Lumberman's Gazette*, September 1873, 69; November 1873, 139; Engberg, "Labor in the Lake States Lumber Industry," 255. Mr. Jerome of Saginaw City sent two teams to work in the woods that fall, four times fewer than the preceding year (*Lumberman's Gazette*, October 1873, 121).

96. Several companies, such as Chaplin and Barber, Pitts and Carnage of Bay City, A. Stevens and Co., Henry W. Sage of West Bay City, and the Tittabawassee Boom Co., advised their workers of lower pay in September. However, none of these companies believed that they would experience problems in finding enough workers. The *Bay City Tribune* urged workers to accept the new wages because, according to the newspaper, they would not find better wages elsewhere (Vander Hill and Warner, *A Michigan Reader*, 48; *Lumberman's Gazette*, September 1873, 69).

97. *Lumberman's Gazette*, March 1874, 1.

98. *Lumberman's Gazette*, May 10, 1877, 325.

99. *Lumberman's Gazette*, October 4, 1877, 212.

100. *Lumberman's Gazette*, October 27, 1877, 260.

101. *Lumberman's Gazette*, April 2, 1879, 6.

102. *Twelfth Annual Review Issued by the Saginaw Board of Trade*, 12.

103. The companies of Rory McDonald and of Samuel H. Webster in Bay City, and also that owned by Henry Gamble and Tolfree E. Simpson of East Saginaw, went bankrupt. Other owners had no choice but to sell. This was the case of the owners of Stevens and Co. and Johnson and McKay, both of Bay City.

104. *Lumberman's Gazette*, November 2, 1881, 3.

105. Woodlands in Canada have interested entrepreneurs since the beginning of 1880. In 1881, Maire Hill, C. W. Wells, and A. T. and L. W. Bliss, all

owners of sawmills in Saginaw City, bought nearly ninety square miles of pineland in the Georgian Bay, in Ontario, to feed their sawmills (*Lumberman's Gazette*, December 28, 1881, 1; June 21, 1882, 5).

106. *Lumberman's Gazette*, April 11, 1883, 1.

107. Henry W. Sage did not find a buyer for his sawmill till 1892. W. R. Burt of Bay City also tried to sell his sawmill without success. Thomas McGraw, who erected his own sawmill in 1873, sold it to Benjamin Birdsall and C. C. Barker for $350,000 (*Lumberman's Gazette*, February 16, 1882, 2; February 22, 1882, 5; June 14, 1882, 2–3; May 1873, 143).

108. In May, the prices were $8–$9.50, $16–$18.50, and $37–$39. At the end of 1884, they were $6.50–$7, $13–$17, and $35–$37 (*Fourth Annual Review of the Saginaw Board of Trade*, 11).

109. *Lumberman's Gazette*, December 17, 1884, 3.

110. *Lumberman's Gazette*, October 15, 1884, 2.

111. Jensen, *Lumber and Labor*, 59.

112. Vander Hill and Warner, *A Michigan Reader*, 49.

113. Benson, "Logs and Lumber," 272; Vander Hill and Warner, *A Michigan Reader*, 49.

114. Engberg, "Collective Bargaining in the Lumber Industry," 207.

115. Kilar, "The Lumbertowns," 314.

116. Engberg, "Labor in the Lake States Lumber Industry," 277.

117. The traditional interpretation is sustained by Engberg, "Labor in the Lake States Lumber Industry"; Goodstein, "Labor Relations in the Saginaw Valley Lumber Industry"; Jensen, *Lumber and Labor*; Vander Hill, *Settling the Great Lakes Frontier*; and the State of Michigan, *Second Annual Report of the Bureau of Labor and Industrial Statistics*.

118. *Fifth Annual Review of the Saginaw Board of Trade*, 24.

119. Kilar, "Community and Authority Response."

120. Kilar, "The Lumbertowns," 315. It was possibly a misunderstanding that persuaded the workers to wait until July 6 to start the strike instead of July 1 when, according to the rumor, the law might be implemented.

121. Jensen, *Lumber and Labor*, 50.

122. *Fifth Annual Review of the Saginaw Board of Trade*, 25.

123. Kilar, "The Lumbertowns," 317–18.

124. Ibid.

125. *Bay City Tribune*, August 13, 1885, 5; August 18, 1885, 1.

126. The prisoners were released on a thousand dollars' bail. The progress of the trials, which were postponed several times, was covered by the *Bay City Tribune*. In May 1886, the trials were still ongoing, but the *Bay City Tribune* stopped covering them (*Bay City Tribune*, August 14, 1885, 1.

127. Engberg, "Labor in the Lake States Lumber Industry," 278.

128. Vander Hill and Warner, *A Michigan Reader*. Sage was the first to state

publicly that for the sake of the industry, the sawmills should remain closed for sixty days.

129. Engberg. "Labor in the Lake States Lumber Industry," 394.

130. Kilar, "The Lumbertowns," 329.

131. Engberg, "Collective Bargaining in the Lumber Industry," 207.

132. Kilar, "The Lumbertowns," 330. One should note that a "blacklist" of workers who participated in the strike circulated in the lumber industry in the region.

133. *Sixth Annual Review of the Saginaw Board of Trade*, 5. From 1885 to 1892, sawmills were regularly destroyed by fires whose origins were mysterious (*Sixth Annual Review of the Saginaw Board of Trade*, 10; *Tenth Annual Review of the Saginaw Board of Trade*, 11).

134. Kilar, "The Lumbertowns," 376; *Annual Review Issued by the Saginaw Board of Trade*, 9.

135. Kilar, "The Lumbertowns," 379.

136. Horace Greely, *Recollections of a Busy Life* (1868), cited in Mentor, "Horace Greely and Michigan Copper," 131.

137. Dersch, "Copper Mining in Northern Michigan," 300.

138. Ibid., 290.

139. Hybels, "The Lake Superior Copper Fever," 102.

140. Lankton and Hyde, *Old Reliable*, 2.

141. Hybels, "The Lake Superior Copper Fever," 107.

142. Hyde, "From 'Subterranean Lotteries' to Orderly Investment," 6.

143. Lankton and Hyde, *Old Reliable*, 2–4.

144. Dunbar, *Michigan*, 297.

145. Ibid., 299.

146. Hyde, "From 'Subterranean Lotteries' to Orderly Investment," 7.

147. Lankton and Hyde, *Old Reliable*, 4. Quincy Mining Co. was created by the merger of Portage Mining Co. and Northeastern Mining Co.

148. Ibid., 3.

149. Copper fever was so high that more than seven hundred permits were allowed in 1845 alone. Dunbar and Jamieson compare the copper fever in Michigan to the gold rush in California. See Dunbar, *Michigan*, 298; Jamieson, "The Copper Rush."

150. *History of the Upper Peninsula of Michigan*, 250.

151. Hyde, "From 'Subterranean Lotteries' to Orderly Investment," 10.

152. Dunbar, *Michigan*, 300.

153. Lankton and Hyde, *Old Reliable*, 11.

154. Hyde,"From 'Subterranean Lotteries' to Orderly Investment," 5.

155. Dersch, "Copper Mining in Northern Michigan," 300.

156. Chase, "Michigan Upper Peninsula," 327.

157. In 1859, the Quincy Mining Co. owned twenty-seven houses, four tene-

ment houses, and three rudimentary houses to host the vast majority of its 217 workers.

158. Dersch,"Copper Mining in Northern Michigan," 299.

159. Gates, *Michigan Copper and Boston Dollars*, 98. This wage system was imported from Cornwall, England, by Cornish miners and applied in the Michigan copper industry.

160. Ibid., 100.

161. The first federal census was made in this region in 1850.

162. U.S. Census Office, *Eighth Census*, table 3, pp. 240–43.

163. Lankton and Hyde, *Old Reliable*, 11.

164. The testimony of O. W. Robinson clearly illustrated the itinerary that those going to Upper Michigan should follow (Robinson, "From New England to Lake Superior").

165. Dersch, "Copper Mining in Northern Michigan," 302.

166. Gates, *Michigan Copper and Boston Dollars*, 95.

167. Ibid.

168. Thurner, *Calumet Copper*, 14.

169. Gates, *Michigan Copper and Boston Dollars*, 95. See also Jopling, "Cornish Miners of the Upper Peninsula."

170. Of all the immigrants, one should note that only the Germans did not want to return home.

171. Gates, *Michigan Copper and Boston Dollars*, 95–96.

172. Ibid.

173. Ibid.

174. The *Portage Lake and Mining Gazette* (PLMG) reported that this organization stimulated the coming of several immigrants during the war, mainly British (PLMG, May 16, 1863, 3; May 23, 1863, 3; September 10, 1864, 2). Few had the expertise for the work they were doing.

175. Recruited this way were 250 Norwegians and 200 Swedes (Lankton and Hyde, *Old Reliable*, 17).

176. Ibid.

177. Ibid.

178. Lankton and Hyde, *Old Reliable*, 18; Gates, *Michigan Copper and Boston Dollars*, 98.

179. Gates, *Michigan Copper and Boston Dollars*, 105. For an excellent study of mining in the Keweenaw Peninsula, the introduction of new technologies, and working conditions, see Lankton, *Cradle to Grave*.

180. For more information, see Wax, "Calumet and Hecla Copper Mines."

181. Ibid., 24; Chase, "Michigan Copper Mines," 484.

182. U.S. Census Office, *Ninth Census*, 3:778.

183. The county of Keweenaw was created in 1861 by a subdivision of Houghton County.

184. U.S. Census Office, *Ninth Census*, 3:778.
185. Pyne, "Quincy Mine," 227. This drill allowed companies to save 30 percent on the cost of drilling and reduced the number of miners by nearly 50 percent while allowing 50 percent more production.
186. Lankton and Hyde, *Old Reliable*, 16.
187. Ibid.
188. Ibid., 12. In 1891, C & H built the Buffalo Smelting Works in the region.
189. Here is an example of continuity in the ethnic composition of the community: in 1870, in Houghton County, the Irish counted as one-third of all foreign-born inhabitants. The British were in second place and Canadians were third. Ten years later, a few changes had occurred; the Irish fell to third place, the British were in first, the Canadians second, and Germans fourth (Gates, *Michigan Copper and Boston Dollars*, 106).
190. U.S. Department of Interior, Census Office, *Report on the Mining Industries*, 15:798. There were 5,447 workers in 1864, 4,188 in 1870 (a loss of more than 1,200), 5,453 in 1874, and 4,986 in 1880.
191. Gates, *Michigan Copper and Boston Dollars*, 107.
192. Ibid.
193. State of Michigan, *Annual Report of the Commissioner of Mineral Statistics* (1889), n.p.
194. For details about this program, see Gates, *Michigan Copper and Boston Dollars*, 109.
195. *History of the Upper Peninsula of Michigan*, 312.
196. Murdock, *Boom Copper*, 153.
197. C & H could count on several devoted persons elected at city hall, the school board, or public services to get the necessary support.
198. Lankton and Hyde, *Old Reliable*, 84.
199. Ibid, 34.
200. The average wage of miners was around sixty-three dollars in 1872 (PLMG, May 9, 1872, 3; August 10, 1871, 2; September 21, 1871, 2).
201. Gates, *Michigan Copper and Boston Dollars*, 112–13.
202. PLMG, May 23, 1872, 3.
203. PLMG, October 1, 1874, 3. It should be added that the construction of a new bridge, at a cost of fifty thousand dollars, was planned, linking Houghton and Hancock (PLMG, November 25, 1875, 3).
204. PLMG, January 17, 1878, 3. The economic crisis had an effect on the newspaper itself and the size of the newspaper was changed to save money (PLMG, October 10, 1878, 3).
205. PLMG, June 19, 1879, 3; November 6, 1879, 3.
206. PLMG, April 3, 1879, 3; March 12, 1879, 3; April 24, 1879, 3; June 5, 1879, 3.

207. Chase, "Michigan Copper Mines," 486.

208. Lankton and Hyde, *Old Reliable*, 99–101.

209. The introduction of the one-man drill profoundly changed the organization of the work and was the main cause of the 1913–14 strike.

210. Between 1888 and 1900 in the mines of Houghton County alone, 327 miners died, an average of 27 deaths per year (State of Michigan, Houghton County, *Inspectors of Mines Report, 1888–1900*).

211. Lankton and Hyde, *Old Reliable*, 82.

212. Gates, *Michigan Copper and Boston Dollars*, 107.

213. Ibid., 106.

214. Lankton and Hyde, *Old Reliable*, 129.

215. For an excellent survey of this strike, see Thurner, *Rebels on the Range*. Like others in this period, the strike was characterized by violence, repression, and the use of strikebreakers.

216. Thurner, *Calumet Copper*, 89. The Western Federation of Miners had been active in the region since 1904.

217. Thurner, *Rebels on the Range* 1; Jensen, *Lumber and Labor*, 275.

218. Thurner, *Rebels on the Range* 113; *Daily Mining Gazette*, July 24, 1913, 1.

219. Jensen, *Lumber and Labor*, 276 and 281; Lankton and Hyde, *Old Reliable*, 129; Thurner, *Rebels on the Range*, 1 and 113.

220. From September to December 1913, approximately 525 strikebreakers were brought into the district, mainly Russians, Poles, and Germans. From August 1913 till the end of the strike in February 1914, C & H used strikebreakers to replace workers refusing to go back to work. See C & H employment files.

221. Jensen, *Lumber and Labor*, 285.

222. Thurner, *Calumet Copper*, 89.

223. Several articles in local newspapers indicated that a number of workers had left the region since the beginning of the strike. Many strikers moved to Detroit; Duluth, Minnesota; or Superior, where they were joined by their families after finding jobs (*Daily Mining Gazette*, July 29, 1913, 3; August 2, 1913, 7, August 9, 1913, 3; Thurner, *Calumet Copper*, 95.

224. Lankton and Hyde, *Old Reliable*, 130.

225. Ibid. Quincy Mine Co., among others, had this problem.

CHAPTER 3

1. These data are based on the enumeration schedules of U.S. federal censuses. Since the censuses do not indicate place of birth, family names were used to identify the target population. This method is, of course, subject to error, and this compilation cannot claim to be complete. The Angli-

cization of names, the absence of wives' maiden names, and the illegibility of certain parts of the censuses all reduce the reliability of this method. Nonetheless, even given these difficulties, I believe that this treatment of the data is as comprehensive as possible. It includes all persons of French Canadian origin born in Canada or the United States. U.S. Census Office, *Sixth Census*, manuscript census, reel no. M 704–210.

2. U.S. Census Office, *Seventh Census*, manuscript census, reel no. M 432–361.

3. Roby, *Les Franco-Américains de la Nouvelle-Angleterre*, 18, citing Télésphore Saint-Pierre, *La marche ascendante de notre race: Trois millions de Canadiens français en Amérique* (1903).

4. According to McQuillan, the agricultural frontier, previously in Michigan, moved to Illinois in the 1850s (McQuillan, "Les communautés canadiennes-françaises du Midwest américain au dix-neuvième siècle," 101).

5. U.S. Census Office, *Eighth Census*, manuscript census, reel nos. M 653–356 and M 653–558.

6. The township of Bangor in Bay County was created (in 1859) and named by Thomas Whitney, who was originally from Bangor, Maine. He built a sawmill on the west bank of the Saginaw River (Foster, *Dictionary of Michigan Place Names*, 16).

7. Including the new Bay County.

8. This reflects previous migration by their parents.

9. The following is an example of this geographical mobility. Dominique Hébert was born in 1817 in Canada. He married a Canadian and the Héberts had their first two children in 1838 and 1840 in Canada. In 1844, they had a child in New York. Four more children were born in that state, in 1846, 1848, 1852, and 1855. Between 1855 and 1858, the Hébert family left New York for Michigan, where twins were born in 1858, probably in Saginaw County, where they were living in 1860. This information comes from the enumeration schedules of the 1860 U.S. federal census for Saginaw County.

10. *St. Joseph Parish, Diamond Jubilee*, 11. This company aimed to stimulate the development of the region.

11. Mills, *History of Saginaw County*, 2:325. This lot is located at the intersection of Washington and Monroe Streets.

12. *Seventy-fifth Anniversary*, 11.

13. Ibid., 10–11. In the history of St. Joseph Parish, the resident bishop was Monsignor Lefebvre.

14. Saint-Pierre, *Histoire des Canadiens du Michigan*, 222.

15. *Seventy-fifth Anniversary*, 11.

16. *St. Joseph Parish, Diamond Jubilee*, 11. Télésphore Saint-Pierre counted fourteen families, most of whom were French Canadian (Saint-Pierre, *Histoire des Canadiens du Michigan*, 222).

17. Briggs, *An Italian Passage*, 272.

18. Particularly St. Joseph Parish in Bay City.

19. Saint-Pierre, *Histoire des Canadiens du Michigan*, 262. The great majority of Michigan's French Canadian parishes were originally mixed parishes, variously including members whose native languages were English, French, German, or Dutch.

20. Saint-Pierre, *Histoire des Canadiens du Michigan*, 263.

21. See ibid., 222–23 and 264–65 on the tensions between the parishioners and the bishop in these two towns; and Magnan, *Notes historiques sur la paroisse de Saint-Jean-Baptiste*.

22. According to the enumeration schedules of the U.S. federal census of 1880 for Bay City, Michigan.

23. *St. Joseph Parish,Diamond Jubilee*, 15. The list of priests who headed the parish after the Reverend Girard is as follows: the Reverends Dalbaire (1872–73) Conters, Zarilli, Van Straellen, Zarilli again, Kemper, Shaeken, Ebert, Thibodeau (1880–86), Vitali, Guérin (1887–89), Roth, Dangelzer.

24. According to the state census.

25. *St. Joseph Parish,Diamond Jubilee*, 15.

26. It is impossible to identify the moment when the specifically Francophone characteristics of this French Canadian parish began to be attenuated. It seems that the process was under way by the late nineteenth century. It should be noted that this parish was subdivided several times. In 1867, St. James Parish was created, and in 1872 another subdivision of St. Joseph led to the creation of St. Mary's in 1874, on the west bank of the Saginaw.

27. According to Saint-Pierre, there were six French Canadian parishes within the diocese of Grand Rapids, which was created in 1882, including one in Bay City, one in East Saginaw, and one in West Bay City (Saint-Pierre, *Histoire des Canadiens du Michigan*, 267).

28. Ibid.

29. *Bay City Daily Journal*, January 30, 1872; February 28, 1872.

30. There has been little research on the specific characteristics of the French Canadian press in the United States—that is, the large number of such publications and their short duration. Newspapers in this period, in the United States as in French Canada, were often founded to put forward a single political idea, which would explain their short life span. In addition, the high rate of illiteracy among the French Canadians probably limited potential readership and created financial problems that caused the papers to fold.

31. Examination of a number of French Canadian newspapers from Michigan showed this clearly.

32. This analysis is based on a detailed study of *Le patriote* and *Le courrier*.

33. Belisle, *Histoire de la presse franco-américaine*, 30. Only a few numbers of the newspaper *Le courrier* are still available in Michigan. The reason for its disappearance is unknown.

34. Ibid., 31. In 1891, *Le patriote* was a weekly, published every Thursday. A year's subscription cost $1.50, and the press run was 2,600 copies. By comparison, the *Bay City Tribune*, an American newspaper published in the same town since 1873, had a press run of 3,500 copies (*Bay City Directory for 1890–1891*, 44).

35. Belisle, *Histoire de la presse franco-américaine*, 33.

36. Saint-Pierre, *Histoire des Canadiens du Michigan*, 249.

37. In the nineteenth century, there was a tradition of solidarity, based on mutual aid and charity, in the rural villages of French Canada. This notion of charity became institutionalized with the creation of charitable organizations such as the Saint Vincent de Paul Society, founded in France in 1837 and established in French Canada shortly before 1867. This charity was especially known for *la guignolée*, a campaign organized by the parishes to collect money and food for the poor. In addition, this period also saw the emergence in the towns and cities of a large number of mutual aid societies, which combined aspects of mutual aid associations, cooperatives, and health insurance companies. Workers who were unable to pay high life insurance premiums sometimes formed mutual aid societies to combat their poverty. The Union Saint-Joseph, established in Montreal in the mid-nineteenth century, was typical of this type of organization. Each member paid dues, and the sum of the dues provided sick members—or their widows—with a modest pension. See Paul-André Linteau, René Durocher, and Jean-Claude Robert, *Histoire du Québec contemporain*, 1:205–6.

38. Briggs, *An Italian Passage*, 142.

39. Vander Hill, *Settling the Great Lakes Frontier*, 8; Saint-Pierre, *Histoire des Canadiens du Michigan*, 224.

40. Vander Hill, *Settling the Great Lakes Frontier*, 8.

41. Saint-Pierre, *Histoire des Canadiens du Michigan*, 225–26. The society promised to provide sick members with two dollars a week.

42. *Bay City Directory for 1890–1891*, 47. The president was I. Obey; the vice president, John Batias; the secretary, Jos. Cusson; the treasurer Narcisse Laporte. Lafayette Hall was on the east side of Washington Avenue, between Second and Third Streets.

43. Saint-Pierre, *Histoire des Canadiens du Michigan*, 224–25; Vander Hill, *Settling the Great Lakes Frontier*, 8.

44. Saint-Pierre, *Histoire des Canadiens du Michigan*, 228, 248. An association called the Union française, about which little is known, was created in Bay

City in 1861 under the aegis of M. J. L. Hébert. It was still active in 1869 at the time of the meeting of French Canadians in Detroit. It is not known when it disappeared.

45. Saint-Pierre, *Histoire des Canadiens du Michigan*, 228.

46. Some were established on the Upper Peninsula in the mid-1880s—at Lake Linden, Houghton, Calumet, and Hancock—but none in the valley.

47. Lanctot was a social reformer from a liberal petit bourgeois background. Influenced by the writings of Marx and Engels, he had sought to aid the workers of Montreal by organizing them. He had also had a go at politics, as a candidate in the 1867 elections in the county of Montréal-Est against George-Etienne Cartier, a strong defender of confederation. He advocated severing the colonial ties and was fiercely opposed to confederation, which he saw as a tool for placing the French Canadians at the mercy of the Anglophone majority (Monière, *Le développement des idéologies au Québec*, 205). It should also be noted that in 1849 an annexationist movement had been launched in United Canada by some members of the economic elite. This movement advocated "an amicable and peaceful separation from Great Britain, and union on equitable bases with the great confederation of sovereign states of North America" (Frégault and Trudel, *Histoire du Canada par les textes*, 1:239.

48. Saint-Pierre, *Histoire des Canadiens du Michigan*, 234.

49. Ibid., 235.

50. These organizations were the Saint-Jean-Baptiste Society of the state of Michigan, the Société de bienfaisance Lafayette de Détroit, the Wayne County Saint-Jean-Baptiste Society, the Association de l'indépendance pacifique du Canada, the Detroit Société de bienfaisance franco-américaine, the Union française of Bay County, and other societies and literary circles based in Chicago, New York, Maine, and Vermont.

51. Saint-Pierre, *Histoire des Canadiens du Michigan*, 238–39.

52. The delegates opposed to these resolutions angrily condemned the process by which they had been introduced. However, incapable of getting a proper hearing, they withdrew from the convention and began forming a new organization, which was independent both from the Saint-Jean-Baptiste Association and from the Société Lafayette. They called it the Union canadienne de secours mutuels. The annexationists now had the latitude they needed to go ahead with their project.

53. The delegates who had supported the resolutions generally represented the Detroit societies, while those who opposed them were generally from the Northeast, Chicago, and, within Michigan, Bay County (Saint-Pierre, *Histoire des Canadiens du Michigan*, 240).

54. As Saint-Pierre described it: "The *Canadiens*, deprived of freedom at home, sought it in the United States. The proof that they have found it is that they remain there, and the proof that it exists only in the United States is that

the *Canadiens* continue to emigrate" (*Histoire des Canadiens du Michigan*, 243–44). *L'impartial* is omitted from Belisle's book on French-language newspapers in the United States, *Histoire de la presse franco-américaine*.

55. Saint-Pierre, *Histoire des Canadiens du Michigan*, 246.

56. Vander Hill, *Settling the Great Lakes Frontier*, 9.

57. Saint-Pierre, *Histoire des Canadiens du Michigan*, 247.

58. In Quebec, the Grand Trunk Railroad followed the north shore of the St. Lawrence as far as Montreal and then followed Victoria Bridge and went on toward St. Hyacinthe and Richmond, from where a branch line led to Sherbrooke and on to Portland, Maine, and another to Lévis and Rivière-du-Loup on the south shore of the St. Lawrence. Indeed, examination of the petitions for naturalization for Saginaw County, in which the means of transportation used by the person seeking citizenship to enter the United States is indicated, suggests that beginning in 1860 the Grand Trunk Railroad was the means of transportation most frequently used to get to the valley (U.S. Department of Labor, Naturalization Service, *Petition for Naturalization* [Saginaw County]).

59. U.S. Census Office, *Ninth Census*, manuscript census, reel nos. M 593–662, M 593–701, M 593–702. It should be noted that beginning with the 1870 census, the data analysis is based on a sample using one household in ten with (at least) one individual of French Canadian origin. The compilation of the French Canadian population was, however, based on the whole population.

60. U.S. Census Office, *Tenth Census*, manuscript census, reel nos. T 9–571, T 9–572, T 9–601, T 9–602, T 9–603.

61. Thistlethwaite, "Migration from Europe Overseas," in Vecoli and Sinke, *A Century of European Migrations*. Thistlethwaite analyzes the migration that leads individuals from place to place as a "continuum," an ongoing series of migratory experiences or migration by phases, none of which are planned as part of a sequence, but which are, on the contrary, set in motion according to the information obtained at certain points and on the basis of economic cycles and family needs.

62. It should be noted in the discussion that follows that it is impossible to know whether the migrants made stops on Canadian soil in the course of their migration to Michigan. These data are based on the years and places of birth of children.

63. Given that the firstborn son was often given the father's name, we may presume either that this was not the couple's first child or that older children had already left home.

64. West Bay City received its charter in 1877 (Partridge, "Bay County History," 335).

65. The general expression "work in sawmill" comes up again and again.

66. These two French Canadian saloon owners were born in Canada and seem to have migrated directly from French Canada to Michigan.

67. The Paquettes had children in Michigan in 1861, 1865, 1866, and 1873. U.S. Census Office, *Tenth Census*, manuscript census, reel nos. T 9–601, T 9–602, T 9–603.

68. These data resemble those in research on the nineteenth century by Hareven and Modell, "Urbanization and Malleable Household"; and Katz, *The People of Hamilton*, (1975) in which 25 to 30 percent of households took in boarders.

69. In Saginaw County, 37.5 percent of household heads were born in Canada, while in Bay County, the figure was 20.8 percent.

70. Lamarre, "Étude d'une communauté canadienne-française de la Nouvelle-Angleterre," 117–18.

71. The data for Bay County are too limited to allow for valid conclusions.

72. *Bay City Daily Journal*, July 16, 1872.

73. *St. Joseph Parish, Diamond Jubilee*, 15; *Bay City Daily Journal*, July 14, 1872.

74. See Lamarre, "L'intégration des migrants canadiens-français à la réalité socioéconomique aux Etats-Unis."

75. This is an estimate based on the statistics available for 1884 and 1894 for Bay County alone, because the 1890 federal census was destroyed and the censuses for Saginaw County are not available.

76. Michigan Department of State, *Census: 1884*, manuscript census, Bay County, reel no. 5637–39; Michigan Department of State, *Census: 1894*, manuscript census, Bay County, reel no. 4834–36. French Canadians represented 11.4 percent of the population of Bay County in 1900.

77. U.S. Department of Interior, *Twelfth Census*, manuscript census, reel nos. T 623–701, T 623–702, T 623–739, T 623–740.

78. It must be said that in the mid-1880s, seeing that the lumber industry was in decline, the political and economic authorities of the valley tried to diversify the region's economic activities, particularly by developing a manufacturing sector.

79. *Le Patriote*, September 11, 1884, 3.

80. *Le Patriote*, March 8, 1884, 3; December 11, 1884, 2. The slogan "Soyons Canadiens en tout et partout" (Let's be *Canadien* in all respects) was also widely used.

81. *Le Patriote*, August 14, 1884, 3. He sold it to Ed Duckett.

82. *Le Patriote*, January 3, 1884, 2.

83. *Le Patriote*, June 19, 1884, 4 ; *Bay City Tribune*, June 21, 1885, 7.

84. Or at least it is not included in the list of organizations participating in the June 24 celebrations in 1884 (*Le Patriote*, June 19, 1884, 3).

85. *Bay City Tribune*, June 21, 1885, 7.

86. The Saint-Jean-Baptiste Society of West Bay City, not to be outdone,

sent Alex Brissette and Constant Plourde to represent it in Montreal (*Le Patriote*, June 5, 1884, 3; March 20, 1884, 3).

87. *Le Patriote*, June 19, 1884, 4.

88. *Le courrier*, October 4, 1884, 2; *Le Patriote*, October 23, 1884, 3.

89. *Le Patriote*, April 10, 1884, 3.

90. The exact figures are: 1.0 percent in Maine, 4.5 percent in New York, and 0.5 percent in Vermont.

91. U.S. Department of Interior, *Twelfth Census*, Bay County, Michigan, reel nos. T 623–701 and T 623–702.

92. Subsequent research may demonstrate more precisely that differences between the economic cycles related to the cotton manufacturing industry in New England and the cycles of the lumber industry in the Midwest had an effect on this migration triangle or on population transfers within this geoeconomic model.

93. In Saginaw County, 57 percent of household heads had already obtained their citizenship, and 14 percent were in the process of obtaining it. In Bay County, the situation was even more obvious: 61 percent of household heads already had their American citizenship, and 8 percent had received their first papers. In 1880, the enumeration schedules of the U.S. federal census do not give this type of information. In 1870, the rate of naturalization was 30 percent.

94. In Bay County, 57.8 percent of household heads were homeowners, and 47.4 percent of these had paid off their mortgages. In Saginaw County, 63.5 percent of household heads had acquired homes, and 60 percent had paid off their mortgages. In 1870, 35 percent of homeowners had paid off their mortgages.

95. Briggs, *An Italian Passage*, 272.

Chapter 4

1. Statistics for the Keweenaw Peninsula include Houghton, Ontonagon, and Keweenaw Counties, unless otherwise indicated.

2. These data are taken from the enumeration schedules of the U.S. federal census for Houghton and Ontonagon Counties. For 1860, it should be noted that relationships between members of the same household are not indicated and must therefore be reconstituted (Houghton County, reel no. M 432–351; Ontonagon County, reel no. M 432–361).

3. Great Northern Route American Lines, *The Ontario and St. Lawrence Steam Boat Co. Handbook.*

4. DuLong, "Roman Catholic Church Records and Cemeteries," 58.

5. The lumber contractor was bound by contract to an employer, often a mining company, to supply lumber. He was responsible for hiring the loggers to fulfil the requirements of his contract.

6. It is impossible to know in what exact field these laborers worked. However, it is reasonable to suppose that preparatory work in the mining sector required some nonskilled laborers.

7. *History of the Upper Peninsula of Michigan*, 313.

8. *PLMG*, June 27, 1863, 5.

9. *PLMG*, March 5, 1864, 4.

10. *PLMG*, October 24, 1863, 5.

11. DuLong, "Roman Catholic Church Records and Cemeteries," 57–58. In fact, there were few French Canadians in the towns of Houghton and Hancock. In 1860, there were 172 French Canadians in Houghton and only 81 in Hancock. The latter attended the parish of Ste. Anne from 1861 to 1884, and in 1889 this parish became Irish and took the name of St. Patrick. French Canadians then moved to the multiethnic parish of St. Joseph in Hancock, created in 1885, which also included Germans.

12. Until 1882, this little hamlet was known as Torch Lake because it was situated at the northern tip of the lake of the same name. Monette, *The History of Lake Linden*, 1.

13. *History of the Upper Peninsula of Michigan*, 311.

14. Monette, *The History of Lake Linden*, 1. Lake Linden was incorporated as a municipality in 1883.

15. Ibid., 2. The region is located within the broad pine belt running from Maine to Minnesota.

16. *St. Joseph Church, Lake Linden*, 37. For further information on Joseph Grégoire, see Saint-Pierre, *Histoire des Canadiens du Michigan*, 274–77. He was born August 5, 1833. According to *Le patriote* (October 30, 1884, 2), he ran as a Democratic candidate to represent Houghton County in the state legislature in the 1884 elections. He died in 1895, at the age of sixty-two.

17. *PLMG*, March 12, 1874, 3.

18. *PLMG*, February 28, 1867, 3; *History of the Upper Peninsula of Michigan*, 313; Monette, *The History of Lake Linden*, 2.

19. Monette, *The History of Lake Linden*, 2.

20. Bourbonnière, *Le guide français des Etats-Unis*, 785.

21. Saint-Pierre, *Histoire des Canadiens du Michigan*, 277.

22. *PLMG*, September 6, 1866, 3. The French Canadians constituted almost half the population of Lake Linden.

23. *St. Joseph Church, Lake Linden*, 25.

24. Ibid.; *History of the Upper Peninsula of Michigan*, 312. The religious authorities indicate that Grégoire paid for the land upon which the church was
built, as well as providing money and materials to build a residence for
the parish priest, with the condition that his name not be revealed as the
benefactor of the parish. The Reverend Héliard lived with the Reverend
Jacker, pastor of Sacré Coeur de Calumet Parish, until August 1871, when
the work was completed (*St. Joseph Church, Lake Linden*, 3).
25. *PLMG*, October 15, 1874, 3.
26. The *PLMG* was the principal publication in which these fairs were announced.
27. *PLMG*, November 19, 1874, 3. This information comes to us from an
article published in French, a first of its kind for this newspaper.
28. Monette, *The History of Lake Linden*, 20; *St. Joseph Church, Lake Linden*,
29.
29. *St. Joseph Church, Lake Linden*, 29.
30. Ibid.; Monette, *The History of Lake Linden*, 22. The new congregation
thus created continued to function within St. Joseph Parish until October
1888, when the construction of the church was finished and the new
parish, named Holy Rosary, was assigned to Father Henn. The population
of Schoolcraft Township in 1874, according to the enumeration schedules,
stood at 1,761 inhabitants.
31. *St. Joseph Church, Lake Linden*, 33.
32. *PLMG*, June 3, 1875, 3.
33. *Lumberman's Gazette*, September 7, 1876, 181; Monette, *The History of
Lake Linden*, 54.
34. *History of the Upper Peninsula of Michigan*, 311.
35. For further details, see Monette, *The History of Lake Linden*, 30 and 66–68.
36. *St. Joseph Church, Lake Linden*, 29.
37. In 1872, the legislature of Michigan passed a law that required all children
to attend public school. Children between eight and fourteen years of age
had to attend school for a minimum of twelve weeks per year, including six
consecutive weeks (*PLMG*, September 3, 1874, 3).
38. *History of the Upper Peninsula of Michigan*, 312. This practice of building a
school and renting it at a low rate to the school authorities of the township
was one of the paternalistic practices of the large mining companies in
isolated regions.
39. Monette, *The History of Lake Linden*, 22.
40. *St. Joseph Church, Lake Linden*, 29.
41. Saint-Pierre, *Histoire des Canadiens du Michigan*, 249.
42. Ibid., 248–49.
43. *PLMG*, April 6, 1871, 3.
44. *PLMG*, April 13, 1871, 3.

45. Saint-Pierre, *Histoire des Canadiens du Michigan*, 250–51.

46. Ibid., 251.

47. Ibid.

48. Ibid.

49. Monette, *The History of Lake Linden*, 37.

50. PLMG, April 22, 1875, 3; May 13, 1875, 3. Bélisle indicates that Charles Thibault was the founder (*Histoire de la presse franco-américaine*, 29).

51. Monette, *The History of Lake Linden*, 37.

52. Saint-Pierre was well known in Michigan. Originally from Lavaltrie, he began his journalistic career in the region of Detroit-Windsor and helped found several Michigan newspapers, including *L'Ouest français*, published in Bay City in 1888–89.

53. *L'Union franco-américaine*, July 9, 1891.

54. Monette, *The History of Lake Linden*, 37. On the whole, the content of these newspapers was quite simple, consisting of dispatches, local news, and a social column. The newspapers were not much interested in the socioeconomic conditions of the region.

55. Monette, *The History of Lake Linden*, 14.

56. Ibid., 45–46. Perreault was one of the first colonists in the region in 1865. This hotel was rebuilt a year after the fire of 1887.

57. Thurner, *Calumet Copper*, 7.

58. Ibid., 22. The Reverend lived with Captain Ryan, sheriff of the community, until 1869, when construction of the church was completed.

59. DuLong, "Roman Catholic Church Records and Cemeteries," 58.

60. PLMG, October 23, 1873, 3.

61. PLMG, July 11 and 18, 1874, 3. Classes began on July 21, 1874.

62. Thurner, *Calumet Copper*, 22–23. It is estimated that in 1896 there were 260 families in the parish of St. Louis, including 900 communicants and 582 noncommunicants (under twelve years of age). St. Louis later became the parish of Ste. Anne. These data concur with my own compilation indicating that 1,492 French Canadians were living there. There was a parish school attached to St. Louis Church with 75 students in 1895.

63. Thurner, *Calumet Copper*, 26.

64. *L'Union franco-américaine*, June 18, 1891.

65. According to the enumeration schedules of the U.S. federal census for 1870. Houghton County, reel no. M 593–674; Keweenaw County, reel no. M 593–683; Ontonagon County, reel no. M 593–696.

66. It may, however, be assumed that a significant number of these laborers worked in the mining sector, which dominated the labor market of the region.

67. Four percent of heads of households worked on the construction of the canal on Portage Lake in 1870.

68. Before 1850, the mining sector in French Canada did not amount to much more than the extraction of sand and gravel from quarries. After 1850, four new sectors opened up: in gold, asbestos, phosphates, and copper. The expansion of the last three sectors was the result of American demand. The first copper mines went into operation in 1859 in the Eastern Townships. In 1871, copper mining activities were being carried out in the counties of Mégantic, Sherbrooke, and Brome. However, these operations were modest and limited to the extraction of raw materials that were then exported for processing. Some French Canadians may have had a certain amount of experience in mineral extraction, but few of them could have become familiar with processing work. See Paul-André Linteau, René Durocher, and Jean-Claude Robert, *Histoire du Québec contemporain*, 364–68; Armstrong, *Structure and Change*, 183. At the end of the nineteenth century, the sector had almost ceased operations. It disappeared entirely around the time of the First World War (Paquette, "Industries et politiques minières au Québec," 575–76).

69. Note that the quality of reproduction is poor for the enumeration schedules of the 1910 census. Users are warned of this in a note. Since the originals were destroyed after being microfilmed, these documents are the only ones now available. It is therefore possible that some elements were not clearly discernible to the researcher. For 1900, Houghton County, reel nos. T 623–714 and T 623–715; Keweenaw County, reel no. T 623–724; Ontonagon County, reel no. T 623–737. For 1910, Houghton County, reel nos. T 624–646 and T 624–647; Keweenaw County, reel no. T 624–658; Ontonagon County, reel no. T 624–667.

70. It should not be overlooked that deaths may have contributed, to a certain extent, to the decline of the population.

71. Cited by Thurner, *Calumet Copper*, 29. See also *L'Union franco-américaine*, June 4, 1891. Some French Canadians were even drawn to the Alaskan gold rush of 1898. Note also that many French Canadians made their way to Arizona, where numerous silver mines were operating at this time.

72. *St. Joseph Church, Lake Linden*, 31.

73. Ibid. Some restoration work, however, was carried out in 1902.

74. Ibid.

75. Monette, *The History of Lake Linden*, 71.

76. Ibid. A December 1916 issue is available at the Library of Michigan in Lansing. The following issue is dated June 1919.

77. "Strike Investigation by the Committee of the Copper Country Commercial Club of Michigan," 57.

78. See the information contained in the employment records of C & H (Thurner, *Calumet Copper*, 16).

Conclusion

1. Ramirez, *Par monts et par vaux*, 170.
2. This estimate takes into account natural growth.
3. Numerous monographs on the manufacturing cities of Fall River and Holyoke in Massachusetts, Lewiston in Maine, and Manchester in New Hampshire confirm that the French Canadians almost always opposed strikes. See Silvia, "Spindle City"; Haebler, *Habitants in Holyoke*; Frenette, "La genèse d'une communauté canadienne-française"; Hareven, *Family Time and Industrial Time*; Roby, *Les Franco-Américains de la Nouvelle-Angleterre*, 188.
4. See Lamarre, "Étude d'une communauté canadienne-française de la Nouvelle-Angleterre," 117–18. The French Canadians of New England were often criticized for being reluctant to apply for American citizenship and for not participating in American social and political institutions. These are, in fact, the two main criticisms formulated by Carroll D. Wright, director of the Bureau of Labor Statistics of the Massachusetts legislature in his report of 1882. On the reluctance of French Canadians to become naturalized citizens, see Roby, *Les Franco-Américains de la Nouvelle-Angleterre*, 199.
5. See Hareven, *Family Time and Industrial Time*, Chapter 8.
6. Ramirez, "French-Canadian Immigrants in the New England Cotton Industry: A Socioeconomic Profile."
7. Haebler, *Habitants in Holyoke*, 68; Roby, *Les Franco-Américains de la Nouvelle-Angleterre*, 68–69.
8. Hareven, *Family Time and Industrial Time*, 125; Roby, *Les Franco-Américains de la Nouvelle-Angleterre*, 79.
9. Roby, *Les Franco-Américains de la Nouvelle-Angleterre*, 135, 143.
10. Ibid., 290ff.
11. Exceptionally, they participated in the Lawrence, Massachusetts, strike in 1912, which was led by the Industrial Workers of the World.

Bibliography

PRIMARY ARCHIVAL SOURCES

Calumet and Hecla Mining Company. Employment files, 1913–14. Calumet, Mich.

Federal Censuses

Bay County: 1860: rolls M 653–536; 1870: M 593–662; 1880: T 9–571, T 9–572; 1900: T 623–701, T 623–702.
Saginaw County: 1840: rolls M 704–210; 1850: M 432–361; 1860: M 653–558; 1870: M 593–701, M 593–702; 1880: T 9–601, T 9–602, T 9–603; 1900: T 623–739, T 623–740.
Houghton County: 1850: rolls M 432–352; 1860: M 653–544; 1870: M 593–674; 1880: T 9–581; 1900: T 623–714, TEcircumflex623–715; 1910: T 624–646, T 624–647.
Keweenaw County: 1870: rolls M 593–683; 1880: T 9–589; 1900: T 623–724; 1910: T 624–658.
Ontonagon County: 1850: rolls M 432–361; 1860: M 653–557; 1870: M 593–696; 1880: T 9–600; 1900: T 623–737; 1910: T 624–667.

Michigan State Censuses

Bay County: 1884: rolls 5637, 5638, 5639, 5640; 1894: 4834, 4835, 4836.
Houghton County: 1864: roll 5216; 1874: 5216.
Keweenaw County: 1884: roll 5217; 1894: 5217.

Parochial Registers

St. Joseph of Bay City:
Baptisms: vol. 1 (1850–67), vol. 2 (1867–80), vol. 3 (1881–1908).
Marriages: vol. 1 (1850–78), vol. 2 (1879–87).
Deaths: vol. D (1879–86), vol. E (1887–1935).

St. Andrew of Saginaw:
    Baptisms: vol. 1 (1862–94), vol. 2 (1894–1921).
    Marriages: vol. 1 (1862–1901), vol. 2 (1901–49).
    Deaths: vol. 1 (1862–1902), vol. 2 (1902–present).
St. Mary of Saginaw:
    Baptisms: vol. 1 (1866–98).
    Marriages: vol. 1 (1866–1947).
    Deaths: vol. 1 (1868–1955).
Houghton County:
    Marriages: vol. 1 (1848–64), vol. 2 (1864–65), vol. 3 (1867–87), vol, 4,
        (1887–99), vol. 5 (1899–1906).
    Deaths: vol. 1 (1867–87), vol. 2 (1887–1900), vol. 3 (1901–10).
St. Ignatius, Loyola of Houghton:
    Marriages: vol. 1 (1877–1913), vol. 2 (1913–46).
    Deaths: vol. 2 (1877–1923).
St. Joseph of Lake Linden:
    Baptisms, marriages, and deaths: vol. 1 (June 13, 1871–December 27,
        1878), vol. 2 (January 12, 1879– December 30, 1891).
    Liber Matrimonium (January 19, 1892–December 31, 1970).
    Liber Baptizatorium (1892–1967).
    Liber Defunctorum (1892–1990).

Primary Published Sources

United States Government

U.S. Census Office. *Sixth Census of the United States, 1840.* Washington, D.C.:
    Blair and Rives, 1841.
———. *Seventh Census of the United States, 1850.* Washington, D.C.: Govern-
    ment Printing Office, 1853.
———. *Eighth Census of the United States, 1860: Population.* Washington, D.C.:
    Government Printing Office, 1865.
———. *Ninth Census of the United States, 1870.* 3 vols. Washington, D.C.:
    Government Printing Office, 1872.
———. *Tenth Census of the United States, 1880.* Vol. 1, *Population;* vol. 2,
    Manufactures. Washington, D.C. Government Printing Office, 1886.
———. *Eleventh Census of the United States, 1890.* Vol. 1, *Compendium on Pop-
    ulation;* vol. 2, *Manufacturing Industries.* Washington, D.C.: Government
    Printing Office, 1895.
U.S. Department of Interior. *Twelfth Census of the United States, Taken the Year
    1900.* Vol. 1, part 1, *Population.* Washington, D.C.: Government Printing
    Office, 1901.

U.S. Department of Commerce, Bureau of the Census. *Thirteenth Census of the United States, 1910.* Vol. 2, *Population.* Washington, D.C.: Government Printing Office, 1913.

U.S. Department of Interior, Census Office. *Report on the Mining Industries.* Vol. 15, 1880, Washington, D.C.: Government Printing Office, 1886.

U.S. Department of Labor, Naturalization Service. *Petition for Naturalization.* Vols. 1–6. [Naturalization Acts, Petition, and Record for Saginaw County, 1906–1920.]

——. *Petition for Naturalization.* Vols. 14, 15, 17, 18, 19. [Naturalization Acts, Petition, and Record for Houghton County, 1906–1908.]

U.S. House Subcommittee of the Committee on Mines and Mining. *Report Pursuant to House Resolution 387, a Resolution Authorizing and Directing the Committee on Mines and Mining to Make Investigation of Conditions in the Copper Mines of Michigan.* 63rd Cong., 2d sess., 1914.

Michigan Government

State of Michigan, Department of State. *Census and Statistics of the State of Michigan: 1854.* Lansing: Geo. W. Peck, 1854.

——. *Statistics of the State of Michigan: 1860.* Lansing: John A. Kerr, 1861.

——. *Census and Statistics of the State of Michigan: 1864.* Lansing: John A. Kerr, 1865.

——. *Statistics of the State of Michigan: 1870.* Lansing: John A. Kerr, 1873.

——. *Census of the State of Michigan: 1874.* Lansing: W. S. George, 1875.

——. *Population of Michigan, 1884 and 1880.* Lansing: Michigan Department of State, 1884.

——. *Census of the State of Michigan: 1884.* 2 vols. Lansing: Thorp and Godfrey, 1886.

——. *Census of the State of Michigan: 1894.* 2 vols. Lansing: Robert Smith, 1896.

——. *Census of the State of Michigan: 1904.* 2 vols. Lansing: Wynkoop Hallenbeck Crawford, 1906.

State of Michigan. *Annual Report of the Commissioner of Mineral Statistics for 1880.* Lansing, 1881.

——. *Annual Report of the Commissioner of Mineral Statistics for 1881.* Lansing, 1882.

——. *Mineral Resources.* Report by Charles D. Lawton. Lansing, 1886.

——. [Houghton County.] *Inspectors of Mines Report.* Houghton 1888–1900.

——. *Annual Report of the Commissioner of Mineral Statistics.* Lansing, 1889–92.

——. *Mines and Mineral Statistics for 1896.* Lansing, 1897–1910.

——. *Copper Handbook.* Vol. 10, 1911. Lansing, 1912–13.

————. *The Mines Handbook and Copper Handbook.* Vol. 12. Lansing, 1916.

————. *Second Annual Report of the Bureau of Labor and Industrial Statistics.* Lansing: W. S. George, 1885.

————. *Third Annual Report of the Bureau of Labor and Industrial Statistics.* Lansing: Thorp and Godfrey, 1886.

————. *Fifth Annual Report of the Bureau of Labor and Industrial Statistics.* Lansing: Thorp and Godfrey, 1888.

Saginaw Valley

Bay City Directory for 1890–1891. Vol. 1. Bay City, 1891.

Boards of Supervisors of the Counties of Saginaw, Bay, Tuscola, Genesee, Midland, Shiawassee, Clinton, Gratiot, Alpena, Isabella, and Iosco, on the Subject of Immigration to the Saginaw Valley. N.p., 1868.

Industries of the Saginaws: Historical, Descriptive and Statistical. East Saginaw: J. M. Elstner, 1887.

Saginaw Board of Trade. *Summary of Business Transacted on the Saginaw River for the Years 1880–1881.* East Saginaw: Courier, 1882.

————. *Annual Review of the Saginaw Board of Trade of the Manufacturing Industries in the Saginaw District . . . for 1882.* East Saginaw: Courier, 1883.

————. *Third Annual Review of the Saginaw Board of Trade of the Commerce, Manufactures, and Material Resources of the Saginaw District . . . for 1883.* East Saginaw: Courier, 1884.

————. *Fourth Annual Review of the Saginaw Board of Trade of the Commerce, Manufactures, and Material Resources of the Saginaw Valley . . . for 1884.* East Saginaw: Courier, 1885.

————. *Fifth Annual Review of the Saginaw Board of Trade, Showing the Commerce, Manufactures, and Chief Business Interests of the Saginaw District . . . for 1885.* East Saginaw: Courier, 1886.

————. *Sixth Annual Review of the Saginaw Board of Trade, Showing the Lumber and Salt Production and Commercial Statistics of the Saginaw Valley . . . for 1886.* East Saginaw: Courier, 1887.

————. *Seventh Annual Review of the Saginaw Board of Trade, Showing the Lumber and Salt Production and Auxiliary Industries of the Saginaw Valley . . . for 1887.* East Saginaw: Courier, 1888.

————. *Eighth Annual Review of the Saginaw Board of Trade, Showing the Lumber and Salt Production and Auxiliary Industries of the Saginaw Valley . . . for 1888.* East Saginaw: Courier, 1889.

————. *Ninth Annual Review of the Saginaw Board of Trade, Showing the Lumber and Salt Production and Auxiliary Industries of the Saginaws . . . for 1889.* East Saginaw: Courier, 1890.

————. *Tenth Annual Review of the Saginaw Board of Trade, Showing the Staple Products of Saginaw River Mills, Including Lumber, Lath, Shingles, and Salt and Auxiliary Industries of Saginaw for 1890.* Compiled by E. D. Cowles. East Saginaw: Courier, 1891.

————. *Annual Review Issued by the Saginaw Board of Trade and Saginaw Improvement Co. of the Manufacturing and Commercial Interests of Saginaw for 1891.* East Saginaw: Courier, 1892.

————. *Twelfth Annual Review Issued by the Saginaw Board of Trade of the Commerce, Manufactures, and Resources of Saginaw for 1892.* Saginaw: Jones and McCall, 1893.

Statistics of the Saginaw Valley for 1864. East Saginaw: *East Saginaw Courier*, 1865.

The Tariff on Lumber: Several Reasons Why the Present Tarif Should Not Be Repealed. East Saginaw: Daily Enterprise Steam Print, 1870.

Keweenaw Peninsula

Committee of the Copper Country Commercial Club of Michigan. *Strike Investigation.* Houghton, 1913.

Government of Canada and Government of Quebec

Assemblée législative. *Rapport du comité spécial de l'Assemblée législative nommé pour s'enquérir des causes et de l'importance de l'émigration qui a lieu tous les ans vers les Etats-Unis.* Montreal: Louis Perreault, 1849.

————. *Rapport du comité spécial nommé pour s'enquérir des causes de l'émigration du Canada vers les Etats-Unis ou ailleurs.* Toronto: J. Lovell, 1857.

Quebec Assemblée législative. "Mémoire du comité spécial nommé le 22 juin 1892 pour examiner les causes du mouvement d'émigration dans certaines parties de nos campagnes." In *Journaux de l'Assemblée législative de la province de Québec*, vol. 27, app. 1, pp. 375–98. 1893.

————. "Rapport du comité permanent sur l'agriculture, l'immigration et la colonisation." In *Journaux de l'Assemblée législative de la province de Québec*, app. 12. 1868.

Newspapers

Bay City Daily Journal (1885–1886).
Bay City Tribune (June 14, 1885–May 25, 1886).
Le courrier, Bay City (January 12–December 13, 1885).
Daily Mining Gazette (October 1899–1914).
Lumberman's Gazette, Bay City, (1872–74, 1874–87).

La Minerve, Montreal (1885, 1913–14).
Le patriote, Bay City (September 6, 1883–December 31, 1884).
Portage Lake Mining Gazette (July 26, 1862–October 28, 1897).
La presse, Montreal (1885, 1913–14).
Saginaw Daily Courier (1885).
L'union franco-américaine, Lake Linden (February–July 1891).

SECONDARY SOURCES

Books

Armstrong, Robert. *Structure and Change: An Economic History of Quebec.* Toronto: Gage, 1984.
Arndt, Leslie E. *The Bay County Story.* Detroit: L. Arndt, 1982.
Auger, Pierre. "La grande mouvance et la route du Bois." In *La grande mouvance*, edited by Marcel Bellavance, 45–62. Sillery, Quebec: Septentrion, 1990.
Belisle, Alexandre. *Histoire de la presse franco-américaine.* Worcester, Mass.: L'Opinion publique, 1911.
Bellavance, Marcel, ed. *La grande mouvance.* Sillery, Quebec: Septentrion, 1990.
Bodnar, John. *The Transplanted: A History of Immigrants in Urban America.* Bloomington: Indiana University Press, 1985.
Bourbonnière, A. *Le guide français des Etats-Unis.* Lowell, Mass.: Société de publication française des Etats-Unis, 1891.
Briggs, John. *An Italian Passage: Immigrants to Three American Cities, 1890–1930.* New Haven, Conn.: Yale University Press, 1978.
Brouillette, Benoit. *La pénétration du continent américain par les Canadiens français, 1763–1846: Traitants, explorateurs, missionnaires.* Montreal: Granger, 1939.
Brown, Jennifer S. H., W. J. Eccles, and Donald P. Heldman, eds., *The Fur Trade Revisited: Selected Papers of the Sixth North American Fur Trade Conference, Mackinac Island, Michigan.* East Lansing: Michigan State University Press, 1991.
Bryant, Ralph Clement. *Logging: The Principles and General Methods of Operation in the United States.* New York: John Wiley and Sons, 1913.
Butterfield, Georges E. *Bay County Past and Present.* Bay City, Mich.: Bay City Board of Education, 1957.
Chaput, Donald. *Hubbel: A Copper County Village.* Lansing, Mich.: self-published, 1969.
Defebaugh, James E. *History of the Lumber of America.* 2 vols. 2d ed. Chicago: American Lumberman, 1906.
Desrosiers, Léo-Paul. *Nord-Sud.* Montreal: Fides, 1931.

Dunbar, Willis Frederick. *Michigan: A History of the Wolverine State*. Rev. ed. Grand Rapids, Mich.: W. B. Eerdmans, 1980.

Farmer, Silas. *History of Detroit and Michigan and Wayne County and Early Michigan*. 2 vols. Detroit: Silas Farmer, (1884) 1890.

Foehl, Harold M., and Irene Hargraves. *The Story of Logging the White Pine in the Saginaw Valley*. Bay City, Mich.: Reg Keg Press, 1964.

Foster, Theodore. *Dictionary of Michigan Place Names*. Dept. of Education, Michigan State Library: Lansing, Mich., 1967.

Fox, Truman. *History of Saginaw County, from the Year 1819 Down to the Present Time*. 1858.

Frégault, Guy, and Marcel Trudel, eds. *Histoire du Canada par les textes (1534–1854)*. Vol 1. Montreal: Fides, 1963.

Fuller, George N. *Economic and Social Beginnings of Michigan*. Lansing, Mich.: Wynkoop Hallenbeck Crawford, 1916.

———. *Michigan: A Centennial History of the State and Its People*. 5 vols. Chicago: Lens, 1939.

Gansser, Augustus H., ed., *History of Bay County, Michigan, and Representative Citizens*. Chicago: Richmond and Arnold, 1905.

Gates, William B. *Michigan Copper and Boston Dollars: An Economic History of the Michigan Copper Mining Industry*. New York: Russell and Russell, 1951.

Goodstein, Anita Shafer. *Biography of a Businessman: Henry W. Sage, 1814–1897*. Ithaca, N.Y.: Cornell University Press, 1962.

Great Northern Route American Lines. *The Ontario and St. Lawrence Steam Boat Co. Handbook for Travelers to Niagara Falls, Montreal, and Quebec*. Buffalo, N.Y.: Jewett Thomas, 1854.

Greer, Allan. *Peasant, Lord, and Merchant: Rural Society in Three [Quebec] Parishes, 1740–1840*. Toronto: University of Toronto Press, 1985.

Gutman, Herbert G. *Work, Culture, and Society in Industrializing America*. New York: Vintage Books, 1973.

Haebler, Peter. *Habitants in Holyoke: The Development of the French Canadian Communities in a Massachusetts City, 1865–1910*. Durham: University of New Hampshire, 1976.

Hamon, Edouard. *Les Canadiens français de la Nouvelle-Angleterre*. Quebec: N. S. Hardy, 1891.

Handlin, Oscar. *The Uprooted: The Epic Story of the Great Migration That Made the American People*. 2d ed. Boston: Little, Brown, 1973.

Hansen, Marcus Lee, and J. B. Brebner. *The Mingling of the Canadian and American Peoples*. New Haven, Conn.: Yale University Press, 1940.

Hardy, René, and Normand Séguin. *Forêt et société en Mauricie: La formation de la région de Trois-Rivières, 1830–1930*. Montreal: Musée national de l'homme, Boréal Express, 1984.

Hareven, Tamara K. "Family and Work Patterns of Immigrant Laborers in a Planned Industrial Town, 1900–1930." In *Immigrants in Industrial America, 1850–1920*, edited by Richard L. Ehrlich, 47–66. Charlottesville: University Press of Virginia, 1977.

————. *Family Time and Industrial Time: The Relationship between the Family and Work in a New England Industrial Community*. New York: Cambridge University Press, 1982.

Hendrickson, Dike. *Quiet Presence: Histoire de Franco-Américains en New England*. Portland, Maine: Gannet, 1980.

History of the Upper Peninsula of Michigan. Chicago: Western Historical, 1883.

Hotchkiss, George W. *History of the Lumber and Forest Industry of the Northwest*. Chicago: self-published, 1898.

The Industries of Saginaw. East Saginaw, Mich., 1887

Innis, Harold A. *Essays in Canadian Economic History*. Toronto: University of Toronto Press, 1962.

————. *The Fur Trade in Canada: An Introduction to Canadian Economic History*. New Haven, Conn.: Yale University Press, 1930.

Jensen, Vernon H. *Heritage in Conflict: Labor Relations in the Nonferrous Metals Industry up to 1930*. Ithaca, N.Y.: Cornell University Press, 1950.

————. "Industrial Relations in the Lumber Industry." In *Labor in Postwar America*, edited by E. Warne Colston, chapter 24. New York: Remsen Press, 1949.

————. *Lumber and Labor*. Toronto: Farrar and Rinehart, 1945.

Katz, Michael B. *The People of Hamilton, Canada West: Family and Class in a Mid-Nineteenth Century City*. Cambridge: Harvard University Press, 1975.

Lanctôt, Gustave. *Les Canadiens français et leurs voisins du sud*. Montreal: Editions Bernard Valiquette, 1941.

Lankton, Larry D. *Cradle to Grave: Life, Work and Death at the Lake Superior Copper Mines*. New York: Oxford University Press, 1991.

Lankton, Larry D., and Charles K. Hyde. *Old Reliable: An Illustrated History of the Quincy Mining Company*. Hancock, Mich.: Quincy Mine Hoist Association, 1982.

Lanman, James H. *History of Michigan*. New York: E. French, 1839.

Lapointe, Pierre-Louis. "L'Outaouais: Une culture en mutation." In *Les régions culturelles du Québec*, 79–108. Quebec: I.Q.R.C., 1983.

Lavoie, Yolande. *L'émigration des Canadiens vers les Etats-Unis avant 1930: Mesure du phénomène*. Montreal: Presses de l'Université de Montréal, 1972.

————. *L'émigration des Québécois vers les Etats-Unis de 1840 à 1930*. Quebec: Editeur officiel, 1979.

Leeson, Michael A. *History of Saginaw*. Chicago: Chas. C. Chapman, 1881.

Lewis, George F., and C. B. Headley, *Annual Statement of the Business of Saginaw*

Valley and "the Shore" for 1868. East Saginaw, Mich.: Daily Enterprise Steam Printing House: Daily Courier Book and Job Print, 1869–1873.

Lewis, Martin D. *Lumberman from Flint: The Michigan Career of Henry H. Crapo*. Detroit: Wayne State University Press, 1958.

Linteau, P. A., Durocher, R., and Robert, J-C. *Histoire du Québec contemporain, 1867–1896*. Vol. 1. Montreal: Boréal, 1979.

Little, J. I. *Nationalism, Capitalism, and Colonization in Nineteenth Century Quebec: The Upper St-Francis District*. Montreal: McGill-Queen's University Press, 1989.

Louder, Dean, and Eric Waddell. *Du continent perdu à l'archipel retrouvé: Le Québec et l'Amérique française*. Quebec: P.U.L., 1983.

Lower, A. R. M. *The North American Assault on the Canadian Forest: A History of the Lumber Trade between Canada and the United States*. Toronto: Ryerson Press, 1938.

Magnan, Jean-Roch. *Notes historiques sur la paroisse de St-Jean-Baptiste à Muskegeon, Michigan et divers renseignements utiles, 1883–1900*. Bay City, Mich.: J. G. Duval, 1900.

Mathieu, Jacques. *La Nouvelle-France: Les Français en Amérique du Nord, XVIe-XVIIIe siècle*. Paris: Belin, 1991.

Maybee, Rolland H. *Michigan's White Pine Era, 1840–1900*. John M. Munson Michigan History Fund pamphlet no. 1. Lansing: Michigan Historical Commission, 1960.

McCallum, John. *Unequal Beginnings: Agriculture and Economic Development in Québec and Ontario until 1870*. Toronto: University of Toronto Press, 1980.

McLaughlin, Doris B. *Michigan Labor: A Brief History from 1818 to the Present*. Ann Arbor, Mich.: Institute of Labor and Industrial Relations; Detroit: Wayne State University, 1970.

McQuillan, Aidan E. "Les communautés canadiennes-françaises du Midwest américain au XIXe siècle." In *Du continent perdu à l'archipel retrouvé*, edited by Dean R. Louder and Eric Waddell, 98–115. Sainte-Foy: Presses de l'Université Laval, 1983.

Mills, James Cooke. *History of Saginaw County, Michigan*. 2 vols. Saginaw, Mich.: Seeman and Peters, 1918.

Monette, Clarence. *The History of Lake Linden, Michigan*. Lake Linden, Mich.: Welden H. Curtin, 1977.

Monière, Denis. *Le développement des idéologies au Québec, des origines à nos jours*. Ottawa: Québec-Amérique, 1977.

Morissonneau, Christian. *La terre promise: Le mythe du nord québécois*. Montreal: Hurtubise, HMH, 1978.

Murdoch, Angus. *Boom Copper: The Story of the First Mining Boom*. New York: Macmillan, 1943.

Ouellet, Fernand. *Histoire économique et sociale du Québec, 1760–1850.* 2 vols. Montreal: Fides, 1971.

Rameau De Saint-Pere, Edme. *La France aux colonies: Etude du developpement de la race française hors d'Europe, Les Français en Amérique, Acadiens et Canadiens.* Paris: A. Jouby, 1859.

———. *Notes historiques sur la colonie canadienne de Detroit.* Montreal: J. B. Rolland, 1861.

Ramirez, Bruno. "Migration and Regional Labour Markets, 1870–1915: The Québec Case." In *Class, Community and the Labour Movement: Wales and Canada, 1850–1930,* edited by Deian R. Hopkin and Gregory S. Kealey, 119–33. St. John's, Nova Scotia: Llafur/CCLH, 1989.

———. *Par monts et par vaux: Migrants canadiens-français et italiens dans l'économie nord-atlantique.* Montreal: Boréal, 1991.

Ramirez, Bruno, Jean Lamarre, et al. *The Emigration from Québec to the USA, 1870–1915: Questions of Sources, Method, and Conceptualization.* Montreal: Université de Montréal, 1988.

Rector, William G. *Log Transportation in the Lake States Lumber Industry, 1840–1918.* Glendale, Calif.: Arthur H. Clark, 1953.

Reid, Richard, ed. *The Upper Ottawa Valley to 1855: A Collection of Documents.* Toronto: Champlain Society, 1990.

Roby, Yves. *Les Franco-Américains de la Nouvelle-Angleterre, 1776–1930.* Sillery, Quebec: Septentrion, 1990.

———. "Un Québec émigré aux Etats-Unis: Bilan historiographique." In *Les rapports culturels entre le Québec et les Etats-Unis,* edited by Claude Savary, 103–30. Quebec: I.Q.R.C., 1984.

Rouillard, Jacques. *Ah les Etats! Les travailleurs canadiens-français dans l'industrie textile de la Nouvelle-Angleterre, d'après le témoignage des derniers migrants.* Montreal: Boréal Express, 1985.

Rumilly, Robert. *Histoire des Franco-américains.* Montreal: self-published, 1958.

Seguin, Normand. *Agriculture et colonisation au Québec: Aspects historiques.* Montreal: Boréal Express, 1980.

Seventy-fifth Anniversary, Saint Andrew's Parish 1862–1937. Saginaw, Mich.: 1937.

Smith, David C. *A History of Lumbering in Maine, 1861–1960.* Orono: University of Maine Press, 1972.

Steer, Henry B. *Lumber Production in the United States, 1799–1946.* United States Dept. of Agriculture, Miscellaneous Publication no. 669. Washington, D.C.: United States Government Printing Office, 1948.

St. Joseph Church, Lake Linden, Michigan, 1871–1971. 1971.

St. Joseph Parish, Bay City, Michigan, Diamond Jubilee, 75th Anniversary, 1850–1925. Bay City, Mich., 1925.

Saint Pierre, Télesphore. *Les Canadiens des Etats-Unis: Ce qu'on perd à émigrer.* Montreal: Typographie la Gazette, 1893.

———. *Histoire des Canadiens du Michigan et du comté d'Essex en Ontario.* Montreal: Typographie la Gazette, 1895.

Tasse, Joseph. *Les Canadiens de l'Ouest.* 2 vols. Montreal: Compagnie d'imprimerie canadienne, 1878.

Thistlethwaite, Frank. "Migration from Europe Overseas in the Nineteenth and Twentieth Centuries." In *A Century of European Migrations, 1830–1930,* edited by Rudolph Vecoli and Suzanne M. Sinke, 17–49. Urbana: University of Illinois Press, 1991.

Thurner, Arthur W. *Calumet Copper and People: A History of a Michigan Mining Community, 1864–1970.* Hancock, Mich.: privately published, 1974.

———. *Rebels on the Range: The Michigan Copper Miners' Strike of 1913–1914.* Lake Linden, Mich.: John H. Forster Press, 1984.

Trudel, Marcel. *Chiniquy.* Trois-Rivières, Quebec: Editions du bien public, 1955.

———. *Initiation à la Nouvelle-France.* Montreal: HRW, 1971.

Truesdell, Leon E. *The Canadians Born in the United States.* New Haven, Conn.: Yale University Press, 1943.

Tulchinsky, Gerald. *La rivière et la forêt: Le commerce du bois dans la vallée de l'Outaouais de 1800–1900.* Montreal: McCord Museum, McGill University, 1981.

Turner, Frederic Jackson. *La frontière dans l'histoire américaine.* Paris: P.U.F., 1963.

———. *The United States, 1830–1850.* W. W. Norton, 1965.

Vander Hill, C. Warren. *Settling the Great Lakes Frontier: Immigration to Michigan, 1837–1924,* Lansing, Mich.: Historical Commission, 1970.

Vander Hill, C. Warren, and Robert M. Warner, eds. *A Michigan Reader, 1865 to the Present.* Grand Rapids, Mich.: W. B. Eerdmans, 1974.

Vecoli, Rudolph J. "Ethnicity: A Neglected Dimension of American History." In *The State of American History,* edited by Herbert J. Bass, 70–88. Chicago: Quadrangle, 1970.

———. "From the Uprooted to the Transplanted: The Writing of American Immigration History, 1951–1989." In *From "Melting-Pot" to Multiculturalism,* edited by Valeria Gennaro Lerda, 25–53. Rome: Bulzoni editore, 1991.

Vecoli, Rudolph, and Suzanne M. Sinke, eds., *A Century of European Migrations, 1830–1930.* Urbana: University of Illinois Press, 1991.

Weil, François. *Les Franco-Américains, 1860–1960.* Paris: Bélin, 1989.

Wood, Richard G. *A History of Lumbering in Maine, 1820–1860.* Orono: University of Maine Press, 1961.

Yans-Mclaughlin, Virginia, ed. *Immigration Reconsidered: History, Sociology, and Politics.* Oxford: Oxford University Press, 1990.

Articles

Bellaire, John I. "Michigan's Lumberjacks." *Michigan History* 26 (1942): 173–87.

Bowman, James C. "Life in the Michigan Woods." *Michigan History* 21 (1937): 267–83.

——. "Lumberjack Ballads." *Michigan History* 20 (1936): 231–45.

Brinks, Herbert. "The Effects of the Civil War in 1861 on Michigan Lumbering and Mining Industries." *Michigan History* 14 (1960): 101–7.

Campbell, James V. "Early French Settlements in Michigan." *Pioneer Society of the State of Michigan, Pioneer Collections*, no. 9 (1901): 241–78.

Catlin, Georges B. "Early Settlement in Eastern Michigan." *Michigan History* 26 (1942): 319–42.

Chaput, Donald. "Some Repatriement Dilemmas." *Canadian Historical Review* 44 (December 1968): 400–412.

Chase, Lew Allen. "Early Copper Mining in Michigan." *Michigan History* 29 (1945): 22–30.

——. "Early Days Michigan Mining Pioneering Land Sales and Survey." *Michigan History* 29 (1945): 166–79.

——. "Michigan Copper Mines," *Michigan History* 29 (1945): 479–88.

——. "Michigan Upper Peninsula." *Michigan Historical Magazine* 20 (1930).

Coon, David S. "The Quincy Mine." *Michigan History* 24 (1940): 91–104.

Courville, Serge. "Un monde rural en mutation: Le Bas-Canada dans la première moitié du XIXe siècle." *Histoire sociale — Social History* 20, no. 40 (November 1987): 237–58.

Danford, Ormond S. "The Social and Economic Effects of Lumbering on Michigan, 1835–1890." *Michigan History* 26 (1942): 346–64.

Darroch, Gordon A. "Migrants in the Nineteenth Century: Fugitives or Family in Motion?" *Journal of Family History* 6, no. 3 (fall 1981): 257–77.

Dersch, Virginia J. "Copper Mining in Northern Michigan: A Social History." *Michigan History* 61, no. 4 (1977): 291–321.

Dessureault, Christian. "Crise ou modernisation? La société maskoutaine durant le premier tiers du XIXe siècle." *Revue d'histoire de l'Amérique française* 42, no. 3 (winter 1989): 359–87.

DuLong, John P. "Roman Catholic Church Records and Cemeteries." *Michigan Habitant Heritage* 11, no. 3 (July 1990): 56–59.

Engberg, Georges B. "Collective Bargaining in the Lumber Industry in the Upper Great Lakes States." *Agricultural History*, no. 24 (1950): 205–11.

——. "Lumber and Labor in the Lake States." *Minnesota History* 36 (1959): 133–66.

——. "Who Were the Lumberjacks?" *Michigan History* 32 (September 1948): 238–46.

Faucher, Albert. "L'émigration des Canadiens français au XIXe siècle: Position du problème et perspectives." *Recherches sociographiques* 5, no. 3 (December 1964): 277–317.

———. "Projet de recherche historique: L'émigration des Canadiens français au XIXe siècle." *Recherches sociographiques* 2, no. 2 (April–June 1961): 243–45.

Ford, Richard Clyde. "The French-Canadians in Michigan." *Michigan History* 27 (1943): 243–57.

Forster, John H. "Life in the Copper Mines of Lake Superior." *Michigan Pioneer and Historical Collections* 11 (1887): 175–86.

Fuller, Georges N. "Settlement of Michigan Territory." *Missississppi Valley Historical Review*, no. 1 (June 1915): 25–55.

———. "Settlement of Southern Michigan, 1805–1837." *Michigan History* 19 (1935): 179–214.

Gedicks, Al. "Ethnicity, Class Solidarity, and Labor Radicalism among Finnish Immigrants in Michigan Copper Country." *Politics and Society* 7, no. 2 (1977): 127–56.

Goodstein, Anita S. "Labor Relations in the Saginaw Valley Lumber Industry." *Bulletin of the Business History Society* 27 (1953): 193–221.

Hansen, Marcus Lee. "The History of American Immigration as a Field for Research." *American Historical Review* 32, no. 3 (April 1927): 500–518.

Hareven, Tamara K., and John Modell. "Urbanization and Malleable Household: An Examination of Boarding and Lodging in American Families." *Journal of Marriage and the Family* 35 (1973): 467–79.

Hybels, Robert James. "The Lake Superior Copper Fever, 1841–1847." *Michigan History* 34, no. 2 (June 1950): 97–119; vol. 34, no. 3:309–26.

Hyde, Charles K. "From 'Subterranean Lotteries' to Orderly Investment: Michigan Copper and Easter Dollars, 1841–1865." *Mid-America: An Historical Review*, no. 66 (January 1984): 3–20.

Jamieson, James K. "The Copper Rush of the '50s." *Michigan History* 19 (1935): 371–90.

Jenks, William L. "Michigan Immigration." *Michigan History* 28 (1944): 67–100.

Jobin, Antoine. "The First Frenchmen in Michigan." *Michigan History* 19 (1935): 231–51.

Jopling, James E. "Cornish Miners of the Upper Peninsula." *Michigan History* 12 (1928): 554–67.

Joyaux, George J. "French Press in Michigan: A Bibliography." *Michigan History* 37 (1952): 260–79.

Kadler, Eric H. "The French in Detroit, 1701–1880." *French-American Review* 6, no. 2 (1982): 296–309.

Kern, John. "A Short History of Michigan." *Michigan History* 60, no. 1 (spring 1976): 3–70.

Kilar, Jeremy W. "Community and Authority Response to the Saginaw Valley Lumber Strike of 1885." *Forest History* 20 (1976): 67–79.

Lalonde, A. N. "L'intelligentsia du Québec et la migration des Canadiens français vers l'Ouest canadien, 1870–1930." *Revue d'histoire de l'Amérique française* 33, no. 2 (September 1979): 163–85.

Lamarre, Jean. "L'intégration des migrants canadiens-français à la réalité socioéconomique aux Etats-Unis: Essai comparatif entre la Nouvelle-Angleterre et le Michigan." In *Prende la route. L'experience migratoire en Europe et en Amérique du Nord au XIVe au Xxe siècle*, edited by Andrée Courtemanche and Martin Pâquet, 155–169. Hull: Vent d'Ouest, 2001.

Lankton, Larry D. "Paternalism and Social Control in the Lake Superior Copper Mines, 1845–1913." *Upper Midwest History*, no. 5 (1985): 1–18.

Leach, Carl Addison, "Lumbering Days." *Michigan History* 18 (1934): 134–42.

———. "Paul Bunyan's Land and the First Sawmill of Michigan." *Michigan History* 20 (1936): 69–89.

Leigh, G. Copper. "Influence of the French Inhabitants of Detroit upon Early Political Life." *Michigan History* 4 (1920): 299–304.

Little, John. "La Patrie: Quebec's Repatriation Colony, 1875–1880." *Communications historiques*, 1977, *Société historique du Canada* (1977): 67–85.

Massicotte, E.-Z. "L'émigration aux Etats-Unis, mais il y a 40 ans." *Bulletin de recherches historiques* 39:21–27, 86–88, 179–80, 228–31, 381–83, 427–29, 507–8, 560–62, 697, 711–12; vol. 40:121.

Mathieu, Jacques, Pauline Therrien-Fortier, and Rénald Lessard. "Mobilité et sédentarité: Statégies familiales en Nouvelle-France." *Recherches sociographiques* 28, no. 3 (1987): 211–28.

McCalla, Douglas. "Forest Products and Upper Canada Development, 1815–1846." *Canadian Historical Review* 68, no. 2 (1987): 159–98.

McQuillan, Aidan D. "French-Canadian Communities in the American Upper Midwest during the 19th Century." *Cahiers de géographie du Québec* 23, no. 58 (April 1979): 53–72.

Mentor, L. William. "Horace Greely and Michigan Copper." *Michigan History* 34 (June 1950): 120–34.

Miller, Albert. "The Saginaw Valley." *Pioneer Collections: Report of the Pioneer Society of Michigan*, no. 7 (1884): 228–305.

Morissonneau, Christian. "Mobilité et indentité québécoise." *Cahiers de déographie du Québec* 23, no. 58 (April 1979): 29–38.

Paquet, Gilles. "L'émigration des Canadiens français vers la Nouvelle-Angleterre, 1870–1910: Prises de vue quantitatives." *Recherches sociographiques* 5 (September–December 1964): 319–70.

Paquet, Gilles, and Jean-Pierre Wallot. "Crise agricole et tensions socio-ethniques dans le Bas-Canada, 1802–1812: Eléments pour une réinterprétation." *Revue d'histoire de l'Amérique française* 26, no. 2 (September 1972): 185–237.

Paquette, Pierre. "Industries et politiques minières au Québec: Une analyse économique, 1896–1975." *Revue d'histoire de l'Amérique française* 37, no. 4 (March 1984): 573–602.

Patridge, B. F. "Bay County History—Its Pioneer Record and Wonderful Development." *Michigan Pioneer and Historical Collections* 3 (1881): 316–38.

Pyne, William. "Quincy Mine: The Old Reliable." *Michigan History* 41 (1957): 219–42.

Quinlan, Maria. "Lumbering in Michigan." *Michigan History* 62, no. 4 (1978): 37–41.

Ramirez, Bruno. "French-Canadian Immigrants in the New England Cotton Industry: A Socio-Economic Profile." *Labour/Le travailleur*, no. 11 (spring 1983): 125–42.

Ramirez, Bruno, and Jean Lamarre. "Du Québec vers les Etats-Unis: Etude des lieux d'origine." *Revue d'histoire de l'Amérique française* 38, no. 3 (spring 1985): 409–22.

Robinson, O. W. "From New England to Lake Superior (1854)." *Michigan Pioneer and Historical Collections* 32 (1902): 387–91.

———. "Recollections of the Civil War Conditions in the Copper Country." *Michigan History* 3 (1919): 598–609.

Silver, A. I. "French Canada and the Prairie Frontier, 1870–1890." *Canadian Historical Review* 50, no. 1 (March 1969): 11–36.

Stevens, J. Harold. "The Influence of New England in Michigan." *Michigan History* 19 (1935): 321–54.

Stocking, William. "New England Men in Michigan." *Michigan History* 5 (1921): 123–39.

Sutherland, Daniel E. "Michigan Emigrant Agent: Ed. H. Thompson." *Michigan History* 59, nos. 1–2 (1975): 3–37.

Sweet, William H. "Brief History of Saginaw County." *Michigan Pioneer and Historical Society Historical Collections* 28 (1900): 481–501.

Vecoli, Rudolph J. "Contadini in Chicago: A Critique of *The Uprooted.*" *Journal of American History*, no. 51 (December 1964): 404–17.

Wax, Anthony S. "Calumet and Hecla Copper Mines: An Episode in the Economic Development of Michigan." *Michigan History* 16 (1932): 5–41.

Ph.D. Dissertations and Master's Theses

Benson, Barbara, B. "Logs and Lumber: The Development of the Lumber Industry in the Michigan Lower Peninsula, 1837–1870." Ph.D. diss., Indiana University, 1977.

Engberg, Georges B. "Labor in the Lake States Lumber Industry, 1830–1930." Ph.D. diss., University of Minnesota, 1949.

Frenette, Yves. "La genèse d'une communauté canadienne-française en Nouvelle-Angleterre, Lewiston, Maine, 1800–1880." Ph.D. diss., Université Laval, 1988.

Kilar, Jeremy W. "The Lumbertown: A Socioeconomic History of Michigan's Leading Centers, Saginaw, Bay City, and Muskegon, 1870–1905." Ph.D. diss., University of Michigan, 1987.

Kovacik, Charles F. "A Geographical Analysis of the Foreign-Born in Huron, Sanilac, and St-Clair Counties of Michigan with Particular Reference to Canadians, 1850–1880." Ph.D. diss., University of Michigan, 1970.

Lamarre, Jean. "Etude d'une communauté canadienne-française de la Nouvelle-Angleterre: Le cas de Warren, Rhode Island, 1880–1895." Master's thesis, Université de Montréal, 1985.

Mcgaugh, Maurice E. "The Settlement of Saginaw Basin." Ph.D. diss., University of Chicago, 1950.

Sylvia, Philip T., Jr. "The Spindle City: Labor, Politics, and Religion in Fall River, Massachusetts, 1870–1905." Ph.D. diss., Fordham University, 1973.

Vicero, Ralph D. "Immigration of French-Canadians to New England, 1840–1900: A Geographical Analysis." Ph.D. diss., University of Wisconsin, 1968.

Index

Albany (New York), 20
American Civil War, 20, 41, 59, 61, 73, 118
American Fur Company, 9, 30, 148
Amerindians, 7, 55
Annexationist Movement, 91–94, 130, 177
Anti-Roman Advocate, 93
Arizona, 69
Aubry, Zotique, 104

Baltic region, 11
Bangor Daily Whig and Courier, 35, 37
Barry, Thomas, 49–50
Bay (county), 78, 97, 105
Bay City (Lower Saginaw), 31–33, 44, 45, 48, 50, 51, 53, 78, 81, 85–90, 95, 97, 102–4, 112, 156
Baye des Puants, 8
Birney, James G., 32
Biron, Alfred, 139
Bliss, A. T., 36
Borduas, Rev. Édouard P., 143
Borgess, Msgr. Caspar, 81, 84
Bouchard, Louis, 105
Boucher, Célestin, 88
Bourbonnais (Illinois), 22
Bourdon, Henri, 106
Boutyette, Régis, 104
Brûlé, Euchariste, 123–25
Buffalo (New York), 35, 120
Burlington (Vermont), 16

Burt, Wellington R., 36
Butte (Montana), 142, 147

California, 15
Calumet (village), 70, 127, 129, 131–35, 141, 143, 144, 145, 146, 148, 158
Calumet and Hecla Consolidated Mining Company (C&H), 61–68, 71–72, 124–34, 144, 147
Campau, Daniel J., 89
Campau, Louis, 30, 76
Carleton (county), 13
Champagne, Jos, 139
Chassell (village), 137
Chaudiere River, 15
Chicago (Illinois), 21, 22
Chiniquy, Charles, 22
Connecticut, 15, 17
Constitutional Act (1791), 2
Convention of French Canadians of the United States (5th), 91
Convention of French Canadians of Upper Michigan, 131
Cook, Albert F., 36
Copper Country Evening News, 142
Copper Harbor, 55, 56
Court Lafayette no. 26, 135
C. P. Williams and Company of Albany, New York, 35
Cushway, Benjamin, 31

203

TITLES IN THE GREAT LAKES BOOKS SERIES

Walnut Pickles and Watermelon Cake: A Century of Michigan Cooking, by Larry B. Massie and Priscilla Massie, 1990

The Making of Michigan, 1820–1860: A Pioneer Anthology, edited by Justin L. Kestenbaum, 1990

America's Favorite Homes: A Guide to Popular Early Twentieth-Century Homes, by Robert Schweitzer and Michael W. R. Davis, 1990

Beyond the Model T: The Other Ventures of Henry Ford, by Ford R. Bryan, 1990

Life after the Line, by Josie Kearns, 1990

Michigan Lumbertowns: Lumbermen and Laborers in Saginaw, Bay City, and Muskegon, 1870–1905, by Jeremy W. Kilar, 1990

Detroit Kids Catalog: The Hometown Tourist, by Ellyce Field, 1990

Waiting for the News, by Leo Litwak, 1990 (reprint)

Detroit Perspectives, edited by Wilma Wood Henrickson, 1991

Life on the Great Lakes: A Wheelsman's Story, by Fred W. Dutton, edited by William Donohue Ellis, 1991

Copper Country Journal: The Diary of Schoolmaster Henry Hobart, 1863–1864, by Henry Hobart, edited by Philip P. Mason, 1991

John Jacob Astor: Business and Finance in the Early Republic, by John Denis Haeger, 1991

Survival and Regeneration: Detroit's American Indian Community, by Edmund J. Danziger, Jr., 1991

Steamboats and Sailors of the Great Lakes, by Mark L. Thompson, 1991

Cobb Would Have Caught It: The Golden Age of Baseball in Detroit, by Richard Bak, 1991

Michigan in Literature, by Clarence Andrews, 1992

Under the Influence of Water: Poems, Essays, and Stories, by Michael Delp, 1992

The Country Kitchen, by Della T. Lutes, 1992 (reprint)

The Making of a Mining District: Keweenaw Native Copper 1500–1870, by David J. Krause, 1992

Kids Catalog of Michigan Adventures, by Ellyce Field, 1993

Henry's Lieutenants, by Ford R. Bryan, 1993

Historic Highway Bridges of Michigan, by Charles K. Hyde, 1993

Lake Erie and Lake St. Clair Handbook, by Stanley J. Bolsenga and Charles E. Herndendorf, 1993

Queen of the Lakes, by Mark Thompson, 1994

Iron Fleet: The Great Lakes in World War II, by George J. Joachim, 1994

Turkey Stearnes and the Detroit Stars: The Negro Leagues in Detroit, 1919–1933, by Richard Bak, 1994

Pontiac and the Indian Uprising, by Howard H. Peckham, 1994 (reprint)

Charting the Inland Seas: A History of the U.S. Lake Survey, by Arthur M. Woodford, 1994 (reprint)

Ojibwa Narratives of Charles and Charlotte Kawbawgam and Jacques LePique,
1893–1895. Recorded with Notes by Homer H. Kidder, edited by Arthur P.
Bourgeois, 1994, co-published with the Marquette County Historical Society

Strangers and Sojourners: A History of Michigan's Keweenaw Peninsula, by Arthur W.
Thurner, 1994

Win Some, Lose Some: G. Mennen Williams and the New Democrats, by Helen
Washburn Berthelot, 1995

Sarkis, by Gordon and Elizabeth Orear, 1995

The Northern Lights: Lighthouses of the Upper Great Lakes, by Charles K. Hyde, 1995
(reprint)

Kids Catalog of Michigan Adventures, second edition, by Ellyce Field, 1995

Rumrunning and the Roaring Twenties: Prohibition on the Michigan-Ontario Waterway,
by Philip P. Mason, 1995

In the Wilderness with the Red Indians, by E. R. Baierlein, translated by Anita Z.
Boldt, edited by Harold W. Moll, 1996

Elmwood Endures: History of a Detroit Cemetery, by Michael Franck, 1996

Master of Precision: Henry M. Leland, by Mrs. Wilfred C. Leland with Minnie
Dubbs Millbrook, 1996 (reprint)

Haul-Out: New and Selected Poems, by Stephen Tudor, 1996

Kids Catalog of Michigan Adventures, third edition, by Ellyce Field, 1997

Beyond the Model T: The Other Ventures of Henry Ford, revised edition, by Ford R.
Bryan, 1997

Young Henry Ford: A Picture History of the First Forty Years, by Sidney Olson, 1997
(reprint)

The Coast of Nowhere: Meditations on Rivers, Lakes and Streams, by Michael Delp,
1997

*From Saginaw Valley to Tin Pan Alley: Saginaw's Contribution to American Popular
Music, 1890–1955,* by R. Grant Smith, 1998

The Long Winter Ends, by Newton G. Thomas, 1998 (reprint)

*Bridging the River of Hatred: The Pioneering Efforts of Detroit Police Commissioner
George Edwards,* by Mary M. Stolberg, 1998

Toast of the Town: The Life and Times of Sunnie Wilson, by Sunnie Wilson with John
Cohassey, 1998

*These Men Have Seen Hard Service: The First Michigan Sharpshooters in the Civil
War,* by Raymond J. Herek, 1998

A Place for Summer: One Hundred Years at Michigan and Trumbull, by Richard Bak,
1998

Early Midwestern Travel Narratives: An Annotated Bibliography, 1634–1850, by
Robert R. Hubach, 1998 (reprint)

All-American Anarchist: Joseph A. Labadie and the Labor Movement, by Carlotta R.
Anderson, 1998

Michigan in the Novel, 1816–1996: An Annotated Bibliography, by Robert Beasecker, 1998

"Time by Moments Steals Away": The 1848 Journal of Ruth Douglass, by Robert L. Root, Jr., 1998

The Detroit Tigers: A Pictorial Celebration of the Greatest Players and Moments in Tigers' History, updated edition, by William M. Anderson, 1999

Father Abraham's Children: Michigan Episodes in the Civil War, by Frank B. Woodford, 1999 (reprint)

Letter from Washington, 1863–1865, by Lois Bryan Adams, edited and with an introduction by Evelyn Leasher, 1999

Wonderful Power: The Story of Ancient Copper Working in the Lake Superior Basin, by Susan R. Martin, 1999

A Sailor's Logbook: A Season aboard Great Lakes Freighters, by Mark L. Thompson, 1999

Huron: The Seasons of a Great Lake, by Napier Shelton, 1999

Tin Stackers: The History of the Pittsburgh Steamship Company, by Al Miller, 1999

Art in Detroit Public Places, revised edition, text by Dennis Nawrocki, photographs by David Clements, 1999

Brewed in Detroit: Breweries and Beers Since 1830, by Peter H. Blum, 1999

Detroit Kids Catalog: A Family Guide for the 21st Century, by Ellyce Field, 2000

"Expanding the Frontiers of Civil Rights": Michigan, 1948–1968, by Sidney Fine, 2000

Graveyard of the Lakes, by Mark L. Thompson, 2000

Enterprising Images: The Goodridge Brothers, African American Photographers, 1847–1922, by John Vincent Jezierski, 2000

New Poems from the Third Coast: Contemporary Michigan Poetry, edited by Michael Delp, Conrad Hilberry, and Josie Kearns, 2000

Arab Detroit: From Margin to Mainstream, edited by Nabeel Abraham and Andrew Shryock, 2000

The Sandstone Architecture of the Lake Superior Region, by Kathryn Bishop Eckert, 2000

Looking Beyond Race: The Life of Otis Milton Smith, by Otis Milton Smith and Mary M. Stolberg, 2000

Mail by the Pail, by Colin Bergel, illustrated by Mark Koenig, 2000

Great Lakes Journey: A New Look at America's Freshwater Coast, by William Ashworth, 2000

A Life in the Balance: The Memoirs of Stanley J. Winkelman, by Stanley J. Winkelman, 2000

Schooner Passage: Sailing Ships and the Lake Michigan Frontier, by Theodore J. Karamanski, 2000

The Outdoor Museum: The Magic of Michigan's Marshall M. Fredericks, by Marcy Heller Fisher, illustrated by Christine Collins Woomer, 2001

For an updated listing of books in this series, please visit our Web site at http://wsupress.wayne.edu